The Officers and Directors of Daniel International Corporation are pleased to present this biography of Charles E. Daniel and the official history of the company he founded.

CHARLES E. DANIEL
1895-1964

CHARLES E. DANIEL
His Philosophy and Legacy

Co-Authors

PART 1

C. R. (RED) CANUP

PART 2

W. D. WORKMAN, JR.

The R. L. Bryan Company
Columbia, South Carolina

MANUFACTURED IN THE UNITED STATES OF AMERICA BY
THE R. L. BRYAN COMPANY
COLUMBIA, SOUTH CAROLINA

Table of Contents

CHAPTER   PAGE

Preface vii

PART 1

Building a Business and the South

1   Philosophy and Legacy   3

2   The Early Years..................................   8

3   A Vision Takes Shape 17

4   A Move and a World War 29

5   The Most Eventful Decade 43

6   The Fortune Story................................ 51

7   Pushing Back the Horizon 64

8   A Pattern for Progress 70

9   A One-Man Magnet for Industry 74

10 His Last Project................................. 81

11 Changing of the Guard 87

12 Reaching the Top 92

13 Entering the '80's............................... 98

14 The Organization 105

15 Life with Daniel 110

    Picture Section 122

Table of Contents (Continued)

CHAPTER   PAGE

PART 2

A Constructive Citizen

16   The Military Mood 137

17   Clemson Connections.............................. 145

18   The Postwar Period 149

19   Senatorial Interlude 154

20   Southern Accent 162

21   The Timmerman Era 166

22   Seaports — Airports 169

23   The Hollings Era 175

24   Black and White 182

25   The Labor Front 190

26   The Local Scene 195

27   Advocate of Good Government 198

28   Textile Teamwork 202

29   Presidential Politics 205

30   Sharing the Wealth 209

31   The Last Rites 216

     Index.. 223

Preface

This book reveals how one man's dedication to success engendered vast improvement in the economic, social and cultural life of the South and projected him to national influence and prominence. It is the story of Charles E. Daniel and his construction company. Charlie Daniel was an entrepreneur with a unique approach, so the reader will find herein the essence of two narratives: one dealing with the history of an international engineering and construction firm, the other depicting the life and works of a man imbued with a driving determination to improve the conditions under which he and his contemporaries lived.

This presentation is designed for that segment of the public that knew him only by reputation, and for past, present and future Daniel employees who have an especial interest in understanding "the boss" and the temperament and philosophies that made him and his company stand out from the crowd. Charlie Daniel was a 20th Century economic philosopher whose thought processes and work performance combined to earn him recognition in the realms of industry, finance and politics. He came on the scene when his native Southland was beginning to emerge from the economic doldrums that had beset the region since the Reconstruction days after the Civil War. Indeed, he might well be credited with having shifted the Southern emphasis to "construction" rather than "reconstruction."

He built into his company an emphasis on youth and occupational opportunity, giving real meaning to the concept that lateral and upward mobility was available to workers who could prove their mettle. True, the proving process occasionally involved a real "chewing-out" by Daniel himself when his quick temper boiled over. But such outbursts more often than not were productive; for the Daniel temper cooled as quickly as it flamed. Such exchanges reflected another Daniel trait — the habit of exerting his management skills "out on the job" rather than from behind a desk. This provided a continuing demonstration of his credo that his was and would ever be a "people-oriented" organization.

Daniel drilled into his co-workers his belief that success had to be based on reliability, which would lead to repeat business, always a major portion of the company's work. This led to many construction transactions that were handled in an almost informal manner, often without written contract and with no more fiscal protocol than a handshake.

vii

To be sure, there were those — both in and out of the construction industry — who regarded Daniel with something less than admiration. Some simply envied his success. Perhaps the strongest censure of Daniel came from politicians who felt, with or without just cause, that they were being "used" by Daniel through his financial contributions and/or his influence. Nonetheless, he constantly preached and practiced the doctrine that self-respecting citizens owed it to themselves and to their society to give at least a tenth of their time and talent to the betterment of their community, state and country.

Along with such presentations of the Daniel personality and practice as an individual, there will be narrative accounts of Daniel Construction Company as a business entity with a personality of its own. The focus, of course, will be on Daniel himself, but due recognition will be given to those other persons — in and out of the Daniel family — who contributed, early and late, to the success of what still is known to many as "Charlie's company."

PART 1

Building a Business and the South

CHAPTER 1

Philosophy and Legacy

Charlie Daniel had parallel goals, and any accomplishment of one enhanced the achievement of another. This is a story about his ambitions, motivations and triumphs; and it is to his lasting credit that his legacy has been perpetuated and expanded, both in the continued growth of his company and in the industrialization of the South. That is what this book is all about.

Date the Daniel scenario back to the beginning of his business career — 1919, when he returned from World War I, and 1934, when he started his company in Anderson, South Carolina, on faith, determination and a loan. In 1920-21, the economically poor agrarian South was further depressed when boll weevils stripped its cotton crops, worsening living conditions and causing bank failures. The national depression of the early 1930's compounded the area's plight; and even up to the beginning of World War II, many were surviving only on government food baskets and jobs created by federal work agencies. Practically no new industry had come to the Southeastern states in a quarter of a century, and unemployment in some areas ran as high as 20 to 25 percent.

World War II kept Southern industrialization dormant for another four to five years except for military and related projects, and there were few available jobs for the tens of thousands of returning servicemen at the war's end in 1945. Charlie Daniel was doubly concerned. His defense contracts had been fulfilled, and there was not enough new work to keep all his craftsmen on the payroll nor to rehire those who were now out of uniform. He addressed the problem in typical Daniel fashion — by means of strategic action. He worked up a list of potential industrial customers and boarded the train for New York and other corporate headquarters centers in the North and Midwest. He knocked on some executive doors that no other Southerner had ever entered. He sold many companies on the benefits of expanding to the South. The results of

3

his numerous day-and-night train rides and his untiring efforts were soon evidenced by the volume of new construction, most of it initially in South Carolina and bordering states.

As industry moved into the Sun Belt, he would show related process or service companies the wisdom of locating in the proximity of these new markets. This led to a continuing march to the South; and as the economy improved and more jobs became available for tens of thousands of previously unemployed and underemployed, business leaders began referring to Charlie Daniel as the "Industrial Ambassador of the South." The influx of new industry required special training and further education for the more complex jobs, and he made technical schools another of his goals.

Robert S. Small, a Greenville textile executive, shared his friend Daniel's enthusiasm and made several industrial excursions with him. Small put that association and experience in these words: "Charlie was a man who, through his infectious personality, ability and originality, literally captivated people. Our own business leaders, and those in the North and Midwest whom he called on, were fascinated with him. He gave a different pitch. He was recognized as the leader of a new, progressive, dynamic section of the United States. He had knowledge, enthusiasm and direction, and a vision to lift up South Carolinians and the whole South, both economically and educationally. He was the Moses who would lead us out of the depressed wilderness. After all, the South then, and to a degree many years later, was looked down on as an underdeveloped part of this country.

"Charlie proved, really for the first time, to the rest of the country that given the proper tools and training the people of this area were superior, or certainly equal, to industrial workers anywhere. Nobody had thought that before because we had always been an agrarian economy, but Charlie did. He would tell any and every responsible person that 'We are on the verge of great industrialization. We're going to throw off Reconstruction once and for all. We're going to correct the South being the lowest paid, the most illiterate, and the most underdeveloped part of the country. We will get in the mainstream of America.' He was determined to put us there, and he did. He was a Billy Sunday of industry."

Industrial evangelist or not, Charlie Daniel was successful; yet succeeding never brought self-satisfaction because he would never back off from new challenges and opportunities. That was his restless nature. A self-made man, he had compassion and a ready hand for struggling entrepreneurs traveling the roads bearing his own tracks. By the same token, he admired bigness in business, appreciative of the fact that growth is achieved through competitive performance. And big business respected him, seeking his advice and friendship long before his company became a leader in engineering and construction.

Corporate presidents and board chairmen, government officials and educators recognized his ability and the sincerity with which he applied his talents in everything he tackled. Moreover, they liked his business philosophy and the ethical manner in which he operated his own company. They knew by reputation, the best judge of a man, that his word was his bond. And they appreciated his labor posture and philosophy, which was, quite simply, that every man and woman, regardless of race, should be privileged to work without paying tribute to any organization. He championed people's rights and the open shop with a passion — in the same dogmatic way he fought government bureaucracy.

Charlie Daniel could not accept all of the major corporate directorships or the college trusteeships offered him, yet he did serve on a number of boards, usually for life. Corporate boards to which he was elected and accepted included: Chemical Bank, 1962; Prudential Insurance Company, 1960; Eastern Air Lines, 1959; Georgia-Pacific, 1957; Southern Bell, 1957; J. P. Stevens, 1952; LaFrance Industries, 1951-1961; Textron, Inc., 1949-54; Graniteville Company, 1947-1963, and South Carolina National Bank, dating back to 1944 with First National of Greenville prior to its 1957 merger with SCN. Other activities outside his company are explained in Part II of this book.

The policies and basic philosophy that earned the company its reputation under Charlie Daniel became known as the "Daniel way" of doing business, and every new employee hears about it the first day on the job. What it means is that the company still observes the policies and philosophies that the founder practiced and preached — they are part of his legacy. While the basic "Daniel way" has not been changed, various policies have been modified to conform to an ever-changing society and modern customs. For example, the founder believed that Labor Day should be a day of labor and that, along with traditional black-eyed peas and collard greens, the new year should be started off right — by working. Those dates have long since been among national holidays observed by the company, but his basic philosophy remains the same.

The "Daniel way" legacy is so sacred in the company that new employees are surprised that it is not in the Employee Handbook in the form of an ironclad code of do's and don'ts. Soon enough, however, they understand that it simply means that the company continues to deal with customers just like Charlie Daniel did — do what you say you will do, and when called for, provide services over and beyond what is in the contract. So in reality, the "Daniel way" is the perpetuation of a reputation. In that sense, reputation is established with each client because no two companies, their representatives nor their projects are alike.

Judge Clement F. Haynsworth, Jr., former Greenville attorney who worked with Daniel on many contracts, recounts two examples of the "Daniel way" in action. One reveals how subtle Charlie Daniel could be in a one-on-one sales effort. The other typifies total teamwork.

Haynsworth said that a major company's general counsel contacted him for assistance in their plans to locate a plant in South Carolina. He suggested that they also contact Daniel because he thought substantial help could be provided in locating a site and working out practical problems. "I assured them," Haynsworth said, "that Charlie would be glad to do it with no idea that they should have any sense of obligation to him. So they did, and about two weeks later the head man of that company said to me:

> " 'You know, Charlie Daniel is the damnedest fellow I ever met in all my life. He has been taking me all around the state, showing me plant sites and producing data about everything in the world that we need to know about each site. I've been with him in the morning, sometimes as early as 5 o'clock, and late at night, and he has not said one word to me about who's going to build our factory.' I asked him if he had any doubt in his mind about who will build it. He smiled and said, 'No sir!' "

On the other specific occasion Haynsworth recalled, a group of Singer Company representatives came to Greenville in early 1951 to confer with him and Daniel about a probable site for a plant in nearby Anderson. "They arranged to meet with us in the morning," Haynsworth said, "and they produced a long list of questions to which they needed answers. Some of the questions were for Charlie, such as cost and engineering; and the Singer team wanted some changes, such as the switching limits on the railroad. As these questions came up, Charlie was on the phone calling his people, and he called one of the head men of Southern Railway and got a verbal commitment that the switching limits would be changed. Meanwhile, they had legal questions that I was answering, sometimes having to call my office when I didn't have the information they wanted. But we did get all of the answers for them.

"About 1 o'clock, after working all morning, one of the Singer people said, 'What do you know? We've run out of questions!' Charlie and I suggested that we go to lunch. As we were about to leave, one of the Singer men said, 'Before we go, there's something we think we should tell you. Coming down on the train last night we got up a little pool and each person put in some money and wrote on a slip of paper how long he thought it would take us to get answers to all of the questions we brought along. The winner of the pool had written down three days, and the rest of us had estimated a week or more. But we got answers to all of our questions this morning.' " Daniel built the Singer plant.

"Needless to say," Haynsworth continued, "they were greatly impressed. But this is the kind of thing Charlie did. He did it so well that people concerned with their building plans would go to him because they had complete confidence in him. And they knew he worked very effectively and very rapidly. As a result, he would build a plant for a company; and when they wanted a second plant, he built it too. No doubt about it, there was no consideration of them going to some other construction company."

More than a decade and half after the founder's death in 1964, there were only a few old-timers still with the company who had worked with him and really knew him. There were many who had come aboard in the early 1960's, but most were not in positions that received his personal attention. One of the old-timers was pleasantly surprised at the 1980 winter marketing meeting when young salesmen were called on to explain the sales approach they would take under a variety of hypothetical situations. After several explained how they would react to various client peculiarities, hostile attitudes and unexpected questions, the old-timer whispered to the person seated beside him: "No wonder these guys can sell. They remind me of Charlie Daniel."

CHAPTER 2

The Early Years

Charlie Daniel never had any doubt about the line of business he would follow after working several summers at Townsend Lumber Company in his hometown of Anderson, South Carolina. Yet he did have opportunities to change his mind. There had been the two years at The Citadel, the military college at Charleston that he attended on a competitive scholarship, followed by service as a first lieutenant in the Army during World War I. He had been exposed to life greatly different from what he experienced in the small town of Anderson, including the bright lights of New York and Paris. Even so, he went contrary to the wartime song that wondered: "How are you going to keep them down on the farm after they've seen Paree?"

It was in the spring of 1919 that he began his construction career with the lumber company, which also provided some design and building services, the latter being what Charlie liked best. He went to work immediately after returning from the service because he believed practical experience would expedite his career, and he wanted to help send his younger brothers to college. Three of them — Earle W., James F. Jr., and Fred A. — were barely old enough to have also served in the just-ended war, and the youngest, R. Hugh, was not yet out of high school. As it developed, Charlie did provide financial assistance in their continuing education; and in the second World War, the family's service-to-country tradition was kept alive when Hugh joined the Navy.

Some journalists have played up the fact that as a schoolboy making wooden crates for Townsend, Charlie was paid only seven and one-half cents an hour. In the modern labor market that would be an incredibly low wage; yet in 1910, at the age of 15, the boy was appreciative of the job and the pay because then many grown men in the South were not making much more, wherever they worked.

Eugene E. Lassiter was one of several schoolboys who worked side-by-side with Charlie at Townsend, and he recalled that "Charlie could make at least three boxes while anybody else was making one. He would take a hammer and some shingle nails and make a box before you could turn around. I've never seen anything like it. He was a hard worker even in his younger days, and you'd never see him when he wasn't in a hurry."

That innate motivation to succeed and his constant high-energy drive were not dampened by Army service. Charlie was 23 when he returned home with ambitious ideas. He was determined to be a builder and began his career at $18 a week. Frank Brownlee, a close friend who was then a young Anderson insurance executive, recalled that "Townsend was doing nothing but selling lumber and building a few little houses from time to time" when the first World War ended. Here is Brownlee's insight into what motivated Daniel:

"Charlie wanted to build more houses, and Keith Prevost, the president of Townsend, was in favor of that, so he was allowed to build houses, one at a time, to get the hang of it. Charlie figured that if he could build 10 houses at a time he could get somewhere with it, and the houses could be completed faster. He called on textile mill owners and sold them on letting him build six, eight or ten of their village houses at a time. He got a crew together, worked right along with them, and proved his point: He could build houses better, faster and cheaper. His next idea was to build 100 houses at a time. He finally did, anywhere he could get a contract in the Carolinas, Georgia and Alabama. That was his start in major construction. He was the only man I knew who was building houses like that; and nobody was competing with him at that volume, so he was getting most of the big housing contracts."

To quote from the *National Cyclopedia of American Biography:* "Daniel's responsibilities were subsequently increased to include the preparation of estimates for building contracts. In 1924, he obtained for his company (Townsend) a contract from a textile company for the construction of 175 houses (a mill village in Anderson), and later he negotiated a contract for the building of 350 homes and a schoolhouse (in Rome, Georgia) for the American Chatillon Corporation, a forerunner of Celanese Corporation."

The Rome project created interesting firsts for Charlie Daniel: it was in the million-dollar range; it started a long relationship with a major engineering firm; and it returned him to his native Georgia for several months.

Elberton, Georgia, is where Charlie was born, on November 11, 1895, to James Fleming Daniel and Leila Mildred Adams Daniel; and it was there that he married Homozel Mickel 29 years and 14 days later (November 25, 1924).

The Daniel family had made an economic move to Anderson, little more than 30 miles across the Savannah River state line, at the turn of the century. The head of the household was a millwright, a person who plans mills or sets up their process machinery. James F. Daniel did not build mills, something his first son would become noted for later, but he did perform maintenance on machinery; and in Anderson, there were more textile mills in need of his skill and service. The father's trade required wooden boxes to transport new and used machinery, and that is how Charlie first became interested in carpentry, the craft that led him into construction.

When Charlie returned to Georgia temporarily to manage the Rome project, which started in 1928, he took his wife with him. As it developed, that would be the first of many trips to construction sites for "Mickey," her nickname, and she would become a full-fledged officer in her husband's company as corporate secretary and an active member of the board of directors.

Charlie Daniel established both personal and business relations with many of the world's major architectural and engineering firms. One such contact is reported by Samuel B. Lincoln, then a senior project engineer for Lockwood Greene Engineers, Inc., and later its president. He recalled it in his 1958 history of the firm:

> "It was in 1928 that Lockwood Greene first became acquainted with Charles E. Daniel. . . . The meeting came about in connection with a housing development in Rome, Georgia, for Dr. D. M. Balsam, head of the American Chatillon Corporation, a rayon yarn manufacturing company having a technical affiliation with the Italian company of that name. After the major part of the plant had been designed by Lockwood Greene and construction and equipment arranged for, Dr. Balsam decided that it was going to be absolutely necessary to have a good number of employee houses."

Four- to six-room frame houses were typical of Southern mill villages in that era. They could be built for about $400 per room. Balsam projected 338 houses for his development at Rome, and he requested that they be constructed with brick walls and have concrete porches and steps. Advised that those modifications would increase the cost substantially, he agreed to spend $600 per room. When the first three bids ran $25 to $50 higher per room, he stood firm. Lincoln's history of the project is picked up at that point:

"Then we received a telephone call in New York from the Townsend Lumber Company of Anderson who said that they had heard there were some houses to be built at Rome, and that they would like to look at the plans and specifications. We told them to come ahead and see them, and shortly Charles E. Daniel arrived in our office. We told him the story. He looked at the plans, studied them for a while and said that he believed he could build the houses for $600 per room. We said, 'All right. If you can, let's go and see Dr. Balsam and you tell him yourself.'

"We went to see Dr. Balsam, who was in the habit of settling things very promptly. Within a very few minutes thereafter, a verbal agreement was made. Lockwood Greene was instructed to draw up the contract — which was done and signed that same day — for 338 brick houses at an average of four and one-half rooms per house, or about 1,500 rooms, for about $900,000. Before the job was finished the Townsend Lumber Company was authorized to add to the contract $51,000 for a brick schoolhouse. With a few other items added at the owner's request, the total contract came to just about $1,000,000.

"Daniel moved to Rome for this operation to take charge of the project in the field. The houses were delivered on time, of excellent quality, and without a single argument with the contractor during the progress of the work, either on the question of speed of performance or quality of workmanship. Thus began our acquaintance with Charlie Daniel. . . . It is a contact which has continued unbroken through scores of building operations all over the Southeastern states, where many large plants today represent the combined efforts of Lockwood Greene and Daniel Construction Company."

In late 1978, 50 years later, Lincoln recalled the project and this history in a letter to Mrs. Daniel in which he wrote: "The brick walls of those houses were not ordinary brick. A brickyard in the area had developed an eight-inch hollow red brick called 'DuBrik' and had demonstrated that an eight-inch wall with proper coating on the inside could be made water-tight, so that was used and turned out well. We in L. G., and the owner's staff too, were so busy with the large and complex manufacturing plant that we scarcely found time to worry about the houses once the construction was in good hands. In fact I saw very little of Charlie during that period but knew he was right on the job because results showed it."

Lincoln inadvertently touched on a prime Daniel philosophy in another paragraph of his letter. He mentioned his continuing relationship with the constructor: "Later, in 1936, he was low bidder on a hosiery mill at Athens, Georgia, for Rodgers Hosiery Company; and in 1938 when the plant was doubled, there were no other builders considered. Charlie was the first and only choice."

Buck Mickel, who joined the company in 1948 and worked up through the ranks to become chairman and chief executive officer, is continually instilling Daniel philosophy throughout the organization. "One thing Charlie always stressed, and we still emphasize it, is that you do what you say you will do. He knew from early experience that if you build a plant right, like you assured the owner you would, then when that plant is to be expanded you will be called back." For many years, more than 75 percent of the company's work has been repeat business, the expansion of the hosiery plant in Athens being one of the first examples of continuous service to clients.

Social life in small Southern towns was rather limited in the 1920's and 1930's. That did not concern Charlie Daniel because the major weekly event was the popular Friday night dance and that was about the only social activity in which he took the time to participate. His box-making friend, Gene Lassiter, later promoted the dances in Anderson. "Going to a dance was just about the most enjoyable thing you could do," he recalled, "and Charlie really liked to dance." Couples and groups would attend from Elberton, other nearby Georgia towns, and neighboring South Carolina communities.

Even though most roads were not paved in that area in the 1920's, creating slippery if not hazardous traveling conditions during rain or snow, the Anderson crowd often went to public dances in Greenville, and occasionally in Spartanburg, more than 60 miles and about three hours away by automobile. It was at the Greenville dances that Charlie and Mickey met J. Mason Alexander, who leased hotels in the Carolinas, managed the old Ottaray Hotel in Greenville, and later took over the famous Poinsett Hotel in that city. As a result of their dance sessions, which attracted big-name bands of that era, the Daniels and Alexanders became lifelong friends.

Friends have said Charlie danced to burn off excess energy even though he worked 10 or 12 hours every day, often seven days a week. His long, hard-driving work schedule paid off early. He purchased stock in Townsend, and became a vice president in 1927. One of his most important contracts was negotiated in 1928 when American Enka Corporation was formed with headquarters in Enka, North Carolina. Charlie built 91 supervisory-type houses for the company while an industrial contractor constructed the first

Enka rayon filament yarn plant just down the mountain. Enka officials were pleased with the housing project, and in years to come Daniel would build several large plants for the company and the headquarters offices at Asheville for Akzona, the parent corporation.

A second Daniel joined the Townsend team in the summer of 1929. R. Hugh Daniel, the youngest brother, had just graduated from The Citadel. Hugh also had worked at the lumberyard during summers, and with that experience he chose to follow construction. His first major field assignment was a timekeeper on the large housing project in Rome, Georgia. Charlie sent Hugh to manage a project in Alabama on November 10, 1934, and he never returned to Anderson to live. Born in Anderson on September 1, 1906, Hugh would become a construction giant in his own right, contributing substantially to the firm through his Birmingham office and later as president, chairman, chief executive officer and treasurer of the company.

Two other men who were to figure prominently in Charlie's future went to work at Townsend in 1930. One of them, Lawrence W. Yeargin, was assigned as Hugh's superintendent and spent several years on various Alabama projects, mostly in commercial building. The other member of the "original superintendents" team was J. Ed Moore. Both he and Yeargin began their construction careers in Anderson County, where each later retired and are now buried. Being from the "old school," they believed in giving their employer a full day's work for a full day's pay, and expected everyone on their projects to do the same.

Yeargin was best known for his supervision on institutional and commercial buildings where finished carpentry and masonry were required. Moore, who was nicknamed "Cussin' Ed" and earned it, was at his best on tougher, and sometimes more critical, industrial projects. Each was often assigned to projects in preference to more available superintendents when management felt that they possessed more experience and drive and could get a specific job completed on time and in the money. They helped develop other superintendents with equal ability, reliability and total dedication to "the Daniel way."

Townsend's corporate secretary was Pearl A. Moore, and by early 1930 her responsibilities had increased to the point that another secretary was needed. It was then that Mary Neese entered Charlie Daniel's business life, and she would become Daniel's oldest employee in years of service and the company's most reliable historian. Her first job lasted only 18 months because Townsend's business, like most others, was affected by the depression of the 1930's. Feeling badly about being unable to keep her on the payroll, Charlie scouted around and found Miss Neese a job before she left Townsend. She was employed as secretary to Wilton E. Hall, publisher of *The Anderson Independent*, a morning newspaper. His need for a secretary developed in 1932 when *The Independent* was awarded a contract to print the *South Carolina Farm Market Bulletin*. He transferred his secretary to *Bulletin* work and replaced her with Miss Neese.

Hall involved himself and his newspaper in politics, and Mary recalls that on many occasions she took dictation in the proverbial smoke-filled room while Hall, Charlie Daniel, James F. Byrnes, then a Spartanburg attorney, and Olin D. Johnston, aspiring governor, mapped political strategy and wrote speeches for Johnston and other candidates. Johnston and Byrnes went on to make state and national political history, and Hall remained an influential Democrat for many years, not always behind the scenes. But just as politics and issues make strange bedfellows, they can also separate friends. Within a few years Hall no longer accepted the political views of Byrnes and Daniel. His break with Daniel finally became so bitter that Hall would not allow the names of Charles E. Daniel or Daniel Construction Company to be printed in his publications.

As the early 1930's moved along, Daniel realized that there would be an ever-increasing market for industrial construction, especially in the South. His partners at Townsend, however, preferred to concentrate on selling lumber and constructing houses and school buildings. Daniel wanted to change that philosophy and often discussed his ideas with his friend Brownlee, because any mention of expansion to Prevost fell on deaf ears. Daniel told Brownlee that "even though Townsend can do industrial work, it's not the same when I try to sell our services to industrial clients. Those I deal with in housing work want a construction company for their industrial jobs, not a lumber company."

Prevost reasoned that the depression had the nation in its grip, many companies had failed, and this was no time to branch out since Townsend's own business was slow. Then, on March 4, 1933, Franklin D. Roosevelt took the oath of president and immediately began priming the nation's economic pump with all kinds of alphabetical aid, such as the WPA, the PWA, etc. He saw the South, depressed since the end of the War Between the States, as the "Nation's No. 1 Economic Problem." And he kept priming the pump. By year's end there were general signs of an economic recovery even though hard times lingered throughout the South.

Charlie Daniel firmly believed that a New South would come into prominence in the wake of the depression. All of his business life he was able to perceive what lay ahead more clearly and quickly than most men, and he parlayed this innate gift into a great business and personal fortune. As he sensed a rising South, he was more convinced that his own future efforts must be directed toward industrial construction. And he was becoming restless.

At 1934 New Year's Eve parties, bands everywhere played Roosevelt's "Happy Days Are Here Again," and everyone welcomed in what they hoped would be the best year since 1928. And Charlie Daniel was even more certain that Townsend should expand into industrial construction. Mary Neese remembers "Mr. Daniel told me that I would not work at the newspaper very long, because some day he would have his own company and he wanted me to come back when that happened." So as he ripped off pages on the 1934 calendar he intensified his persuasion for an industrial construction division at Townsend or a new company, but Keith Prevost still would not agree.

However, Prevost did change his mind before the end of the year, and in early December he and Daniel worked out financial arrangements for a new company. Others within Townsend, along with Frank Brownlee, who carred the firm's insurance, had helped convince Prevost. As a matter of fact, Brownlee, a close and lifelong friend, recalled: "Charlie said that I talked Keith into going into business with him; and if it hadn't been for me, he didn't think there would ever have been a Daniel Construction Company."

Another friend, Beaty Jackson, formerly vice president of South Carolina National Bank and a lifelong resident of Anderson County, was closely involved in the financial affairs of Daniel from the beginning. "Keith Prevost was a very conservative and good businessman," Jackson recalled. "He was extremely conservative and he didn't like to borrow much money to get those larger jobs, which had to be financed, that Charlie was seeking. So Charlie decided, I think, just to go out on his own and establish Daniel Construction Company. But there was no break between Charlie and Keith. It was just a difference of opinion, and Prevost was not as young as Charlie. He was ambitious, but he didn't want to move as fast as Charlie did. They kept up their relationship as long as Keith lived. It was always a congenial relationship." As a matter of fact, Prevost bought a significant amount of stock in Charlie's company to help him get started.

As for establishing the new company, Jackson said, "I have a very vivid recollection of that. Charlie brought his statement to the bank and talked with Jeff Shumate, then vice president and cashier of the bank, and me. His statement showed $20,000 in the bank and $5,000 in equipment. As long as I stayed at SCN, Charlie remained a good customer. At times, through the volume of business he did on limited capital, he was rather pressed for money, but any bank was always glad to make a loan to him. They respected his judgment as well as his ability and integrity. At the end of each year, while I was connected with the bank, he would bring his statement in there in person, and it showed a profit every year." That was something Daniel did all his life with his numerous bankers even when he did not need to borrow.

CHAPTER 3

A Vision Takes Shape

The records show that the company's application for a South Carolina charter was filed December 17, 1934, by F. K. Prevost and Charles E. Daniel. The charter noted that "the name of the proposed corporation is Daniel Construction Company; that the principal place of business is Anderson, South Carolina." It showed that the amount of capital was $25,000 and that the stock was divided into 250 shares with a par value of $100.

The charter also explained the general nature of the business to be conducted by the new company: "That of a general construction business; buying, selling, owning and in such other manner as the corporation may deem desirable, dealing in real estate, lumber, building materials and supplies and merchandise of any and every kind; building and constructing houses and structures of every nature and kind; constructing or to cause such houses and such structures to be done and constructed."

The charter was signed and issued by South Carolina Secretary of State, W. P. Blackwell. It was recorded in the Anderson County courthouse at 9:50 a.m., December 18, 1934, in charter book No. 2, page 553, as noted by Bogue C. Young, clerk of court. Young's son, Joseph, for many years a salesman at Sullivan Hardware Company in Anderson, was a close friend of Daniel and often assisted in estimating hardware costs on major projects.

Two interesting points about that charter:

— It is the official confirmation of 1934 as the year that Charlie's company was established; many stories have listed the founding year as 1935.
— "Industrial construction" was not spelled out in the description of the company's proposed business, yet that service was inconspicuously covered in the all-encompassing clause: "Building and constructing houses and structures of every

17

nature and kind." Daniel has in fact constructed industrial facilities of every nature and kind throughout the United States and in many foreign countries.

The by-laws provided that the business and property of the new corporation be managed by a board of directors elected by stockholders and that each director own company stock. The shareholders held their first meeting December 11, 1934, "for the purpose of organizing Daniel Construction Company." They elected Charles E. Daniel, F. Keith Prevost, R. Hugh Daniel, Charles F. Dunham and Pearl A. Moore directors for 1935, all except Hugh Daniel being officers and stockholders in Townsend. Between them they owned all of the new company's stock. Banker Jackson said, "For the shares they held in Daniel, the same were held in reverse in Townsend."

With Prevost acting as chairman of the board, the directors immediately elected the following officers for the new year: Charlie Daniel, president and assistant treasurer; Prevost, secretary and treasurer; and Hugh Daniel and Dunham, vice presidents. A year later, minutes of a December 31, 1935, board meeting showed Charlie Daniel serving as both chairman and president and noted that the company's capital stock had been increased to $50,000, the first of numerous increases in the company's capitalization.

Board meetings were held conveniently in the Townsend building because the integrated directorship agreed there was no need for Charlie to move to another location and thus increase his operating costs. He continued to work out of his old office and used the secretarial services of Pearl Moore. Since there was, in fact, no visible change at Townsend, clients and the public found it rather difficult to distinguish between the two companies. They solved the problem by simply referring to the firms as Townsend and "Charlie's company."

So Daniel Construction Company was known from the beginning as "Charlie's company;" and that is what many still call it even after the founder's death in 1964, the public sale of the company's stock in 1969, its corporate name change in 1971, and its acquisition by Fluor Corporation in 1977.

Perpetuation by yet another generation and tens of thousands of new employees of one man's personality and business philosophy has been widely accepted as a tribute to his reputation and as a lasting testimonial to the "Daniel way" of doing business. This respect first became evident in the summer of 1936 when the growing company needed more space. Daniel added a second floor to the

Townsend building and moved upstairs. Even so, separate offices and a company sign left it nontheless "Charlie's company."

Both Daniel and Townsend had enjoyed a profitable year in 1935, even though the South had not completely shaken loose from the depression. At any rate, Daniel's volume of business was such that Charlie could afford his own secretary and he rehired Mary Neese in the summer of 1935. He was soon to add three new men: C. A. (Doc) Thrasher, chief engineer; Carl Englund, engineer and estimator; and T. Ree McCoy, an experienced superintendent. Ed Moore was unable to supervise all of the work in South Carolina, and Lawrence Yeargin was staying busy in Alabama, where Hugh Daniel was making noises about opening a Daniel division. The year ended with the company showing net earnings of $3,000. It received a $6.05 tax credit from the Treasury Department because its $484.80 tax payment was in excess of the amount due.

1936 was a significant year. The company completed its first major project — four barracks for nearby Clemson College — and the buildings were dedicated November 14, three days after Charlie's 41st birthday. Even so, the volume of work for the 12 months was down from the previous same period; but a year later, with money coming in from construction started in 1936, earnings rose to $9,000. Taxes increased too, with the beginning of Social Security. The minutes of a 1936 board meeting noted that the company had over a million dollars of contract business for the immediate future.

1936 was an expansion year. The Daniel brothers agreed to establish the first regional division, Daniel Construction Company of Alabama, with headquarters in Birmingham. Englund was transferred there to assist Hugh Daniel. The corporate office was also flexing its expansion muscles, crowding the Townsend-Daniel quarters. This prompted construction of the second floor and the move upstairs.

1936 was a tragic year, too. Daniel was constructing a school building in Gainesville, Georgia; and on April 6, a tornado struck that town. It left death and destruction in its wake and next struck Anderson with fatal and destructive force. The damage to Daniel was light. The steel in the new Gainesville school was twisted; the timekeeper's shack on the site was blown three blocks without serious injury to the occupant; and a large tree smashed the garage at the Daniel residence on the Boulevard as the tornado swept on to Anderson. Weeks later, empty Daniel pay envelopes, scattered by the Georgia storm, were found in Walhalla, South Carolina, about 60 miles east of Gainesville.

The storm wreaked considerable property damage in Anderson County as well as in the Gainesville area, and Daniel helped restore the buildings in both states. The most critical jobs were repairing or replacing roofs on industrial and commercial structures; and since Daniel was not then nor is now in the roofing business, that portion of the work was subbed out to J. Roy Martin & Company. That roofing firm was established in Anderson in 1928, and it became one of the South's largest. Much of its roofing over the years was applied to many buildings and plants constructed by Daniel.

The JRM Roofing Review recorded the company's history in the 1978 spring issue and made this reference to Daniel: "Two major events marked the decade of the thirties. In '31, J. Roy acquired the assets of John T. Burris and Son, and moved two blocks down the street into their shop at 305 West Market Street. . . . The second event was the formation of Daniel Construction Company just three blocks down Tower Street from the shop. This was the beginning of the giant corporaton which is now among the largest construction companies in the world. . . . The war years were busy ones. The tie with Daniel Construction Company was close. The two companies worked together for several years at the Charleston Navy Yard. A tire cord plant which they built at Clemson, South Carolina, marked the first time the company used women on a roof. The post-war years produced a rapid expansion in the textile industry in the Southeast. The company applied the roofs on many new plants (constructed by Daniel) ranging from Virginia to Florida, and as far west as Alabama and Mississippi."

The Daniel-Martin association had meant much to both companies over the years; and on the occasion of the roofing company's 50th anniversary dinner June 2, 1978, Buck Mickel was the principal speaker. He reviewed the relationship between the two owners and their firms and told of the total confidence Daniel and the senior Martin had in each other. "When Charlie established his company he found people who could run with him," Mickel said, "and that's how our two companies got together. In those early years there was no such thing as a purchase order. They simply shook hands to close a deal, and to them that was more binding than a piece of paper."

As close as they were, however, Martin and Daniel would "rant and rave," Mickel recalled. "Charlie would tell Roy that there was no way he could lay 100 roofing squares in the prescribed time. Roy would tell Charlie he didn't know anything about roofing and to go lay his bricks. On one such occasion Charlie offered to bet Roy a new hat. Roy told him, 'It will have to be a $20 hat, and you can't afford it.' They were all business in their work, but they were also great friends, having their fun as well as their arguments."

A fire in the Daniel office on Christmas Eve 1963 destroyed some historical company records, and a few others have been lost over the years. Therefore, information on the company's revenues prior to 1944 is incomplete; yet the substantial yearly increases in net earnings, net worth and total assets during the first decade indicate significant volumes in both construction and maintenance work. Any reference to Daniel's growth and its continuing success would be incomplete without inclusion of its maintenance and mill-wright (mechanical) services, which it has always provided. It should be noted that these services were performed by the construction divisions for the first 27 years, and it was not until 1961 that this specific operation received its own identity. The Maintenance & Millwright Department (M&M) was established that year, and grew to divisional status within three years. In 1975, with the addition of regional offices in several southern and southwestern states, it became the M&M Group, one of the company's major profit centers with more than 8,000 skilled craftsmen.

M&M represents a broad term by Daniel's definition because of its contract flexibility and its wide range of services to practically every type of industry. It is generally agreed by both the company and its clients that there is no job that M&M will not tackle in any industry. Basically, its services extend to construction, mechanical, electrical and instrumentation disciplines, as well as relocation, repair and the continuing maintenance of process machinery and equipment. As for actual construction work, M&M makes minor plant additions, but it does not build grass-roots plants.

When Daniel began knocking on doors to obtain industrial work for his new company, he had to convince plant managers and owners that he could produce. So his first projects were relatively small and consisted of little more than the type of work M&M performs. Contracts in 1935 included odd jobs at textile plants in South Carolina; and because he produced as he promised, that work led to the construction of grass-roots plants when the textile industry began expanding. Along with the increasing amount of industrial work, Daniel continued to do a substantial volume of commercial and institutional building, the largest contract during the first two years being the barracks at Clemson. They were built adjacent to Riggs Field, where the Clemson Tigers played their home football games, and were an added convenience for cadets and their guests who could watch the games from their barracks windows during inclement weather.

The young company, coming off a lean fiscal 1936, experienced its first corporate realignment in early 1937 when the Daniel brothers acquired the stock held in the company by Dunham and Moore. At the same time, Charlie Daniel assumed additional responsibilities as treasurer, a title previously held by Prevost, who became an assistant treasurer. This was reported in the minutes of the January 14, 1937, board meeting along with the approval of salaries for the top officers for the year: $18,000 for Charlie and $7,600 for Hugh Daniel, the then-manager of the Alabama Division and corporate vice president and assistant treasurer.

The company reached major milestones in the next three years. One was its first million-dollar project, the Jefferson Hospital in Birmingham (1938). The other was its first multimillion-dollar job (1941), the sprawling Reynolds Metals plant in Sheffield, Alabama, which cost approximately $8 million. Each of those contracts was cause for celebration both in the Alabama Division and at corporate headquarters.

Additional work meant increased employment. With Carl Englund staying busy estimating jobs for the Alabama Division, the decision was to leave him there; and C. W. Thomas was hired in Anderson in 1938 as chief estimator in the corporate office. W. E. (Gene) Watt had come aboard a year earlier as the first full-time bookkeeper, and J. Blake Moose joined the company in 1938; each of them was destined to play important roles over the next three decades.

As result of its work on the "quad" barracks, Daniel received additional projects on the Clemson campus, including the Sirrine Textile Building, and Watt joined the company just in time to help estimate them. He recalls, "We worked night and day, and Mrs. Daniel would come to the office in the evening and make coffee for us." He had agreed to go to work for $135 a month, but his first paycheck was for $150. "I received a raise before I was ever paid," he said, "and that extra amount was enough for me to get married on." (Another Clemson barracks was built in 1938.)

Everyone who had any contact with Charlie Daniel was familiar with his incessant drive and with it, his impatience. They respected his ability to get the job done and his bulldog tenacity, which accounted for Daniel's obtaining some work that otherwise would have gone to other contractors. Watt recalled a prime example of such tenacious action: "The boss asked me to make an inspection trip to our Oconee Mills project in Westminster, about 45 miles northwest of Anderson. That was sometime in 1938. He said he would drive to Pickens, just a few miles out of the way, to inquire when bids would be let for a plant planned there by Poinsett Lumber & Manufacturing Company, a subsidiary of Singer Company. I stayed in the car while he was in the office at Pickens; and when he returned, I could tell he was upset. He told me Daniel had not been placed on the bid list, as he was assured it would be. He drove on to Westminster, rather fast, I might add. We stayed at the site there only a few minutes and returned to Anderson. He couldn't get that Pickens job off his mind; and before we reached our office, he told me he was going to Singer's office in New York and see about that bid."

Watt said Daniel rode the Southern Railway from Greenville to New York that Thursday night and visited Singer's offices Friday morning. He was advised that there must have been a mix-up on the bid list; and if he could have his bid in by the next Monday morning when they were to be opened, his price would be considered along with the others. "Mr. Daniel telephoned Doc Thrasher in our office and told him to go to Pickens and get all of the plans available on the new building. He called Hugh Daniel in Birmingham and told him to come to Anderson and to bring Carl Englund with him. He called a steel company, I don't remember the one, and asked that it send a man to our office to estimate the cost of steel to be used in the building. Keep in mind, that was on Friday. Mr. Daniel rode the train back from New York, and we worked all weekend, day and night, and finished the estimate. Mr. Daniel caught the train in Greenville Sunday night, and on Monday morning he was in the Singer office with his bid. And we got the job. Or I should say, he got the job. He was a hustler, there ain't no doubt." Records show that it was a $236,253 project, or well over a million dollars if built in 1980.

Watt joined the company on October 4, 1937, and retired on February 28, 1969. He lived an exciting part of Daniel's history, more than three decades, during which time the company never had a bad year, with net earnings rising from $9,000 in 1937 to $3,751,000 during the fiscal year of his retirement. He was more than a bookkeeper — his first assignment — and much more than corporate assistant secretary and assistant treasurer; he was a person in whom Daniel had complete confidence, a 100-percent loyal employee. He respected the authority of others, yet he always knew that "the man I reported to was Mr. Daniel."

Even after his retirement, Watt refused to discuss some matters, taking what may be called the Daniel fifth amendment. To certain questions, he would say, "I think that is something Mr. Daniel wouldn't want me to talk about." To him, "Mr. Daniel was the boss as long as he lived; and he ran the company, all of it." To make his point, Watt said, "Mr. Daniel would call me into his office and tell me that we should write the minutes of the directors' meeting. I would tell him the meeting was still two or three days away, and he would tell me he knew that, but he also knew what would be done in the meeting, so let's get on with the minutes. I would write them, and he would read them at the meeting, and that was that. He was the boss. It was his company."

Blake Moose also helped make company history for 31 years. He joined Daniel on December 4, 1938, and this is how he recalled the occasion: "I had worked at Potter-Shackelford Construction Company and later at Liberty Life in Greenville. I left Liberty Life because me and their manager got into an argument. He decided the company didn't need me, and that was okay with me, and I told him so. Since I had some construction experience, I went to Anderson to see if I could get a job with Daniel. They didn't need me there, but told me their Birmingham office was about to start a job in Columbus, Mississippi, and to contact Carl Englund. I knew Carl, so I wrote him a letter. He telegraphed me, asking when I could come to work and what salary did I expect. I wired back that I could come immediately for $35 a week. He wired me that he would pay me $25 a week. I simply wired him back, advising that I would take it."

Moose had the privilege of staking out Daniel's Birmingham office building, the first of numerous company-owned offices to be built in several states. "I staked it out on Saturday afternoon before going to Columbus," he said. "In those days we didn't know what 40 hours a week meant, or eight-hour days. There was no such thing. If we had something to do, we did it." For the next seven years Moose held a variety of jobs in the Alabama Division, including timekeeper, superintendent, purchasing agent, and expeditor. During that time he built a reputation. He cursed suppliers and union business agents alike over the telephone or in person. He was the buyer of all materials on the large Southtown Housing project in Birmingham in the early 1940's; and at one time, about 40 brickmasons were standing around one day waiting for the ready-mixed mortar trucks. Moose got on the telephone and ranted, raved and cursed, but could get no action from the cement company; so he went to the plant and asked for a Mr. Brown, with whom he had dealt on other jobs. When he confronted the oft-harrassed supplier, Brown roared: "You s.o.b. little runt, if I'd known you were no bigger than that, I'd been over there and beat hell out of you a hundred times." Moose said later, "He could have squashed me with one hand if he had wanted to. I weighed only 130 pounds."

Suppliers in Alabama were relieved, Moose felt, when he was transferred to the home office on March 4, 1945, to be Daniel's first full-time purchasing agent. George Ross, acting purchasing agent during the war, returned to his building supplies business in Greenville. Moose was the whole purchasing department at that time; but as the volume of business grew he added agents and secretaries and even "tried a woman as a purchasing agent one time, but she didn't work out." He was appointed director of purchasing, again the company's first; but years later he had forgotten the date, and there was no record. It was typical of the simple manner in which Charlie Daniel operated. "Mr. Daniel told me time and again that I was his director of purchasing," Moose recalled, "but what date he walked into my office and told me to sign my letters and purchase orders as the director of purchasing, I couldn't say." Nor did he remember when he was appointed vice president, purchasing — again Daniel's first.

Charlie Daniel believed in young people and felt that they should be given responsibilities. He reasoned that, "If a man doesn't have responsibilities and the opportunity to make mistakes, then how is he ever going to do anything?" His philosophy also made provisions for human error: "If a man makes a mistake and you clobber him, what have you accomplished? You sit down with him and go over it, yes; but you don't stomp on him and kill his spirit. If the spirit isn't there, you've lost the man."

In that vein, Mickel recalls: "When Charlie felt that somebody had it, he concentrated on working him to death, his theory being that a good man could not be overworked. Unless you crowd the man you believe has what it takes to advance in the company, how are you going to know how good he really is? That was Charlie's philosophy all of his life, and it holds true today. I believe in it, and it is still practiced throughout this company."

One of the first young men to experience the Daniel philosophy, or more aptly "the Daniel way," was Langdon Cheves, a spirited redheaded engineer. He was a student employee during part of the construction of the Clemson barracks; and when he graduated from that college in 1936, he was given a full-time job, working either for Daniel or Townsend, depending on the workload. In March 1939, he quit his $20-a-week job with Townsend, not knowing if Daniel could use him. Daniel could, and started him as a $35-a-week project manager on a state hospital complex at Milledgeville, Georgia. The larger salary prompted Cheves to buy a new car for $750 for the trip to Milledgeville.

Cheves was a second lieutenant in the Army reserve, having been commissioned upon graduation from Clemson. As Adolf Hitler's Nazis began blowing war clouds over Europe, there was talk in the United States of calling up the reserves. After two other projects following Milledgeville, Cheves knew he would be called for active duty; so he decided to go ahead and put in what he thought would be only one year of military training. As it developed, of course, World War II changed the personal plans of millions of young men. So Cheves, who reported for duty in January of 1941, did not rejoin Daniel until 1946.

Cheves served with the Corps of Engineers as a full colonel and was assigned to the Alaskan Highway defense project. He and a young Canadian bridge engineer, George E. McDougall, became close friends; and by the time VJ Day was celebrated and GIs were trying to get home for Christmas 1945, Cheves had talked his friend into coming to the States and joining Daniel. It was a wise decision, because by 1968 McDougall had worked his way up to the position of vice president and general manager of Daniel Construction Company International. Cheves, too, progressed rapidly in the post-war construction boom, and his associates believed he would have become president of Daniel except for his fatal automobile accident January 3, 1955. His three sons now work for Daniel.

Roger Milliken, another young redhead of strong character and untiring drive, entered Daniel's life in 1939. They had so much in common and complemented each other so well that they became key figures in the industrialization of the South — each in his own way, but often together. What initiated the relationship was the Millikens' decision to expand their textile business into woolens. A run-down bankrupt cotton mill in Union, South Carolina, was chosen as the place to begin. When Roger Milliken inspected the old mill that he and his father had purchased, he knew that a considerable amount of construction would be required both inside and outside to prepare the building for the installation of a new woolen manufacturing equipment system. Milliken was new to the area, so he asked about leading contractors who could do the job. Daniel was among those recommended.

When Daniel visited the plant looking for Milliken, he saw a fellow with a broom sweeping out what had once been an office. After introductions, Daniel helped Milliken finish the cleaning chore. Then they sat on the porch of the office and discussed what needed to be done to refurbish and restore the building to production status.

Milliken said later, "It was obvious that this had to be a cost-plus job because there were all sorts of unknowns about what we'd find when we dug up the floor and so forth. The other contractor with whom I had talked offered to do the work at cost plus 10 percent. Charlie Daniel said he was prepared to work on a cost-plus-eight-percent basis in the interest of developing a relationship with our company. It was on that basis that we said, all right, we'd go ahead; and this was the first of many, many jobs that Daniel has done for us over the years. When they have been on a cost-plus basis and not a bid job — and there have been many of each — we always just proceeded with a discussion of the job and a handshake. This proved to be a very outstanding arrangement, and I am not aware that we have ever had any problems of any kind in so doing." That arrangement between the two companies continues.

Elaborating on the Milliken-Daniel relationship, which has now resulted in Daniel's building 44 grass-roots plants or major expansions to existing facilities, Milliken explained: "We always awarded our business to Daniel when it was the case of building something that we wanted in a hurry and couldn't put out for bids. It was on complicated jobs; and this was to the despair of his competition in neighboring states who couldn't understand why we didn't want to bring in other people. I think one of the reasons for this is because we knew Charlie and his organization. We had a relationship where he assigned outstanding construction superintendents to our jobs. We believe that the ability of the superintendent assigned to the job is of paramount importance in building. As we got to know them and had confidence in them, the same men over and over again were assigned to our jobs. They knew how we worked, and they knew our engineering personnel. It's turned out to be a very excellent, effective and happy arrangement."

Milliken was one of the first major companies to move its main offices to the South, locating its headquarters in Spartanburg, South Carolina, in 1958. He explained: "As I was getting into business, I found that I was spending two weeks in the South where our plants were located, where the majority of the people were located, and two weeks in New York where I was born and brought up. One out of those two weeks was largely taken up with dealing with mail and administrative things that could be handled anywhere I had an office. So it became rather obvious, I thought, that the headquarters of our operations, of our company, should be where the majority of the people were located, and not in New York, which for historical reasons had been the place where the company had grown up. We also at that time had a vision of building a research organization, and it was obvious that this belonged as close to the manufacturing operations as possible." Daniel also built the Milliken headquarters and research complex.

Many of the weeks Milliken spent in the South those first few years were spent in Greenville. He stayed at the Poinsett Hotel and worked out of an office in the new Daniel headquarters established in the city in early 1942. At the time, Milliken and Daniel were working with Sirrine engineers on a tire cord plant to be constructed near Clemson College. It was one of America's early defense projects. The manufacturing facility, known as DeFore, and still in operation, was the first in the South to be fully air-conditioned and completely enclosed without windows. It established a trend, and Daniel has built numerous similar facilities.

Daniel devoted its full time and all of its resources to the defense program and to the total war effort. Military projects included the Army Air Base (later named Donaldson) in Greenville; shipyards at Charleston, Savannah, and Brunswick; and thousands of housing units at Navy yards and other military bases in South Carolina, Georgia and Alabama.

In that time frame, the company had become an exclusive Daniel firm and Charlie had begun to weigh the advantages of moving the corporate offices from Anderson to Greenville, a larger city about 30 miles away on U. S. 29 North. The move did not interest Prevost; but just as he had helped Charlie start a business of his own, he would not try to discourage a move that might well accelerate the company's growth. Prevost's reasoning was that he was not getting any younger; he was satisfied with being president of Townsend Lumber Company; his sons were preparing to pursue other careers; and he enjoyed living in Anderson.

So at Daniel's October 6, 1939, board meeting in its offices on the second floor of the Townsend building, Prevost explained why he did not want to be included in Charlie's future plans. An exchange of Townsend and Daniel stock was negotiated, and Prevost resigned as corporate secretary, assistant treasurer and director of Daniel, thus freeing himself of all responsibilities except those of managing Townsend.

Homozel Mickel Daniel, elected a director earlier that year, succeeded Prevost as secretary. She, her husband and Hugh Daniel remained the officers and directors without further change in the organization until 1955, at which time Charlie assumed the official position of chairman of the board and Hugh was elected president and treasurer. Board membership was increased to four in 1962, with the election of Buck Mickel, who had been promoted to executive vice president in 1960.

The directors voted at their January 1941 meeting to expand operations into North Carolina and Tennessee, and at the July meeting they changed the end of the fiscal year to September 30. The most important decision reached at that meeting, however, was the purchase of an office building lot on North Main Street in Greenville either for a branch office or to "change the company's principal place of business."

CHAPTER 4

A Move and a World War

As it developed, the Reynolds Metals plant in Alabama became the first of many Daniel defense projects. The job was placed on a crash program in early 1941 and was completed in 179 24-hour workdays, including the installation of diversified and heavy equipment to convert ore into metal. It was recognized at the time as a world record for construction and equipment erection of a plant of this kind. The schedule was so pressing that work had to be started before the Sirrine Company completed detailed drawings and was continued without delay and in step with the progress of engineering and architectural plans. This exemplified the teamwork between owner, engineer and contractor. The Singer plant at Pickens, completed two years earlier, was a late-classified defense project since it eventually manufactured parts for rifles.

Daniel was awarded 72 separate contracts by the Bureau of Yards and Docks for six major projects at the U. S. Navy Yard in Charleston in 1941. Among the time-pressing construction jobs were drydocks, shops, warehouses, piers, railroad lines and yards, a hospital, cafeterias and other structures of a permanent character. One of the outstanding projects was a $3.5 million permanent outfitting dock large enough to handle several ships at one time; and perhaps the most unusual was a complete underground fuel supply system that covered yard requirements, including bunker-oil loading of a considerable number of ships simultaneously. The variety of structures called into use every item of equipment the company owned, including pile drivers, cranes, compressors, dirt movers, pumps, welders and concrete mixers. Design and supervision were a collaboration of the Bureau of Yards and Docks and Sirrine engineers.

Almost at the same time as the Charleston projects, Daniel was working with Sirrine for the Southeastern Shipbuilding Corporation at Savannah. Southeastern had to provide more than just a shipyard. Over 2,400 housing units with all of the utilities of a city

29

were required, and Daniel worked with Cletus W. Bergen, architect, on that project. While the two major operations were separate contracts, they were interlocked in the same time schedule; and both contributed to the array of "firsts," which were achievements undisclosed to the general public at the time because of tight government security. Daniel was never in a position to determine the status of primacy in any of its wartime operations. The company later learned that Southeastern Shipyard was credited with the lowest cost per shipway, the shortest time for completion per way, and an extremely low cost per ton of completed shipping. Also, the housing operation was designated as the first completed in point of time and as the lowest in cost.

Donaldson Air Force Base in Greenville was a joint construction project, with Daniel working in association with A. H. Guion & Company and with the Army performing the engineering. The runways and buildings called for $21 million of fast, substantial construction. The base has since been developed into an industrial park, and Daniel has erected two large facilities there following its conversion. Several of the original military buildings constructed by Daniel have been converted to commercial or industrial use, and the nine-hole golf course built for Army personnel is now open to the public.

Construction of the air base coincided with Daniel's move to Greenville in February 1942. The minutes note that the last board meeting held in Anderson was on February 16 of that year. Two weeks later on March 2, the directors met for the first time at their new headquarters in Greenville. The minutes of the June board meeting made the first reference to the word "Incorporated" being added to the corporate name.

Only four people were working in the corporate office when Daniel Construction Company left the second floor of Townsend Lumber Company in Anderson and occupied the new offices in Greenville. Making that historic move were Charlie Daniel, Gene Watt, "Doc" Thrasher and Mary Neese. C. W. Thomas, the fifth member of the staff, had already moved to Charleston as project manager on the Navy Yard work.

Those four had been busy in Anderson for several months working up air base project estimates, and in early January the three men set up temporary offices in the new building in Greenville. A makeshift move, it nevertheless eliminated numerous trips to Greenville and expedited the estimating. Daniel was awarded the air base contract in late January, and Englund was named project manager. A few weeks after the signing, Charlie Daniel walked into the Anderson office and told Miss Neese, "Well, it's time to move."

The decision that particular day was typical of his quick reaction to developments. The new offices were ready for permanent occupancy, and there was much work to be done.

The major moving task fell to Miss Neese. It was the secretary's responsibility to see that each box of material accumulated during the first full seven years of business was properly marked. It was she who would also make certain that all those boxes were emptied into the proper files and desk drawers in the new building; so, having completed the first phase of the transfer, she went to Greenville to meet the moving van.

The van arrived at 10 p.m. Ordinarily, the job of unpacking would have been put off until the next day. But those were not ordinary times. A war was on, and Daniel was charged with a substantial volume of defense work. The men were busy getting the air base project organized while movers unloaded the boxes of letters, contracts, drawings and other material. As the tired secretary began assorting the contents, a stranger stepped up and introduced himself as J. C. Keys, Jr. He told her he was a printer and that his company, Keys Printing, had done some work for Daniel in recent weeks, and "I just wanted to be here when the truck arrived so that I could help you unpack."

That was the beginning of a lasting friendship, because Keys continues to be Daniel's primary printer. He is not the company's exclusive printer, yet so little of the business goes elsewhere that other printers think he is. "I learned from the beginning," Keys said later, "that Mr. Daniel stressed quality, speed and service. That is what he gave his customers, and that is what we gave him. Doing that, we have been able to serve the company all of these years." When Keys Printing expanded from its downtown headquarters in 1973, nine years after the death of his good friend Charlie Daniel, there was never any doubt about who would design and construct the new plant off I-385. Daniel had it ready for occupancy in December of that year.

With Keys' help, Miss Neese had the transfer boxes emptied into the new files and desks by midnight. She and her three equally weary associates drove to their homes in Anderson. At 8 o'clock the next morning, all four were back at work in the new headquarters. "We were young then," Miss Neese said, "and nobody really thought anything about working late at night, or on Saturdays and Sundays. We had so many defense projects going in Charleston, Savannah and Brunswick, among other places, that our work kept piling up. As busy as all of us were, Mr. Daniel worked harder than we did. He set the pace and we tried to keep up. He was that way all of his life."

Moving the corporate offices did not stop the round trips for a while, because the four staff people still lived in Anderson. Joseph E. Sirrine, head of the architectural and engineering firm bearing his name, and Daniel were close friends; and Sirrine offered to share his residence with Mr. and Mrs. Daniel until they found a house. Daniel built a house on Crescent Avenue and occupied it in April 1942. His associates had moved to Greenville in the meantime, so when Mr. and Mrs. Daniel took over their new house, the corporate transfer from Anderson was complete.

Many of the craft and mechanical employees joined Daniel's move to Greenville. Ray Fant, one of them, is singled out because he was the first of thousands of blacks to be employed by Daniel and one of the most popular and respected of all employees. Fant first worked for "the Captain," as he referred to Daniel, in 1932 at Townsend and immediately hired on as a laborer when the new company was established two years later. He was not a laborer for long because he could drive trucks and anything else on wheels. Herman Case, traffic manager in the Equipment Division, estimates that during Fant's 42 years on Daniel's payroll he drove approximately three million miles. Fant was never involved in a motor vehicle accident, one reason why he so often chauffeured Mrs. Daniel, even up until a few years after his retirement in 1976.

Fant was also chosen to drive "the Captain's" car on various business trips, but summed up that brief experience as having ridden in the back seat more than behind the steering wheel "because I just didn't drive fast enough to suit the boss." For many years he was assigned to the "Green Monster," a chrome-trimmed green road tractor that pulled an equally decorated low-boy to numerous Daniel ground-breakings throughout the Southeast. He treated the vehicles assigned to him as his own, including Mrs. Daniel's limousine; and his name was printed on the doors of the tractor, a token of respect by Equiment Division management. Such respect was shown further at his retirement party attended by Mrs. Daniel and other directors and officers of the company.

The Greenville move carried much significance in that it placed the company in the heart of the expanding textile industry, nearer several engineering firms, and ended the joint venture enterprise between Townsend and Daniel with the closing of its offices in the Townsend Building. Oddly enough, four years later, Daniel became a major stockholder in Ross Builders Supplies, a newly established company headed by George Ross, the former part-time purchasing agent. That company purchased Townsend and several other similar businesses in the Piedmont and was in turn eventually bought by

Wickes, a national lumber and building supplies firm. Wickes later became a Daniel client.

During the legal transaction of conveying Townsend to Ross, the former was declared a defunct company with Mary Neese and Gene Watt appointed secretary and treasurer, respectively. On August 31, 1946, Miss Neese married Anthony A. Rubino, but her maiden name remained on the legal documents until the Townsend-Ross transaction was completed later that year. During her brief honeymoon trip the first week in September, Daniel telephoned Mrs. Mary Rubino to tell her how nice it would be for her to hurry back to work. He explained that the government had just cleared the defense project photos that had delayed publication of the company's first sales brochure originally planned in May 1942. She had worked on it with the Ullman Advertising Agency of Philadelphia; therefore, she could appreciate the urgency of his call. Even so, she let the brochure wait a few days longer. In years to follow, Ullman prepared other sales books, designed the company's first logo and handled its advertising until shortly after Daniel established its own in-house public relations and advertising services in January 1964.

That original brochure featured black-and-white photographs of the first 36 major projects constructed by Daniel up to the beginning of World War II. The pictures of defense installations that delayed publication because of wartime security included the 1941-42 Quartermaster Port of Embarkation at Charleston, a variety of military housing in Alabama, and the Reynolds and Singer plants. The engineering firms with which Daniel worked during that period and the number of projects for each included: Sirrine, 14; Chas. H. McCauley, 8; Warren, Knight & Davis, 5; J. P. Stevens and Lockwood-Greene 2 each; and single projects with Edward F. Sibbert, Miller, Martin & Lewis, Odis Clay Poundstone, Coleman Engineering, W. S. Schultz, Alfred M. Marks and Barker & Turoff.

Twenty of the projects were located in Alabama: in Birmingham there were a Sears store, the original Daniel office, Jefferson County Hospital, First National Bank, Southtown Housing and Noland Warehouse; high schools in Haleyville, Gordo and Vergon; a county jail in Marion; industrial plants in Sheffield, Gadsden, Jasper and Anniston; a hospital at Cullman; and a University of Alabama dormitory and a Kress store in Tuscaloosa.

The 13 projects located in South Carolina were mostly industrial. Among them were the Industrial Mills and boiler house at Rock Hill; the Appleton Mill addition in Anderson; two separate jobs for Ware Shoals Manufacturing Company; a substantial amount of expansion work for Graniteville Manufacturing Company and Gregg Dyeing and Finishing in Graniteville; the Singer and Charleston Navy Yard projects; a high school in Easley; and the company's original office building in Greenville. Rounding out the Daniel construction shown in the brochure were two projects in Georgia — Rodgers Hosiery at Athens and Rome High School — and one North Carolina job — Beacon Manufacturing Company at Swannanoa.

Daniel received several other defense contracts before the Germans surrendered on May 7, 1945, and two atomic bombs were dropped on Japan in August, ending the war. The larger projects included an in-transit depot and supply depot at the new Army Air Base in Moncks Corner, South Carolina, and an Air Force training base built for Southern Airways at Camden, South Carolina. The Moncks Corner facility was a takeoff point for overseas travel and a stopoff point in long-flight training, especially during the earlier period of the war. At this particular base, special equipment for overseas flying was installed in "the birds of passage." This outfitting required that more or different warehouses, shops, railroad trackage, and testing and control laboratories be installed than would be done for a training field. The runways were longer, and the barracks were different, in that part of them were for transient use. In summary, it was a big job spread over a wide area and built under wartime pressure.

Other Alabama projects during the war included defense housing in Talladega and a supply depot at the Gadsden Air Base. The Alabama Division also was heavily involved in the Savannah project, Hugh Daniel having moved there as project manager. He later handled the combined shipyards and housing (2,000 units) project at Brunswick until he went into service as a naval procurement officer. Daniel also was called on to expand industrial plants for wartime materials: at the Beacon mill for storage of its blankets for the Army; and at Judson Mills in Greenville, which manufactured fabric for officers' coats.

Numerous official commendations were bestowed upon Daniel for its wartime efforts, tokens of recognition for thousands of craftsmen that spurred them on through the long succession of projects. Their pride in serving their country in this manner and their seven-day workweeks made it possible for Daniel to complete all of these contracts ahead of schedule and below estimated cost.

Gene Watt, looking back on the wartime projects, recalled, "We had been working like hell; all of us. They just closed the Birmingham office, except for a secretary, and the men there went to the Savannah or Brunswick jobs.

"All of them moved to some defense project. Hugh Daniel was busy on them until he went into the Navy. Charlie Daniel was all over the place, keeping up with current work and taking on more as the government stepped up its building program."

Watt said, "When the war ended, I thought well, thank the Lord, now we'll get some rest. But, you know, every industrial company, it seemed, had their expansion plans drawn; and they brought them out as soon as the war was over. We just went to work again. Never did slow down. That is when Daniel began making money — real money — after the war."

The retired assistant treasurer remembered, "A lot of people thought Mr. Daniel made his money during the war. That's not so. We had our best year by far in 1948, and it stood as the best year until 1957."

The records bear him out. The greatest amount the company earned during the war years was $235,000 in 1943. That was more than doubled in 1947 with net earnings of $558,000 on revenues of $16,302,000. The big year Watt referred to, 1948, marked the real takeoff of the industrial boom in the South. Revenues jumped to $25,207,000; and the company was getting closer to its first million-dollar year, showing earnings of $869,000, which, as Watt said, "Is mighty darn close to a million." Yet the first actual million-dollar year was a decade away.

What happened immediately after the war and has never really let up is what Charlie Daniel had anticipated when he was building textile houses in the Carolinas and Georgia: that the textile business would have to grow to meet the increasing demand for fabrics in the U. S. and abroad. In 1946, the first full peace-time year after World War II, revenues reached $7,446,000, and there was not a multimillion-dollar project among the 53 contracts awarded Daniel that year. Yet the bulk of the work was industrial, with the two largest projects totaling just over a million. The others, mostly of a maintenance nature, ranged from a few thousand dollars to $200,000 in capital expenditures.

The cost of the individual projects indicates the limited type of work being performed that year. Textile mill owners were upgrading their equipment, buying new material as it became available, and repairing or expanding existing facilities. Much of the work then was of a mechanical nature, including some air conditioning; and along with controlled temperature came the bricking up of windows in the two- and three-story plants. Also, in anticipation of the boom to come, the more enterprising mill men were building new warehouses or enlarging old ones. That, generally, was the kind of work Daniel did the first year after the war.

The million-dollar jobs came along in 1947, but even then they were not common. And they were not even all industrial, because the commercial and institutional businesses also had remained fairly dormant during the war. One project was the new Atlanta Constitution newspaper building in Atlanta at a cost of $1,385,000. Another was the Bob Jones University campus in Greenville, which ran $2,835,485.92 in unrounded figures. The only other two-million-dollar-plus projects were for Lees Cochran Company in Glasgow, Virginia, and the Dunean Mills expansion in Greenville. Fees from part of the 1947 work completed near the end of the year contributed to the "biggest year yet" earnings in 1948.

The 1948 industrial building boom for Daniel was spreading the company into new Southern territory with a substantial number of new clients. Often referred to as "a little country contractor," Daniel was gaining a reputation that would continue to spread. Much of the work that year continued in the same repair and expansion pattern as the earlier contracts following the end of the war. Yet there were new plants for Milliken, additions for J. P. Stevens, which developed into another regular customer, and an unusual amount of commercial construction. Most of the action was in South Carolina, yet there were major projects in Alabama, North Carolina and Virginia too. The million-dollar and two-million-dollar jobs were beginning to show up more often.

J. P. Stevens & Co., Inc., headquartered in New York, was well into its Southern expansion program in 1948; and Chairman Robert T. Stevens was awarding his friend Charlie Daniel contracts to remodel recently acquired mills and to construct new plants. They had first met in Anderson in the mid-1930's when Stevens, then president of the textile firm, was making frequent trips to the Greenville area. Reflecting years later on that association, which developed into a warm friendship, Stevens recalled that Daniel was awarded his first contract with the company as a result of the "bottom-dollar bid and guaranteed fast delivery." That established Stevens' confidence in Charlie and his construction company, and he began negotiating contracts with Daniel "because one of the most impressive things about Charlie was that he did what he said he would do." On one occasion Stevens needed a new mill in the shortest possible time, and arrangements for Daniel to build it were made in a telephone conversation.

The Bob Stevens-Charlie Daniel association extended beyond the construction of mills. They had much in common. Each had served as an Army officer in World War I, and they swapped stories. And in the early 1920's they were shaping their careers, separately but in the same fashion: Stevens learning the textile manufacturing business at Dunean Mills in Greenville and Daniel breaking into construction with Townsend, just 30 miles from the Dunean village. During World War II, while Daniel was busy on numerous defense projects, Stevens served as a colonel in the office of the Quartermaster General, later becoming deputy director of purchases.

Both men were respected for their drive and leadership by friends and competitors alike. Colonel Stevens was reminded of that after his retirement during a conversation with R. D. Mitchell, manager of Daniel's New York sales office. He brushed aside any remarks about himself, but reiterated that "Charlie was a great salesman. He always had a smile, and I don't know of anyone who didn't like him. He was a fast thinker, a good man to have on your team."

The colonel welcomed his constructor friend to the Stevens team in 1952 when Daniel was elected a member of the major textile firm's board of directors. However, Stevens resigned as chairman of the board at the end of that year after being designated secretary of the army by President-elect Eisenhower. Even so, their paths continued to cross, more often during the few months in late 1954 when Daniel's appointment as an interim U. S. senator also placed him in Washington. In September 1955, Stevens returned to the textile industry and rejoined his team as president of the firm.

Colonel Stevens was invited to the Daniel Building ground-breaking ceremonies in June 1964, and he attended to show his admiration for a lifelong friend. Charlie Daniel lived for only three months after that occasion, and the colonel remembered it "as our last public meeting together." For many years the Stevens company occupied three high-level floors in the Daniel Building.

As the South's postwar industrial boom continued to gain momentum through 1948, Daniel's field and office staffs grew with each project. No personnel recruiting campaign was necessary, because talented service men and women returning from overseas duty and U. S. bases were cluttering the job market. Daniel employed a substantial number of them, and many became the management and craft nucleus in the company's continued growth. Through it all, it remained "Charlie's company," and as Gene Watt explained earlier, "Mr. Daniel was the boss." That is spelled out, for example, in a 1949 company brochure.

Only three names were listed in that brochure under "Executive Personnel." Along with the founder were R. Hugh Daniel, vice president and assistant treasurer; and H. M. Daniel (Mrs. C. E. Daniel), executive secretary. The listing of Charles E. Daniel as president and treasurer carried this additional information: "General supervision over all phases of the company's operations, maintaining active contacts with all departments." There isn't a person alive today who would challenge that, nor did anyone then. At the time, Hugh Daniel was identified as being "in direct charge of the Birmingham office and all work estimated and constructed in that area." Nobody challenged that authority, either.

That "statistical" brochure, updated periodically until it was discontinued in the late 1960's, supplemented the company's marketing material. It contained such information as the current financial statement, key office and field personnel, insurance and bank references, equipment, and a list of cost-plus-fee projects. Its purpose was to show that Daniel had the manpower, tools and experience to perform any type of industrial and commercial construction; and it identified the chief executives of Daniel-built plants.

Many of those clients were textile leaders who had awarded Charlie Daniel the early projects that contributed to his crews' experience and his company's reputation for the industrial expansion boom that followed World War II. Most were in the Anderson area, and Daniel had built village houses for them while he worked at Townsend. They included C. B. Nichols, J. M. Cathcart, Charles Gibson, G. H. Emory, Ralph Marshall, Lawrence Hammett, Wilbert and Henry Wood, Carey Page and Andrew Calhoun, along with S. H. Swint of Graniteville and Charles Owen of Swannanoa. One of the most influential business associates in Charlie Daniel's early career was D. D. Little, a Spartanburg textile executive. He was older than Daniel, but they developed a warm friendship and he opened doors to numerous prospective clients.

Much credit for Daniel's fast-building reputation goes to its general superintendents, and those in that time frame were duly recognized in the brochure. They included E. R. Davis, I. R. Brown, James Coker, J. K. Elliott, Max Ellis, George Hardy, Joe Isbell, E. W. Moore, O. R. Oakley, Will Rowland, Don Shelton and Carl Thrash, all working out of the corporate office. The Birmingham group included Eddie Allen, Harry Cambron, George Wells, William Welch, Jim Rice, B. F. Jones, J. H. Gilbert and H. H. Garland. They ran their jobs and they were rugged and tough; but each had crews that followed him from job to job, year after year. Hub Outz and Albert Bolt, masonry superintendents, worked with many of those field bosses as well as with Lawrence Yargin and Ed Moore. Of Charlie Daniel's construction proverbs, this one stuck with Bolt: "The size of the brick pile determines the speed of the laying."

The returning servicemen and others filling new positions in the company's expansion were crowding the corporate office space, and the warehouse built in the rear of the office was overflowing with construction equipment. These conditions resulted in the warehouse being converted into offices and the equipment being moved to a new location at the edge of town on Piedmont Road, with Earle Daniel in charge. A connecting, enclosed breezeway was built between the office and the converted warehouse. The original three-story office building had project managers on the upper floor, the corporate staff on the ground floor and all of the estimators in the basement.

The increasing volume of business, and with it the growing number of key personnel, led to the establishment of departments during the first two postwar years. C. A. Thrasher was promoted to chief engineer in charge of construction in the Greenville office, and Carl Englund was given the same title in the Alabama Division. Second in command to them were Joe Dentici and Leslie Longcrier, Sr., in Birmingham, and Langdon Cheves and Claud Calmes in Greenville.

The Mechanical Department was established in 1946 with Walter Houseman in charge, having been promoted from mechanical foreman. The Purchasing Department had become a reality that same year, when Blake Moose began taking on additional agents and appointed W. W. Hollis manager of mechanical purchasing, and James Craig, Sr., manager of construction purchasing. Jimmy Brazell had joined C. W. Thomas in estimating; and as that segment of the business continued to grow, John Clendenin was named manager and chief estimator in 1949. Barrington King, who had been labor representative for Daniel on the wartime projects in Savannah and Brunswick, was transferred to the home office in 1948 as the company's first personnel manager. S. Garry Smith was moved into the Birmingham office, after several years of field experience, as office manager.

Daniel had moved heavily into mechanical work by 1947 as more complex and sophisticated manufacturing plants were being built in the South. The jobs that year included a worsted spinning mill and a wool finishing plant for Milliken, each one story, totally enclosed and air conditioned. Of the 10 major projects listed in 1947 eight were air conditioned in manufacturing areas, the largest being a 190,000-square-foot facility for James Lees and Sons Company in Glasgow, Virginia, for the manufacture of Lees rugs and carpets.

Textile jobs continued to be Daniel's bread and butter, but the company expanded into pulp and paper construction in the late

1940's. With that beginning, it developed into a leading paper mill constructor in several parts of the country. The first two such projects were new plants for Southern Paperboard Corporation at Port Wentworth, Georgia, and Coosa River Newsprint Corporation in Childersburg, Alabama. Those plants cost $15 million and $25 million, respectively. The Coosa River project for Kimberly-Clark Corporation was the beginning of a substantial volume of work for that company. On the Alabama job, Daniel erected the equipment in addition to constructing the plant, which had a daily capacity of 300 tons of newsprint, 250 tons of ground pulp and 200 tons of sulfate pulp. The company's largest project going into the booming 1950's was the Celanese Corporation of America plant at Rock Hill, South Carolina. It cost $40 million, and introduced Daniel to synthetic fibers, another field in which it would become the leading constructor in the South.

With the popularity of totally enclosed and air-conditioned plants spreading over the South, a considerable volume of Daniel's work began to be almost a duplication of previous mills built for the same owner or other clients. Up until 1949, there had been no apparent need for a cost department, but now there was — not only for similar work, but for every project. The person chosen to head the department was Mary Rubino. She was the unanimous choice because of her complete knowledge of the company and its projects. She continued in that capacity in the Southeastern Region into the decade of the 1980's.

From that humble beginning, Daniel's Cost Department has proven invaluable. What it does, quite simply, is to keep track of costs on all phases of a project for comparison with the definitive cost estimates on material and labor. Labor costs are tabulated weekly on a per-unit basis. Upon completion of the project, the department makes an overall actual cost breakdown, a copy of which is provided to the owner for information in establishing the property tax status of the facility. Its work is so thorough that no tax department in any state has ever turned down Daniel's project cost information. When computers became popular, Daniel used owners' cost codes as well as its own so that clients might have instant information on an ongoing or completed project.

Wesley Davis, of Greenville, formerly an engineer with Sirrine, formed the Bryant-Davis Electric Company in 1949 and was a major subcontractor on many of Daniel's projects until his retirement in 1965. His partner was Hubert Bryant, then an officer of Bryant Electric Company in High Point, North Carolina. Five years later, as more and more manufacturing plants, commercial and institutional buildings began to include HVAC (heat, ventilation and air conditioning) as part of the design, Davis restructured his firm into Davis Mechanical Contractors, Inc., and provided both electrical and HVAC disciplines.

Davis Mechanical grew rapidly with the extra HVAC discipline because Daniel had decided to subcontract its HVAC work, except for the mechanical (piping) phase that it continues to perform. Davis and Charlie Daniel developed both a close personal and business relationship. In 1965, a year after Daniel's death, Davis retired. He sold his company to key employees. Thomas L. Ayers, James B. Stephens, Wesley V. Harrison and James F. Harrison established Davis Electrical Constructors, Inc., with Ayers as president, and moved into the original Daniel Greenville offices, which were being vacated upon completion in 1966 of the 25-story Daniel Building one block up North Main Street. The Harrisons established their own firm in 1974. Harold Gillespie headed up the purchase of the mechanical portion of the original Davis company and retained the name of Davis Mechanical Contractors, Inc. The separate Davis companies continued to do business with Daniel.

Royal Little helped Daniel popularize the totally enclosed and air-conditioned plant concept during the 1940's and 1950's. The Textron magnate recalled that "Charlie would find our plant sites, make all of the necessary arrangements with the communities where they were located, and then his engineers and I would sit down and design the facilities. Within six months or so a 200,000-square-foot plant would be ready for us to occupy."

Little described all of Daniel's work for Textron as "a very informal" business relationship. No contracts were written, and no progress payments were made. "Charlie gave us complete turnkey jobs," he said, "and we paid him when the projects were completed." Daniel designed and built many Textron manufacturing facilities, primarily in the Carolinas and Georgia, and an office building for one of its units at Aberdeen, North Carolina, in 1957.

It is interesting from a Southern viewpoint that Royal Little's informative 1979 book *How to Lose $100,000,000 and Other Valuable Advice* referred to the excellent productivity of employees in Textron's Daniel-built facilities in the South. He noted that their average age was 23, whereas the average age of the company's workers in its New England mills was over 55.

Little was impressed with the "Daniel way" of doing business, and Charlie was elected a Textron director in 1949. "He was a fabulous salesman with tremendous charisma," Little said, "and he knew the South. That was where we were expanding, and we needed such a man on our board. I imagine that is why other corporations elected him to their boards. Without Charlie, a lot of industry would never have gone to South Carolina. He started industrial diversification in his part of the country by his ability to approach people who were looking for Southern locations."

International industrialists agreed with Royal Little that the person to see about locating a plant in South Carolina, or anywhere in the South, was Charlie Daniel. Among the first to be introduced to Southern hospitality in the Daniel manner were Paolino Gerli and Albert A. Prouvost, and they in turn helped other Europeans discover the Sun Belt. Gerli was known as the silk king of the world, and Prouvost contributed to the diversification of industry in the state with a wool combing plant. The wool business is mentioned in the 1954 *Fortune* magazine article about Daniel (Chapter 6).

CHAPTER 5

The Most Eventful Decade

Charlie Daniel directed his company through 30 highly successful years. The decade of the 1950's was the most eventful of all, thanks to the momentum that had been generated during and immediately after World War II.

Daniel's net earnings topped a million dollars in 1958 for the first time and reached almost two million the next year; the net worth of his company doubled and redoubled, and three more divisional offices were established.

The "Builder In and Of the South," as the company slogan read then, was no longer the "little country contractor" without a reputation, for in the 1950's both he and his company became known from coast to coast and border to border, as the radio commentator Walter Winchell would have described it.

It was in the decade of the 1950's that Charlie Daniel knew for a fact that he had built the groundwork of a company whose horizons were unlimited. Yet he did not slow his pace. He still worked seven days a week, and went to the post office every Sunday morning to pick up the mail and distribute it to his staff.

The "Charlie Daniel Sunday School Class" grew in size during that decade, too, because more members became available. Sunday morning was a good time to discuss the business of the past week and map strategy for the week ahead. Key personnel knew the boss would be in his office just about every Sunday morning, and they knew that would probably be the best time to get things off their chests and to receive guidance for the days ahead. The three young sons of Langdon Cheves thought for a long time that their father was attending a real Sunday School class in the Daniel office, because on their way to church he would get out of the car there, and their mother would drive on to church. She explained to her curious children that "your father is attending Charlie Daniel's Sunday School."

43

The continuing success in the 1950's reflected more of Daniel's philosophy. Just as he had reasoned that after the depression there would be a building boom in the textile industry and there was, he now looked further down the road for industries that provided products and services to the new textile, woolen and synthetic fibers mills. The textile business had begun to concentrate in the South, and his newly adopted headquarters city of Greenville had become "the textile center of the world."

It behooves any industry to locate manufacturing facilities in the proximity of its major customers, so it behooved Daniel to call on those industries and help them become acquainted with the South. Also, his company provided any construction services required, from selecting a site all the way to building the plant and installing equipment. In short, Daniel now had the capabilities, plus the manpower, to give any owner a turnkey job and to do it better, faster and more economically.

With that capability, plus his foresight, he began knocking on doors he had not knocked on before. The textile industry would need paper and boxes in which to ship its goods. He convinced pulp and paper mill owners that they should expand to the South with new facilities. He showed chemical companies the wisdom of building closer to mills using dyes and bleaches. To any business leader he would say, "If you sell your product or your services to the textile industry, I will place all of the resources of my company at your disposal to help you locate a plant near those mills." Daniel's new business grew.

Returning from one of his numerous marketing trips to New York and other cities, Daniel handed his secretary a piece of paper on which he had written: "When we build, let us think we build forever." Mrs. Rubino said he told her he thought that would be a fine motto for the company, and that the inspiration had come to him from something he had read on a billboard visible from the railroad. That original note is still in her files.

One new friend of that era was Elmer R. Oliver, who for 28 years was vice president of marketing for Southern Railway. Daniel had met him soon after moving to Greenville when Oliver toured the entire Southern system seeking new business for industrial sites that could be served by a Southern spur track. Since Daniel, too, was looking for new business that would need such service, they worked closely together with numerous prospective customers.

Mrs. Rubino recalls that "Mr. Daniel came to my office one day after lunch and asked me to smell his breath. I did, and told him that he must have eaten something sweet. He explained that he had eaten lunch with Mr. Oliver in the office car and that Mr. Oliver wanted him to sample some peach brandy." She said since there was a strict rule against anyone in the company having any alcoholic beverage during working hours, "Mr. Daniel wanted to make sure there was no odor of brandy on his breath."

Daniel works with many railroads throughout the country in the location and development of industrial sites, as well as with other industrial, commercial and institutional firms and agencies. This is accomplished handily both by the corporate headquarters marketing staffs and the company's regional divisions. Charlie Daniel established those guidelines, which have been expanded and are still followed in all states and countries where the company performs engineering and construction services.

The increased volume of work and the extended geographical range of projects finally reduced Daniel's personal involvement in each facet of his company's operations; he could no longer visit all job sites as was his practice until shortly after the war. Even so, he continued to visit as many as he could, and superintendents never knew when "the boss" would show up on their jobs. This kept them on the alert and ready for such drop-ins. Yet the superintendents were not always around when some of those trips were made, because he and Mrs. Daniel spent many Sunday afternoons riding to nearby projects.

Hugh Daniel recalled that his brother often came to a job site near quitting time, and when the workers left he would say: "All right, Hugh, it's time for you and me to go to work." With that they walked the site, picking up materials the men had left to go to waste. "We would stack the stuff in piles so that the material would be available for them the next day," Hugh said. The Daniel philosophy has always been that it is the client's money being spent, so be sure it is spent wisely, with a minimum of waste and delay.

In a people-oriented company, the business philosophies inherited from the founder relate to people in a broad term. He emphasized that "people include those within the company, those you work with and for, those who sign contracts, and those who recommend you to other people." Further, as an open-shop contractor, he preached and practiced his convictions that an employee's first loyalty is to himself and herself, and with that comes pride and ambition.

Charlie Daniel believed, "If we can get the individual to understand that through his/her personal pride and ambition there is no limit to what he can do or how far he can go in this company, then we have his loyalty, both to the company and to his specific job." He insisted that every person be treated equally; that working and sanitary conditions on the projects be kept safe and clean. Employees knew that, because on frequent visits to job sites he would quickly put things in order if a supervisor had allowed his crew to become lax. As a matter of fact, until there were so many projects that he could not get around to all of them, he knew most of the employees by their first names.

Buck Mickel, expounding on the people philosophies still governing the company, said, "The boss taught us that a corporation has no life span, but that an individual does. The very nature of the business we conduct and of the people for whom we work is most interesting. Many of our clients' officers are at the station in life where they have probably 10 years at the maximum in their jobs before they retire. That is a transitional basic fact. So Charlie always insisted that we don't talk just to the top man but also to the man under him, because that No. 2 fellow will take his job someday. Be sure that the man in the second spot understands what you're doing, and give him the full, honest-to-God treatment both as a man and the position he holds, because he will remember you if you did a good job. If you don't do a good job, if you fail to do what you say you will do, he will remember that, too. We continue to preach that philosophy just like Charlie did."

As for taking care of employees and seeing that those who apply themselves receive recognition and promotion, Mickel said, "The boss recognized in the human nature of things that there are some people who will not be motivated to go beyond a certain point in their responsibility. So why should you push such a person? When you push a person into a job which he is incapable of doing, whose fault is it? It's not the man's fault. It is the supervisor's fault. He is guilty of putting that person in a job above his head. Don't condemn the person; instead, make it possible for him to return to the job he was doing with pride, so that he will not have a sense of failure."

Continuing, Mickel declared, "If there is anything in this company that irritates me beyond belief it is someone losing sight of our 'people are people' philosophy. Now and then, someone will lose sight of that and is ready to fire a person for not living up to expectations after a change of assignment. Are you going to fire a man you've known for 15 years, and you know his capabilities, and replace him with a person off the street? You don't know who in the hell is outside that door or what he can do; you don't know a thing about him. So you move the fellow, and you promote from within as quick as you can. Charlie built a great company on that philosophy, and we have grown greater by preaching it and living it."

As has been alluded to time and again, Daniel had an uncanny knack of sizing up people as to their sincerity, loyalty, honesty and ambition. This perceptiveness became even more obvious in the decade of the 1950's, because in the growth and expansion of his company he was dealing with many more clients and prospective customers; and he was beefing up his managerial staff. His belief in youth became more apparent in that decade, too. He was surrounding himself with young, inexperienced men, training them in his own way. They are now directing the company's daily operations.

E. Smythe Gambrell, the well-known Atlanta corporate attorney and past president of the American Bar Association, who had known Daniel from boyhood, made this sage observation: "It interested me that he not only discovered Charlie Daniel himself, and brought Charlie Daniel up from a simple start, but he seemed to be putting his finger on other Charlie Daniels scattered around the country, wherever he could find them. I was impressed by the fact that he could so successfully pick up comparatively unknown young fellows and develop them into exciting and successful business people. He had lots of them on his team, and they did a great job together. They were happy to recognize him as their leader, and he had a flavor in his organization that I don't believe existed in any other organization in the world. People everywhere, in all lines of business, respected him and were anxious to be identified with him and to have his cooperation."

In order of seniority, the first three key people in that assemblage of "other Charlie Daniels" were Hugh Daniel (1934), Langdon Cheves (1936), and Buck Mickel (1948). Joining them in top administrative or operations positions in their individual time frames as the company grew during the 1950's and early 1960's were George E. McDougall (1947), T. C. (Ted) Johnson (1950), Charles W. Cox and John P. Odom (1956), and Currie B. Spivey (1963). All experienced the personal influence of Charlie Daniel; and, with one exception, Cheves, they composed the major portion of the management team that later directed the company. With one other exception, Daniel, they are the nucleus of the executive committee leading it into the decade of the 1980's. Cheves died in 1955 and Hugh Daniel retired in 1977.

None of the "other Charlie Daniels" ever posed as the founder's successor regardless of title or authority. When a newspaper reporter intimated that Mickel in fact had succeeded him, he immediately and emotionally set the record straight: "Nobody will succeed Charlie Daniel. He was a one and only. He founded the company and gave his life to it. He left us a legacy and a lasting image, and what we achieve both as individuals and as a management team will be predicated on how well we listened to him and how closely we follow his guidelines and business philosophies. In any future growth we may help his company achieve, we will have succeeded, yes, but in any such success there will never be a successor. No way."

Cheves, whose career was cut short, and Daniel had much in common. They had exciting personalities that enhanced their sales efforts, they were gluttons for work, and, being ambitious and often impatient, they displayed their tempers, many times to each other. A secretary recalls them arguing about a telephone call Cheves made to New York. Daniel contended that a three-cent letter would have been sufficient.

Cheves' widow remembers an occasion in 1952 when "Lang took me to Atlanta on a business trip. He and Charlie had been in one of their arguments, and Lang was talking about resigning. That evening we had dinner at one of the clubs, and the more Lang talked about it, the more determined he became about resigning. Before we finished dinner he made up his mind and wrote his resignation on a napkin. But when he returned to the office the next day to turn in his keys and clean out his desk, Charlie talked him into staying; so their disagreement couldn't have been too important, like probably most of their arguments."

Daniel was on the Southern train en route to New York on the evening of January 3, 1955. A telegram, advising him of Cheves' death, reached him while the train was still in North Carolina. He chartered an airplane and hurried back to Greenville. Some reports have it that this was his first flying experience, but he had flown three times previously: once in Anderson; again during an American Legion convention at Myrtle Beach; and on a private plane flight from Anderson to Orangeburg for a Chamber of Commerce meeting. He simply preferred trains for long trips and automobiles for the shorter ones. Even so, the geographic spread of projects prompted him and Hugh to purchase the company's first airplane in 1956, and Charlie used it frequently.

Upon reaching Greenville, Daniel went directly to the Cheves residence. As he and the widow were discussing the accident of a few hours earlier, he told her, "I loved him like a son. I wish I had told him." Repeating the conversation years later, she noted that Cheves had lost his father when he was a small boy and that "Charlie and Lang, I don't know; the two of them just sort of seemed to have a real close tie. Lang knew how Charlie felt about him."

The *Greenville News* report of the death noted that it had been announced a few days earlier that Cheves, in addition to his other duties, would also be in charge of sales for all the Daniel divisions.

The story pointed out that as the company's business grew, "Cheves handled a multitude of administrative, sales and nonengineering problems. He was forever going to New York and New England to talk with clients that Daniel was trying to bring to the new industrial South. He once commented that the Crescent Limited (Southern Railway) was almost like home to him." A vice president, Cheves was 42 years old at the time of the fatal accident.

Like his boss, Cheves championed the South wherever he went. Daniel sent him to a three-month executive management school at Harvard University in 1953. At the graduation night banquet, attended by students from throughout the country and their guests, the master of ceremonies told them there was an important announcement: "Langdon Cheves is having Harvard moved to the South." Again like the boss, he was able to convince just about anybody that the South is the only place to be.

Somewhat questionable recognition was given another Ivy League school five years earlier when Yale graduate Ed Taylor looked around Greenville for a job nearer home after working several months as a petroleum engineer in Texas. "Almost without exception," he recalled later, "every person I talked to said I should see Charlie Daniel. Also without exception, almost everyone I talked to asked me what college I attended. When I told them Yale, they immediately asked: 'What in the hell is wrong with Clemson?' They meant it, too, and I've come to agree with them."

A mutual friend arranged an appointment with Daniel, and Taylor said, "I braced myself for his reply when Mr. Daniel asked me where I went to school. But when I said Yale, he just said, 'That's fine, how did you stand in your class?' I told him, and his next question was, 'When do you want to come to work?' After a few minutes I walked out with a job, and was so impressed I didn't even ask him how much I was going to make. He was quite a dynamic person."

Taylor joined Daniel in March 1948, worked up to project manager, and was assigned to assist Cheves in sales in 1954. He was riding with Cheves at the time of the fatal accident and escaped with a few broken ribs. Taylor became a full-fledged salesman, receiving on-the-job training from Daniel himself; but after four years of constant travel, he asked to be transferred back to the field. By 1963, he had ideas of going into business for himself, and became a successful contractor in Greenville.

Taylor valued his experience with Daniel and never ceased to be amazed by his former employer, explaining, "When he turned on his personality he could charm a snake. When he met somebody, that person would think he had known him all of his life and that Charlie Daniel was the closest friend he ever had."

Robert Yeargin was a project manager with Daniel nine years before opening his own construction business in Greenville in 1959, and he frankly admits that he adopted his former employer's philosophies and policies. "What I learned there is the way I set up my company and started operating it," he said. "I didn't see any reason to try to reinvent the wheel."

Yeargin "appreciated the independence of operation that Mr. Daniel gave all of his people. He let you run your job. You knew he had built his company on reputation, so you knew that your job must be run properly. You are always interested in your client's as well as your own skin, so it just makes for good discipline to run your job well."

Howard Suitt, former project manager who was promoted to division manager, is another Daniel alumnus who had admiration and respect for his employer. He, too, is now operating his own successful construction company in Greenville. Suitt "put into practice every Charlie Daniel philosophy and policy I could think of." Further evidence of his regard for his former boss is a picture prominently displayed in his office. It shows Daniel on a project site in a photo made for the cover of the January 11, 1964, edition of *Business Week* magazine. Suitt was the manager of that project.

CHAPTER 6

The Fortune Story

The magnitude of Daniel's growing business interests was graphically and glowingly illustrated by a significant milestone in 1954 — the appearance of an in-depth article on Daniel in the October issue of *Fortune* magazine. The Daniel story of industrial enterprise had been told from time to time in other publications and would subsequently be recounted in still others, but the *Fortune* account was by all odds the most prestigious publicity thus far accorded the man and his firm.

Written by Freeman Lincoln and amply illustrated with representative photographs of Daniel and Daniel projects, the feature story bore the intriguing title: "The Northerners Surrender to Charlie Daniel."

Because of the full treatment given Daniel not only as an industrialist but as an individualist, the entire article seems worthy of reproduction within the text of this volume, even though some of its content may repeat — or anticipate — material dealt with elsewhere.

What follows is the complete article by Freeman Lincoln, reprinted from the October issue of *Fortune* magazine by special permission; © 1954 Time Inc.

THE NORTHERNERS SURRENDER TO CHARLIE DANIEL

By FREEMAN LINCOLN

Thinking of moving your northern plant? If Charlie Daniel hears about it there's an excellent chance you'll wake up some morning soon in South Carolina with a fine new factory built for you in jig time by Charlie himself. And you'll be friends for life.

Charles E. Daniel of Greenville, South Carolina, is a living denial of the ancient myth that building contractors get no reward for honest toil except a brisk kick in the pants. A big man of fifty-nine, with thinning sandy hair, a subdued speaking voice, and a sudden, luminous, boyish smile, Charlie Daniel is a builder whose postwar success in persuading has brought him out of small-town obscurity and caused him to be greatly honored in his own land.

As everybody in the region knows (and only a few competitors resent), what has been good for South Carolina, and for the South in general, has also been good for Charlie Daniel. Today, Daniel pays about 5,000 workers more than $1 million each month. He did about $40 million worth of work in fiscal 1954 for a profit, before taxes, of about $1,300,000. Operating in all the southeastern states, excepting only Kentucky, he is one of the largest builders in the region, and is by far the largest in South Carolina.

Daniel builds office buildings, schools, hospitals, churches, and the like, but he specializes in industrial plants. In 1943 he built the textile industry's first one-story, windowless, air-conditioned plant, and he has since done more of this type of construction than anybody else. Since the war he has built more industrial plants than any other contractor in the Southeast, and more in South Carolina than all other builders combined. He is modest in remarking that "our company was of assistance in bringing most of these plants into the state." All together he has put up $250 million to $300 million worth of plants in the last ten years.

For Daniel's work in pushing his agricultural region along the road to industrialization, and thus in the opposite direction from the poorhouse, South Carolina is deeply appreciative. Among the leading citizens of the state it is unanimously agreed that Daniel has done more than anybody else for the progress of South Carolina since the war. Governor James F. Byrnes, for whom Daniel has deep respect, says that he is happy he can count on the Greenville builder for advice and help. The Citadel, military college of South Carolina, gave Daniel an honorary degree of doctor of science in 1952, citing him in part as follows: "Charles Ezra Daniel . . . leader in the industrial, economic, and cultural renaissance of the South, who through his courageous faith in his homeland . . . played a major role in the expanding industry of the region. . . ."

Daniel's stature as a contractor is impressively endorsed by his clients, who are important, competent business executives. They say that he does superior work at low cost and incredible speed; that he is a magnificent salesman, a hard driver, an organizer and expediter second to none. They say that he is not only trustworthy but he gives services far beyond those specified in his contracts.

Among Daniel's important clients are J. P. Stevens & Co., Deering Milliken, and Textron, for which he has done tens of millions of dollars of construction work in the past ten years. For Stevens, Daniel has built three new plants and a number of mill additions. He also built the giant cotton mill at Clemson, South Carolina, that the Stevens company recently acquired when it bought Utica & Mohawk. Charlie Daniel and Secretary of the Army Bob Stevens, who was formerly board chairman of J. P. Stevens, are great friends, and Daniel was made a director of the Stevens company several years ago. He built six mills for Textron and was made a member of that board too.

Over the same period Daniel has done practically all Deering Milliken's construction work, including ten new mills and a number of plant additions. This construction, worth some $20 million, has been done without a contract, formal agreement, or any line of writing. Roger Milliken, president of this family-owned concern, trusts Daniel's judgment as much as his honesty. Milliken merely says what kind of plant he wants, and lets Daniel go ahead on a basis of cost-plus. (On two occasions Daniel's fee was not even discussed until the job had been finished.)

Smile-and-All

Roger Milliken, who works as hard getting jobs for Daniel as if he were on Daniel's payroll, sums up his feeling about him as follows: "There are just two men with whom we do business whom I would unhesitatingly recommend to someone whose good opinion I want to hold. One of those men is Charlie Daniel." (The other is a lawyer.) Charlie Daniel is liked by almost everybody. One of his clients says that he has "a modest and engaging personality." Businessmen he has done favors for point out that he never asks a favor in return. (This, seemingly, is a virtue remarkable among contractors.) Some think that Daniel has a strong personal magnetism. "I guess," says a Daniel supplier, with a shrug, "it's that sweet kind of a way he has — his smile, and all." As a matter of fact, Daniel is an intensely impatient man and occasionally explosive of temper. The explosions, however, are confined to his own staff; among clients or prospects he never permits himself to stray from sweet reason.

Charlie Daniel is a worker who knows, cares about, and does almost nothing but work. He has no hobbies, sports, or pastimes. He collects no stamps, plays no bridge, builds no birdhouses in the cellar. He belongs to the Augusta National Golf Club and the Biltmore Forest Country Club in Asheville, but he plays no golf. He has a swimming pool on the grounds of his big house in Greenville, but this is used by his wife (the Daniels have no children) and their friends. In New York, he talks business at the Merchants or Links Club, avoids night life.

In South Carolina, he is as often away from Greenville as in it. He is apt to drive his big, air-conditioned Cadillac to Charleston and back (four hundred-odd miles) in a single day, and when he is not inspecting a Daniel construction job along the way, his foot is heavy on the accelerator, his hand is heavy on the horn, his passengers are weak in the knees. On Saturdays, Daniel works. On Sundays, when most of the good people of the Bible Belt go to church, Daniel works. He empties the company mailbox at the city post office, and carts the bundle to his office. There he opens, reads and sorts every letter, bill, or other notice addressed to himself or his staff of about fifty. He says this keeps him in touch with what goes on.

It may be that vacations were devised with the idea of bedeviling Daniel, but so far he has managed to avoid all but two or three, and from these he returned with an arm-long hand-written list of things to be attended to forthwith. He agrees that his staff should have adequate time off so long as it does not interfere with their work, but he cheerfully admits that "around here we don't let vacations get in the way of business."

Daniel has a compelling built-in drive that makes him the pluperfect expediter, whether of an order of nails from a tardy supplier, or of an entire factory for an impatient customer. It is generally thought that the record of Daniel Construction for terrific speed in building is the direct result of Charlie Daniel's personal drive. The fact is, however, that although his drive does contribute to his speed, Daniel builds fast because he long ago figured out that it is smart tactics.

Daniel believes that after quality of workmanship, speed is the thing that builds a reputation for a contractor. He reasons that before the customer breaks ground for a major new plant he has probably pondered its location and layout for years. Once construction has begun, the owner tots up how many thousands of dollars per day his efficient new factory will save him, and he develops a burning impatience. Catering to this impatience by meeting or beating time schedules is good business.

Daniel leaves as few things as possible to chance. Moreover, he lays plans as far in advance as he can. After the war, for instance, it appeared certain that more and more industry would move south. Daniel was not content to sit around and wait.

The Favorable Climate

The southward movement of industry after World War II obviously would have taken place without any help from Charlie Daniel. Because of him, however, the movement was probably accelerated; and there appears no doubt that he has done more than any other individual to bring the state of South Carolina its share.

Like any other educated Southerner, Daniel had always been aware of the South's acute need for industry to balance its poverty-stricken agricultural economy. (Even as late as 1945, South Carolina had the smallest per capita income of any state except Mississippi.) Like most Southerners, he had watched closely when a few textile mills were built below the Mason-Dixon Line in the late 1930's. Like a few other Southerners, Daniel made a careful appraisal of a favorable situation, and then did something to further it.

The advantages of the southeastern states as the locale for new factories were plenty of cheap, desirable land and water, cheap power, a mild climate, lower construction costs, and a favorable labor situation. In South Carolina there was a surplus of labor due to the decrease of cotton growing and the mechanization of farming, as well as a high birth rate. This potential labor force was made up almost entirely of the direct descendants of the Protestant Scotch, Irish, English or German settlers of the original colony. Mostly ex-cotton farmers hungry for work, they were opposed by temperament and training to the idea of trade unions. Whereas there is union strength in neighboring southern states, South Carolina remains the least unionized state in the nation. Only 6 or 7 percent of South Carolina's workers belong to unions; of the 200-odd major plants in the South Carolina Piedmont, fewer than half a dozen are organized by unions.

To Daniel's way of thinking, the great weakness of the northern states was that their governments were either hostile to industry, taxing it unfairly, or indifferent to its welfare. In the South, particularly in South Carolina, there was no hostility to business, and the tax situation was generally favorable to it. What Daniel was anxious to see, however, was a South Carolina government conspicuously friendly to industry, aggressive in working to bring in new business, and capable of inspiring businessmen with confidence in its stability.

Working for the long pull, Daniel and a group of other influential South Carolinians set out on a successful postwar campaign to replace "jackleg" delegates to the legislature with men who would provide "good" government — meaning, in this case, government favorable to business. In recent years the state legislature has pleased industrialists by passing a "right-to-work" bill, of the kind already adopted by sixteen other states, which outlaws the closed or union shop. It has put in a retail sales tax that eventually will pay the entire state school bill, previouly met by the proceeds of county property taxes, which fell most heavily on industry. To lighten further the burden on industry, Daniel helped get all manufacturing machinery and materials used in the processing of finished goods exempted from the sales tax. He was instrumental also in rescinding a franchise tax that discriminated against out-of-state corporations. New plants are assessed for property taxes on only 40 percent of their book value, so that the owners are not penalized because of present-day inflated costs.

Charlie Daniel was a strong supporter of Strom Thurmond, who was Governor of South Carolina from 1947 to 1951 and the Dixiecrat candidate for President of the U. S. in 1948. (In 1952, Daniel was all out for Eisenhower.) Daniel was influential in getting his good friend Jimmy Byrnes to take over the governorship after Thurmond, and he worked hard for George Bell Timmerman, who will become Governor next January. Both Thurmond and Byrnes (Timmerman will follow suit) have been strong supporters of business, and neither has been above going north, hat in hand, to ask industry to come south. "The businessman doesn't live," says Daniel, "who doesn't appreciate this sort of thing."

In 1945 the state established a Development Board to supply vital statistics about South Carolina to anyone interested, and to promote the state's industrial potential. This agency has been supported with such vigor by Charlie Daniel that Daniel's business rivals have become bitter. They say that the board is so thoroughly in Daniel's pocket that he gets unfair advance information about companies that are thinking of building in the state. The evidence, however, is that more information goes from Daniel to the Development Board than the other way around.

While the cynics can say, with truth, that Daniel is not in the contracting business for his health, they must admit that he goes beyond self-interest to work for what he considers the best interests of South Carolina, i.e., to make it a pasture for contented industrialists. He is pleased when he puts up one of his typical, functional, windowless, air-conditioned, single-story, handsome plants in the middle of a South Carolina meadow, miles from a town or even a stop light. He likes to think that he has thus created from 400 to 1,000 jobs for the people who mysteriously emerge from the hills in their cars to come to work, and who scatter in the evenings to their farms. The notion pleases him that each direct job he creates, creates two or three indirect jobs.

Daniel wants to avoid building factory or mill towns, and instead would like to scatter small plants across the South Carolina map, at every little crossroads, so that the people don't have to be entirely dependent on their farms for a living. He would like to have diversified industries as a hedge against bad times in any one industry. However, he would discourage the "wrong kind" of company from coming to South Carolina.

To Daniel the wrong kind of company would be one that pays substandard wages or is operated under union contract. This does not mean that Daniel is above building a plant for a unionized company, for he has built many. But in the state of South Carolina, so far, there are very few unionized shops, and Charlie likes it that way, and will do his best to keep it that way.

"Without any Obligation"

Daniel put in a lot of work and played an influential part in getting the Du Pont company to build an Orlon plant at Camden, South Carolina, even though he knew that Du Pont did its own construction and no profit would come to him. He is glad Du Pont was well enough pleased with its first plant to have bought the site for another in his state. Most of the time, however, he sells for profit, which is fortunate, for his artistry should have material reward.

By some mysterious method, Daniel learns that a northern manufacturer is planning to build a southern factory almost before the man realizes it himself. When this happens, Daniel appears in the executive's office, bearing an urgent invitation to visit Greenville and learn, "without obligation of any kind," the virtues of setting up shop in South Carolina.

If the customer permits himself to be lured into Daniel's hometown, he is a gone goose. On the first night he will probably be the guest of honor at a dinner in the private Statesman's Room at the Poinsett Hotel, where he will inspect and be inspected by Greenville's leading businessmen, and be "made to feel welcome." The next day he will be whisked by Cadillac to inspect as many as he likes of the twenty-five completely modern new mills, all built by Daniel, that lie within forty miles of Daniel's handsome pine-paneled office. He can discuss mutual problems with plant managers, each of whom is convinced that Daniel is the greatest of all builders.

If the customer is at the proper stage, Daniel will show him a number of likely sites for his plant. If it seems indicated, he will offer to negotiate the purchase of one of these, or perhaps try to get it for the customer as a gift from the people of the county. In the meantime Daniel or his staff will be glad to answer any number of highly technical questions that may come up.

The Full Treatment

All this time, it must be emphasized, no mention is made of Daniel Construction and no suggestion that Daniel would like any work. But by the time the client is ready to sign a contract, it would scarcely occur to him to consider anybody but Daniel.

While the client's plant is turning from dream to reality at phenomenal speed, Daniel Construction attends to the following as a matter of course: It arranges with the county for water and sewer facilities and with the railroad for a siding. It gets the authorities to build access roads. It arranges for disposal plants and for power and telephone extensions. It makes labor surveys. It helps with the housing of employees. It arranges with state officials for tax assessments comparable to those of existing plants. The manager of the Anderson, South Carolina, Fiberglass plant, recently built by Daniel, notes that months after the building was completed Daniel arranged for him to go the State Fair football game with Governor Jim Byrnes. "Once Charlie's got you, he doesn't drop you."

Charlie Daniel's biggest job of all was the 1948 construction of a $62-million acetate plant at Rock Hill, South Carolina, for the Celanese Corp. The building cost alone was about $22 million. Daniel performed a number of extraordinary services in connection with the Rock Hill job. He was influential in having removed from the South Carolina books an old blue law that prohibited women from working on Sunday and thus would have blocked the necessarily continuous Celanese operation. Daniel went to Washington and obtained the essential allocation of steel, which Celanese hadn't been able to get. According to Celanese's chief engineer, Daniel built the Rock Hill plant faster and cheaper than anyone else could have done it, and more than earned his $300,000 fee. (He picked up an additional $200,000 fee when Celanese permitted him to install the highly secret machinery.) After the job was finished, Daniel, although under no obligation, stepped in and helped settle a mix-up in the Celanese tax assessment.

Mill-Town Housing

Charlie Daniel was born on November 11, 1895, in Elberton, Georgia, but he and his four younger brothers grew up across the

Savannah River in Anderson, a county seat in the South Carolina Piedmont. (The Blue Ridge Mountains lie just over the horizon to the north.) Charlie's father, a freelance millwright in the textile mills, earned enough so that his family was never in want, but he could not raise the money to send his boys to college.

Charlie took competitive examinations in high school and won a scholarship at The Citadel. After two years at this state-owned military college in Charleston, he served in the Army in World War I, and after a walking tour of Europe as a second lieutenant with the "Sight-seeing Sixth" Division, he came home to Anderson to work.

In earlier years Daniel had improved his school and college vacations by working as a 7½-cent-an-hour laborer in the Anderson yards of the Townsend Lumber Co., large retailer of building supplies, and it was with Townsend that he took his first full-time job at $18 a week.

Almost the first responsibility young Daniel had was looking after Townsend's small activity of erecting modest residences for Anderson citizens who bought their materials from Townsend. This sort of contracting brought little profit, however, until the early 1920's, when textile mills and other industrial plants from the North began to move into South Carolina.

Townsend went in heavily for building mill villages, which were typical of the textile industry in those days. In 1924, with Daniel doing the estimating for the competitive bid, Townsend won a contract to build 175 mill houses for $250,000. When Charlie, who was construction superintendent on this job, was awarded his first bonus, $3,500, he promptly married a girl from his Elberton, Georgia birthplace. ("I thought I was a wealthy man.") Still larger jobs followed, until in 1928 Daniel, then a Townsend partner, landed a better than $1-million contract to build 350 houses and a schoolhouse for American Chatillon Corp., a forerunner of Celanese.

Faster, Cheaper, Better

In January of 1935, Charlie Daniel resigned from Townsend and set up Daniel Construction Co., using $25,000 of borrowed money for capital. A conservative who thoroughly disapproved of government in business, Daniel was realistic enough to grab all the PWA jobs that were offered.

In addition, he built five barracks and a textile building at Clemson College. He built a woodworking factory that made cabinets for Singer sewing machines. Most important, by repeatedly living up to his promise to build faster, cheaper, and better than competitors, Daniel earned the favorable attention of a Greenville textile engineer, Joseph Sirrine.

"Captain" Joe Sirrine is still remembered in the Piedmont as the "daddy rabbit" of the South Carolina textile industry. Although Sirrine never owned or ran a cotton mill, he was so wise in the trade that at one time he served simultaneously on the boards of directors of thirty-odd textile and other companies. His sponsorship brought Daniel a number of important clients, most notably J. P. Stevens and Deering Milliken.

By 1938 Daniel Construction Co. had achieved an annual volume of more than $1 million. Charlie was able to send his younger brother Hugh (whom he had put through college at The Citadel) to Birmingham, Alabama, to open a company branch. In 1942, Charlie Daniel moved himself, his wife, his office, and about $300,000 of accumulated earnings from Anderson to a new stand at Greenville, South Carolina. Greenville is only thirty-two miles north of Anderson, but in traveling that short distance Daniel moved a long way.

Ahead of Schedule

Daniel acquired a more than local fame as a contractor during the war. In 1942 he won a contract for all the building construction at the Donaldson Air Force Base in Greenville. Completion was promised in ninety days, and the weather was bad, but Daniel delivered on time. Daniel's company handled a total of seventy separate projects in building the port of embarkation and the Navy Yard at Charleston, South Carolina. It built an aluminum plant in the southern part of the state, two airfields, a huge government warehouse at Gadsden, Alabama, and two six-way shipyards at Savannah and Brunswick, Georgia. Much of its reputation as a tremendously fast worker was the result of help it gave the Federal Housing Authority on a 1,400-unit job at Brunswick that had been fumbled by another contractor. Telephoning Daniel in September, 1944, the FHA said it had to have completion on the project in eight to ten months. Figuring fast, Daniel replied, "I'll have it for you on February 1." FHA was incredulous. "In four months? You're nuts!" Daniel: "If I don't deliver, I'll take no fee."

The upshot was that Daniel dropped the keys of the completed project on FHA's desk on December 24, nearly five weeks ahead of his own fast, four-month schedule. From then on, Daniel all but had to hide in closets to avoid more government work than he could handle.

Daniel's organization is extremely good. The 500-man core of his work force can handle as many as forty jobs at one time, has stuck together for long years largely because Daniel has supplied continuous employment. Certain bricklayers have followed certain foremen from one job to another, and certain foremen have followed certain superintendents. This has made for teamwork in the field. The superintendents, trained by Daniel himself, are supported in the home office by project supervisors, all of whom are engineers. Charlie Daniel admits that he has a top crew. "They're not only good," he says, "but willing to put up with me."

For the Long Run

Perhaps more important even than Daniel's technical skill is his long-range planning for South Carolina and the South. An example is his most recent accomplishment — the bringing to South Carolina of two of the biggest wool processors in the world: Arthur O. Wellman, owner of the Boston wool firm of Nichols & Co.; and a subsidiary of Peignage Amedee Prouvost et Cie. of Roubaix, France. For Wellman, Daniel has just completed a $3-million plant near Charleston capable of processing 80 million pounds of wool a year, and he will build a similar one for Prouvost forty miles away. These are the first commercial wool scouring and combing plants in the South, and getting them there from Rhode Island was contingent on Charleston's being made a port of entry for wool — a project in which Daniel took a leading part.

The port development and the new processing plants may be the nucleus of an integrated wool industry in the South. Burlington Mills, Stevens, and Deering Milliken already have extensive spinning and weaving mills there, and others will undoubtedly follow. Roy Little of Textron, which has control of American Woolen, is sure to extend his group's southern operations. It is significant that Wellman and Charlie Daniel were both recently put on the board of American Woolen.

Wellman, manifestly delighted with his new adventure, says that Daniel was recommended to him by Roger Milliken, and that since Milliken doesn't feel that it is necessary to have a contract with Daniel, he doesn't have one either. "This is the first plant I ever built," Wellman admits, "and Charlie has guided me like a daddy. Because of him, everybody is making a fuss over me, and everything is made easy. I'm sending two or three good prospects to this man Daniel."

Low Bid, High Value

The practically unanimous nomination of Charles E. Daniel as "man who has done most for South Carolina since 1945" is not due entirely to the amount of industry he has lured into the state. His work for Clemson Agricultural and Mechanical College has added greatly to his stature. The fact is that in the five years since his election to Clemson's board of trustees Daniel has contributed more in the way of ideas, energy, and money than anyone else in the history of the college. Daniel's major projects at Clemson include:

Textile Equipment
— Daniel wanted to make the Clemson textile school the most modern in the country. He donated $150,000 in cash and got his textile friends to contribute new machinery worth $400,000. Twenty-five percent of all U. S. textile students now study at Clemson.

Clemson House
— Daniel made all the financial arrangements and his firm did the construction on this hotel (and also on 100 campus houses). Originally, Clemson House was to have been FHA financed, but Daniel persuaded the legislature that it was cheaper to issue $2,500,000 of revenue bonds at 2¾ percent than to borrow FHA money at 4½ percent, and that the investment could be amortized ten years sooner. In the six months before the legislature approved, Daniel backed the project with $2 million of his own money.

New Barracks
— Two weeks before this appears, Daniel Construction will have completed a Clemson dormitory and dinning hall. Daniel's bid of $4,700,000 was lower than the next bidder's by $300,000, and beat the second bidder's completion date by more than six months. In building this structure Daniel used the lift-slab method. He figures he saved Clemson about $400,000 and at least six months in construction time.

Agricultural Program
— To the surprise of many who had thought of him only as an industrial builder, Charlie Daniel recognized the importance of agriculture to South Carolina by pushing through a building program for the agricultural department. The buildings, on

which Daniel Construction was again the low bidder, are due to be finished in April, 1955.

Charlie Daniel's work at Clemson has caused a certain amount of grumbling by some of his contractor competitors, who protest the fact that as a Clemson trustee he has been given millions of dollars worth of Clemson buildings. Clemson Business Manager Jim Littlejohn is contemptuous of this criticism, says that in every contract except one (and that a special case) Daniel made the low bid; that far from making a big profit on his Clemson work, he has contributed thousands to the college by putting more value into the structures than the specifications called for. "That being the case," says Littlejohn, "let the dogs howl."

On September 6, Daniel was appointed to the U. S Senate by his good friend Governor Byrnes. He will fill out the term of the late Senator Burnet Maybank, which expires on January 2. Although his many admirers would be happy to vote for him, there is little likelihood of Daniel's running for election to the full term. There isn't much chance of his retiring from the construction business. He does not have to go on working for money, but he probably has to go on working to satisfy his fierce drive.

While there are more industrial plants to be built in the South a Daniel probably will go on building them. Charlie's brother Hugh has built the Alabama part of the business into the biggest construction company in the state. He is eleven years younger than Charlie and well-equipped to carry on the Daniel business when Charlie retires — if he ever does.

CHAPTER 7

Pushing Back the Horizon

Daniel had greatly strengthened its position in Southern industrial development by the mid-1950's. Revenues reached a new high of $58 million in 1955, and the 3,000 craft employees that year doubled the number on Daniel jobs in 1950. Those statistics were enhanced by the opening of two more regional construction offices, the Northeastern in Richmond, Virginia, in 1954, and the Southern in Jacksonville, Florida, a year later. Also, the New York sales office was established in 1958. Project managers in Alabama were promoted to manage the new divisions: H. L. Longcrier, Sr., was appointed to head the office in Virginia and Harry Stellman in Florida. At that time, it was decided to place projects managed by the corporate office under a South Carolina Division, and Carl Englund was transferred from Birmingham to direct it.

The new divisions were the result of additional projects in those areas. Daniel had added a large Allied Chemical contract to its Virginia business in 1952, and a $10-million Prudential Life Insurance Company office tower contract in Jacksonville in 1955. The Prudential job was soon to be followed by a contract to construct the Atlantic Coast Line building, another Florida landmark. The Jacksonville skyscrapers represented milestones in the company's commercial work and coincided with major contracts with Chemstrand (Monsanto) on sites that Daniel has never left; Decatur, Alabama, in 1952, and Pensacola, Florida, in 1955. By 1979, Daniel was on eight Monsanto sites in the United States, and Mickel was serving on the Monsanto board of directors.

Another milestone was recorded at Monsanto-Pensacola in 1955 when Daniel assembled its first B&W boiler. The company had piped numerous boilers, but this was its first complete field erection. Fred Davis, with the company since 1951, was a boilermaker on that project and recalls the day: "Mr. Daniel brought a few Bowater officials there to show them our capability in assembling boilers. Ernie Grisby was our field superintendent, and he helped Mr. Daniel convince those men. I'm satisfied that got us the Bowater paper mill job at Catawba, where Ernie supervised the field erection of two boilers in 1957." Two others were erected in 1959 at the Continental Can project in Augusta, Georgia, and many others followed. This additional capability, which placed Daniel further ahead as a turnkey constructor, was the forerunner of the company's becoming heavily involved in the power-generating field.

Ted Johnson, who had been supervising mechanical work on numerous projects, was promoted to manager of the Mechanical Department in 1955, a position he held for the next five years until he was elected a vice president and corporate staff assistant. He was active in operations and marketing and was appointed executive vice president of construction in 1977. Johnson has been involved in all of Daniel's pulp and paper mill construction, as well as its numerous synthetic fibers projects and many others.

The team of young executives that Charlie Daniel began putting together in the late 1940's to assist him and his seasoned field supervisors was given added responsibilities by the mid-1950's. The founder was then spending much of his time on sales and activities outside the company. In 1955, he relinquished the presidency, retaining the chairmanship and chief executive positions.

Hugh Daniel was appointed president and treasurer. Buck Mickel, having been given more authority over operations, was named assistant to the chairman in 1956. On November 6, 1960, Daniel delegated additional responsibility and authority, naming Mickel executive vice president of the company.

Charles W. Cox brought a new dimension to the company in 1957 when he resigned his top engineering position with Chemstrand and moved to Greenville. He arrived at the time Daniel was ready to broaden its construction services to include design for a combined total project responsibility base. He promoted the idea and became a leader in the company's design-build program, placing heavy emphasis upon its further development while serving as marketing manager, then as general manager and later as president. Later still, as corporate vice chairman, he continued to promote design-build and saw the company's engineering capabilities expand into energy, chemicals, pharmaceuticals, food processing and all types of industrial and commerical projects.

Cox was in the home office only a short while, because when the company opened its New York sales office he was asked to go there for a few weeks until a sales manager could be assigned. The weeks became months, the months became years, and Cox finally returned from that temporary assignment in April of 1968 when he was promoted to general manager of engineering and construction in the United States, a newly created position. At the same time, Daniel Construction Company International had been established with headquarters in Brussels, Belgium, and George McDougall was appointed general manager of all international construction.

Cox had been in Greenville long enough to impress his boss before going to New York. His first assignment was as project manager on the Firth Carpet plant at Laurens, South Carolina. It was a guaranteed-maximum-cost contract, meaning that Daniel was gambling on its ability to save money or, if it went over the guarantee, to lose money. Keeping close watch on actual cost versus estimated cost, Cox advised Carl Englund, division manager, that there would be a $183,000 saving. Englund told Cox shortly thereafter, "Mr. Daniel is upset. He says that he doesn't think you can save $183,000. You should go see him." Cox, recalling the meeting, said, "If Charlie Daniel could chase you in a corner, that was his way of finding out whether you really were a red-blooded Indian or not. He would lean on you pretty hard, and if you yielded, he would work even harder at it."

Cox said when he walked into Daniel's office, the boss was red-faced and told him, "I don't see any savings in this project." Cox replied, "Boss, you don't know what you're talking about." With that appraisal of his knowledge of the project, Daniel's face became redder and he said, "I hope you're right. Now convince me." Cox said he did convince him of the saving. "And from that day on Charlie Daniel never questioned any statement I made to him, and I think it's a way he measured people. It was an interesting part of his makeup, probably the one thing that gave him a great deal of strength among people. He always endeavored to surround himself with decision makers, and that translates into a decision-making capability."

Cox went into marketing in 1958 pretty much like Ed Taylor did in 1952 — without prior experience or formal training. This is how he explained his indoctrination: "Being the type fellow I am, I just went to New York, put my hat on, and Buck and Charlie would call me and tell me of leads they had received from various sources. I would go meet the prospective clients and endeavor to carry the total sales responsibility myself, and I think there's a little joke that goes with this. We started getting contracts, and I wouldn't even bother calling them. I just took the responsibility of executing the contracts myself. Charlie called one day back in 1961 and said, 'You know, you are not allowed to sign contracts. You are not an officer.'

I told him he had better resolve the problem, and it wasn't many days later that the problem was solved." Cox was elected a vice president.

The New York office has never been just a sales office because it gradually broadened into a control area as other divisions were opened. From its inception, as more contracts were established with numerous industries, leading to an ever-increasing number of contracts, the New York sales manager was the central interface for each of the divisions. This involved him directly with all of the divisional managers and the total operation of the company. In the 10-year period after Daniel set up in New York, five more regional construction offices were opened; the company moved into Europe, the United Kingdom, the Caribbean (Puerto Rico), and Spain; and it established an Engineering Department and staffed a Midwest sales office in Chicago. Total involvement by the New York manager with all of the company's operations began to change as Daniel entered the 1970's, expanded into corporate construction groups and increased its sales staff from a half-dozen to approximately 50, with most operations segments having their own marketing specialists. Even so, both the New York and later the Chicago sales offices continue to interface with all engineering and construction operations, contributing substantially to the company's continued growth.

Reviewing Daniel's expansion during its first 45 years, Cox said, "If you really wanted to look for the single mechanical ingredient which has allowed our geographical growth, it would have to be our jet airplanes, because for the first time they gave us the speed and the range to reach out to areas that heretofore had been unavailable to us. Our total marketing configuration within the company exploded. You find us in Wyoming, Colorado and on out to the west coast. I have no question that we are going to further broaden these operations in strength in Canada, and by 1990 I think Daniel will be as strong throughout the Midwest and Northwest as we have become in the entire South and East."

Daniel purchased its first jet airplanes in 1966, 10 years after piston-driven aircraft were put into use, to expand its marketing and operations horizons. Even though he was able to reach his destinations much quicker by air, Charlie Daniel's traveling habits remained about the same. For the pilots, it was often like flying the dawn patrol when he scheduled a flight.

Richard K. Young, Daniel's first full-time pilot and manager of the Aviation Department, said that when company personnel first began flying, he received a call from the boss: "Mr. Daniel wanted to know what time could he take off the next morning. I don't remember where he was going, but I told him we could leave any time. He asked if 6:00 a.m. would be too early. I assured him that would be fine. So he said since that was the case, we may as well leave at 5:00 a.m. And sure enough we did. He never wasted a minute."

The Aviation Department, instigated by Hugh Daniel, was established April 26, 1956, with the purchase of a twin Beechcraft. When someone proposed that the company first buy a single-engine plane, Charlie stated that he wanted two engines and two pilots to take him where he was going and to bring him back. Young's first copilot was Wesley Holcombe, a mechanical engineer, but within a few months a second full-time pilot was hired because Holcombe was spending more time flying than engineering. The company bought another Beechcraft in 1957 for the Alabama Division, and a 10-passenger Lockheed Lodestar Howard 250 was added later. The Howard was sold when two DeHavilland jets were purchased, one based in Greenville and the other in Birmingham where Hugh Daniel continued to maintain his office.

George McDougall did not share Daniel's opinion about single-engine planes. He was a licensed pilot, and he knew how much valuable time could be saved by flying a light plane to remote job sites instead of traveling by car. Without specifying the type of aircraft he had in mind, George broached his idea to the boss and convinced him. He asked Dick Young to buy a little Cessna, and he used it frequently for a couple of years until Charlie Daniel saw it at the Greenville airport and ordered that it be sold immediately. It was.

By 1980, the Aviation Department had six aircraft based at Stevens Hangar at the Greenville-Spartanburg airport and 13 pilots to fly them. In addition to the two medium-range DeHavillands, the fleet consisted of a 2,700-mile-range Lockheed Jet Star with a speed of 500 mph; a Beechcraft King Air and Barron; and a Bell 206 L-Ranger helicopter. They had a combined passenger capacity of 44. Total miles flown by all Daniel planes from 1956 to 1980 was estimated by Young as being more than 15 million.

The company and its pilots have received numerous safety awards because no Daniel plane has been involved in a serious accident. In addition to the mileage logged by its own aircraft, Daniel's personnel have flown several more million miles on domestic and international commercial flights on trips to clients' headquarters and project sites. Young, who flew "the hump" during World War II to supply British troops in the China-Burma-India theater, was a pilot for two other corporations before joining Daniel

April 10, 1956. He estimated that he had flown well over 5 million miles from then until 1980.

An early prime example of how air travel made new territory more accessible and brought additional business to the company is Daniel's experience with the Eastman Chemicals Division of Eastman Kodak Company. Charlie Daniel, Buck Mickel and Ted Johnson began making frequent trips to Kingsport, Tennessee, in the late 1950's in an effort to sell Daniel's construction services to Tennessee Eastman Company, the division's manufacturing unit. Those visits led to the first contract with Tennessee Eastman in 1960, and since then the company has served Eastman almost continuously in construction and maintenance work. In addition to major projects at Kingsport, Daniel constructed the Carolina Eastman plant in Columbia, South Carolina, and the Arkansas Eastman facility in Batesville, Arkansas. The most recent award in this series is a 1980 contract to construct facilities at Kingsport that will produce industrial chemicals from coal. By then, Daniel was heavily involved in the synfuel industry.

In addition to performing a significant portion of the major industrial construction in his state in the 1950's as well as expanding into other states, Daniel became personally involved in a substantial volume of institutional construction. He was practically forced to build Bob Jones University in Greenville when President Bob Jones refused to take no for an answer in the late 1940's. His involvement in this type of construction, and his personal interest, was magnified on the enlarged Clemson campus and the new Furman University campus, which began taking shape in 1954. By 1958, when Furman had completed its move from downtown Greenville and dedicated its new campus, Daniel had performed all the principal construction, in addition to miscellaneous buildings and services. It has constructed additional buildings there in more recent years as Furman has continued to grow. Soon after completion of the Furman dining hall in 1958, the building was named in honor of Charles E. Daniel; and another facility dedicated to the Daniel family is the Homozel Mickel Daniel Music Building completed in 1976.

Daniel closed out the decade of the 1950's with revenues during the 10-year period totaling more than one-half billion dollars, the majority of which represented construction in South Carolina. The Alabama Division continued to obtain a substantial volume of work, and the Virginia and Florida Divisions were growing into prominence; yet Charlie Daniel's influence in bringing new industry into South Carolina and in expanding existing plants was evidenced in the more than 360 home office projects. The momentum gathered in those 10 years carried the company into 1960 with record-breaking revenues that year of $137 million.

CHAPTER 8

A Pattern for Progress

Charlie Daniel applied practical psychology in developing young executives to manage his company. On a marketing trip to New York he used the Empire State Building to make a point to one of them. "Look, Buck," he said, "given enough time and money, we can move that damn building to Greenville, brick by brick. Don't ever forget it." His theory was simple: Lay out your plans, keep your objective in sight, move ahead step by step, and you will reach your goal. "Applying that philosophy," Buck Mickel has since told his own young executives, "we grew into one of the world's largest construction companies, both in services and unlimited geographical range. We still abide by it, and we are still growing."

The company's growth pattern, laid out in the post-war industrial boom years and developed one step at a time, began taking definite shape in the decade of the 1960's. In that 10-year time span, 16 additional major units were established; and the company expanded to the Gulf Coast, across the Mississippi River, into the heart of the Midwest, to Puerto Rico and across the Atlantic Ocean. Its slogan was changed from "Builders in and of the South" to "Building a Better Future" in recognition of its numerous clients in other parts of this country and the world. This was the growth pattern of the 1960's:

1960 — Two project managers in Alabama were promoted to managers of new regional offices: James F. Daniel, III, in Atlanta, and E. F. Matteson in Greensboro, North Carolina. The Georgia unit merged with other divisions in 1969. Harry M. Payne, Jr., was appointed the first manager of Daniel Engineering.

1961 — Claud C. Calmes was promoted to manager of the New Maintenance & Millwright Department.

1964 — The European Division was opened at Brussels, Belgium with Norman Smyth as manager. Roger M. Scovil, who had succeeded Calmes in M&M, was placed in charge of all projects in the Caribbean, with headquarters in San Juan, Puerto Rico. Daniel Realty Corporation was established with offices in Birmingham under Garry Smith and Caldwell Englund. A Midwest sales office was opened in Chicago, and Clifton P. Coleman, formerly in Southeast sales, was appointed manager. Construction of the 25-story Daniel Building in Greenville was begun on June 29. Charles E. Daniel died on September 13.

1965 — The Louisiana Division was opened in New Orleans under the supervision of Thomas Sutter, a veteran construction man who had retired from another firm in that city. The next expansion was across the Mississippi, and Marcus G. McCoy, an Alabama project manager, was promoted to manager of the Arkansas Divsion in Little Rock. Near the end of the year, the Kentucky Division was opened in Lexington, and Joseph Stroud was appointed manager of operations in Kentucky and adjoining states. Stroud, manager of the South Carolina Division at the time of his new assignment, was succeeded by Harry L. Cunningham, Jr., who was promoted from chief project manager. The Louisiana and Kentucky Divisions were later merged with other divisions.

1966 — The Daniel Building in Greenville was dedicated.

1967 — Additional overseas work necessitated further expansion. The United Kingdom branch was opened at Irvine, Ayrshire, Scotland. Monroe Durham, a project manager in the European Division, was given responsibility for that new operation. Work in Spain prompted the establishment of Daniel Navarra, S. A., at Pamplona, and Calmes was named manager.

1968 — Corporate Projects, a headquarters-based task force construction group, was established to manage the increasing volume of the larger and more complex projects. Wilfred Jones was appointed group manager. In the developing stages, there were four divisions. The original Corporate Projects divisional managers were Howard McCall, Power; L. W. Donnelly, Chemical; Sam Duvall, Industrial; and C. R. Cox, Textile & Fibers, a division that was later merged with Industrial and Chemical. The Corporate Projects Group was renamed Corporate Construction in 1975, with each of the three current entities becoming a separate group. Richard Dean was appointed group vice president of Industrial; L. G. McCraw, group vice president, Chemical and Fibers; and Howard McCall was elevated to president, Power.

An interesting sidelight to the establishment of the Power Group, which became a leader in nuclear, fossil fuel and hydro-electric construction in the 1970's, is that Daniel's South Carolina Division constructed the first nuclear power plant in the Southeast at Parr, South Carolina. Construction began in May 1960, and the 17-megawatt prototype plant went into operation in March 1963. It was closed in November 1967 when the experiment was completed. Harry Cunningham was the project manager. The owners were Duke Power, South Carolina Electric & Gas, Carolina Power & Light, and Virginia Electric Power, which formed the Carolinas-Virginia Nuclear Power Association, Inc., for that experimental project.

The purpose of the experiment at Parr was "to develop ways to produce power economically from atomic energy, and to construct and operate a prototype nuclear power plant." Daniel has since performed major construction for each of those pioneers, including four 900-megawatt units for CP&L, a project scheduled for completion in the early 1990's. Daniel's Power Group entered 1980 with 10 active projects representing a total capacity of 15,175 megawatts. The plants, located in the South and Midwest, will cost more than $13 billion upon completion.

1969 — Daniel Construction Company, Inc., became a public-held corporation just before the end of the decade when the directors of the family-owned firm agreed to make the first public offering of the company's stock and convertible debentures, a move spearheaded by Hugh Daniel. The first quarterly report to shareholders was submitted May 14, 1969, and the letter read in part: "We are pleased to welcome you as shareholders, and enclose the quarterly dividend payable to holders of record on April 30, 1969. Results for the six months' period ended March 31, 1969, showed a 96 percent increase over the comparable period of 1968. . . . New awards remain at a high level, and we look forward to the balance of our fiscal year with optimism." At that time, the company's fiscal year ended on September 30.

Directors made another major decision before the end of calendar year 1969. They decided to diversify the company's activities. The long-range plan was to increase revenues through acquisitions and company-established businesses so that nonconstruction operations would eventually match earnings from construction. This plan has never been realized because of the continued significant growth in construction. The first acquisition is described in the 1969 annual report, which went to press just before the end of the first quarter of fiscal 1970:

"On December 1, 1969, the company entered into an agreement in principle to acquire all of the outstanding capital stock of Applied Engineering Company of Orangeburg, South Carolina. Applied Engineering is an international designer and manufacturer of factory-assembled process plants. It is a leading supplier of propane-air standby systems, and recently entered the fields of packaged hydrogen, carbon monoxide, carbon dioxide and other process plants, including various phases of liquefied natural gas. In addition, it is a large distributor of industrial boilers, and has a substantial maintenance business. Applied Engineering is also extending its capabilities into the area of air and steam pollution." The company was purchased from its founders, R. Park Newton and W. W. Dukes, Jr., who continued to operate it.

Two key officers joined Daniel in 1968 to help direct the transition from private to public ownership, to guide it in legal matters, and lead it into diversified activities that would be compatible with construction. Robert P. Stirm became the company's first vice president-law and general counsel, and Greg W. Rothe was elected vice president-finance. Stirm established Daniel's first Legal Department, and in 1977, Rothe was appointed president of Daniel Industrial Services, one of the two newly established principal divisions. He was in charge of 20 subsidiaries and divisions, most of which he recommended acquiring or establishing. Rothe died September 10, 1979.

CHAPTER 9

A One-Man Magnet for Industry

Almost 10 years after his initial exposure to national publicity (in the *Fortune* magazine article of October, 1954, reprinted in Chapter 6) Daniel was back in the limelight of big-name publications. This time, the vehicle was the January 11, 1964, issue of the highly reputable McGraw-Hill magazine, *Business Week*.

As in the case of the earlier *Fortune* article, appropriate photographs supplemented the written word. But not only were there illustrations, the front page of the magazine itself bore a cover picture of Daniel, hard hat in hand, in a typical pose at a plant site. The title of the article likewise typified Daniel: "A One-Man Magnet For Industry."

At this stage of the Daniel career, both his name and his likeness were far more familiar on the national scene than had been the case 10 years earlier. He had achieved some prominence when thrust unexpectedly into the political world as an interim U. S. senator in the last few months of 1954. That in itself gave him a recognition factor that distinguished him from his colleagues and competitors in the construction field. More important, however, was the ever-growing reputation he and his company were achieving as contractors of regional, national, and, by then, international stature.

Additionally, publicity had come his way over the last few years with increasing frequency and intensity. As would be expected, the South Carolina media were attentive to his personal and professional achievements, as was reflected by continuing news stories and occasional in-depth coverage. In the latter category were such articles as the March, 1956, "Palmetto Profile" on Daniel in the *South Carolina Magazine*, which had done an earlier feature on Daniel Construction Company in October of 1951.

In neighboring North Carolina, the *Charlotte Observer* devoted a full-page Sunday spread on January 8, 1961, to Daniel, captioning Rolfe Neill's article with the catchy headline: "He Could Shave A Day Off Creation."

74

From time to time, his speeches were reprinted in their en-
tirety in magazine form as well as capturing newspaper coverage.
The 1960 spring issue of *South Carolina City*, official publication
of the Municipal Association of South Carolina, carried the text of
his January 11 address to the association, entitled "Commitments
for the Future of South Carolina." And in September of 1961,
America's Textile Reporter reprinted Daniel's eyebrow-raising
speech delivered at the Hampton Watermelon Festival of July 1, in
which he challenged South Carolinians to improve the educational,
employment and economic opportunities of the state's Negro citizenry. Then too, on October 17, 1957, there had appeared in another
McGraw-Hill publication, the *Engineering News-Record*, an article
describing Daniel as "A Construction Man with Sales Appeal."

Against that background, it was quite natural that a cover-
story article in *Business Week* would catch the eye of hosts of
Americans who had come to recognize the name Charlie Daniel over
the span of his three decades of hyperactivity in the construction
field.

What follows on the next few pages is that article, reprinted
from the January 11, 1964, issue of *Business Week* by special permission; ©1964 by McGraw-Hill, Inc., New York, N. Y. 10020. All
rights reserved.

A ONE-MAN MAGNET FOR INDUSTRY

Greenville builder Charles E. Daniel has talked hundreds
of companies into putting up plants in the Southeast,
mostly South Carolina – and has built 400 of them himself.

Probably no single individual has worked harder and more
successfully to draw industry to the Southeast — and grab a big
share of it for his own native soil — than a Greenville (S. C.) builder
named Charles E. Daniel (cover and pictures), chairman of Daniel
Construction Co.

Shortly after he started out as a builder, Daniel went to a South
Carolina textile manufacturer and asked to build his next plant.
"Why should I give the job to you?" the man asked. "Because," said
Daniel, "I can build it faster, cheaper, and better than anybody
else." He got the job — and more later on from the same executive.

Through all the great postwar industrial development of the
South, he has been tirelessly pursuing U. S. corporations on behalf
of the state of South Carolina and Charles Daniel. With a disarming
manner, relentless drive, a talent for turning important people into

lifelong friends, and a top-flight building organization, he has persuaded hundreds of companies, including dozens of blue-chip outfits, to let him build their new plants — in South Carolina when he can, in another Southern state when he must.

Incalculable

"He has been of incalculable benefit — the nearest thing I know to perpetual energy for sparking industry in South Carolina and the South," says South Carolina Gov. Donald S. Russell.

Along the way, his unflagging efforts have made him the largest industrial contractor in the Southeast and one of his state's two or three richest, most powerful men. The plants he has built are worth around $2-billion — and he's working on 104 projects totaling some $271-million, the largest volume he has handled in a decade of growth.

Contractors aren't usually thought of as industrialists. But last Nov. 11, his 68th birthday, Daniel received at the Waldorf Astoria in New York — from his friend Richard M. Nixon, on behalf of the National Assn. of Industrial Realtors — an award as "industrialist of the year." Previous recipients included such men as Alfred P. Sloan, Jr., Benjamin F. Fairless, and Thomas J. Watson.

I. OUT OF THE DITCH

Daniel admits with a smile: "They say I divide plants equally, one for South Carolina and one for the rest of the South. Actually, I have to serve the interest of the client."

Clearly, he serves it as often as possible in his native state. The divisional head of a major company says: "He certainly influenced our choice of South Carolina. He gave us six or eight site locations, five of which were in South Carolina. This was sort of loading the dice — but they were good sites."

The actual score:

— 250 major industrial plants in South Carolina.
— 400 plants in all the 12 Southen states where he operates.

Textile mills are his specialty, but he also puts up office buildings, hotels and motels, apartments, stores, shopping centers — almost anything except roads and dams.

The plants he has helped locate and build, Daniel estimates, have provided some 150,000 new industrial jobs for the region, twice that many supporting and supply jobs. "Seeing the South climb out of the ditch," he says, "gives me more pleasure than anything else."

New Deals

The company is currently building 54 new industrial plants, including a $30-million nylon plant for American Enka Corp., a $14-million tissue mill for Georgia-Pacific Corp., and "the most modern textile mill in the world" for J. P. Stevens & Co., Inc.

Daniel expects to complete over $150-million worth of work in the coming year. On this he will draw about 3.5% gross fees, and net, after taxes, between $2.2-million and $2.6-million. Daniel, his wife, and his younger brother Hugh, the company president, own the business completely.

Daniel is now looking further afield. He'll soon open a Chicago sales office to add to the one in New York. In 1962 he started an "experimental" office in Brussels to supervise some European work for a client. Other companies he builds for are looking overseas, and he is deciding whether to make it permanent.

II. STALKING THE PLANT

Daniel's approach while plant hunting can vary, but the basic situation is the same. He has so many friends in the state and among businessmen elsewhere that he soon hears of plans for expansion — and about the time a company starts thinking about a new plant, Daniel appears in its offices.

Some years ago, for example, he and a friend dropped by unannounced at the New York headquarters of a major corporation while a board meeting was in progress. When the directors learned that Daniel and his companion, former Secretary of State and Supreme Court Justice James F. Byrnes, then governor of South Carolina, were outside, they adjourned temporarily.

During pleasantries, Daniel offered to find a good site for a new plant he had heard the company was planning. The upshot was that the company decided in a few months on a plant in South Carolina. The builder: Charles E. Daniel.

Getting at It

Once company officials agree to let him help find a site, Daniel supplies all kinds of cost comparisons, taxes, utility rates, labor surveys. He puts one of his airplanes (he now has three) at company executives' disposal, invites them to Greenville, perhaps to a small dinner with the governor and leading businessmen.

He may visit sites with the company president, but he's careful about that: "When I walk through town, the price of land goes up."

The Prize

All this while, there's no mention of building the plant. In fact, Daniel worked to help DuPont locate in South Carolina, knowing it does its own building. Though he explains his services, he doesn't come right out and ask for the job. But he can get the point over.

Once he found a site for a company, with no commitment to build. But one day the company president found Daniel's grading equipment on the job — showing his eagerness, and discouraging competitors. He won.

III. WEIGHTY VOICE

Not surprisingly, Daniel's personal standing has risen steadily as his business has grown. Estimates of his personal fortune run from $20-million to $40-million. He is one of South Carolina's major employers. Long-standing friendships with businessmen and politicians, especially Byrnes and Sen. Strom Thurmond, give his conservative voice added weight. Daniel himself served in the U. S. Senate in 1954, on a short interim appointment by Gov. Byrnes.

Daniel's influence has gone to help create what he believes is a nourishing climate for business. He worked to get laws that are beneficial to business — tax exemption, for example, on production machinery and materials. His efforts include keeping out elements he regards as discordant, especially strongly unionized companies. "I have occasionally asked companies not to come to South Carolina," he says, "when I felt they wouldn't fit in."

He has run afoul of the National Labor Relations Board himself. He won, by a 3-to-1 vote, an NLRB-sponsored election in his Mechanical Dept. in 1961, but the union appealed on the ground the company used coercion. The case is still pending.

Outspoken

On one controversial issue, Daniel shows outspoken liberalism. He believes in helping Negroes economically and educationally. Two years ago, at a festival in the Black Belt town of Hampton, he told startled listeners:

"The desegregation issue cannot continue to be hidden behind the door. . . . We have a definite obligation to increase the productivity of our Negro citizens, to provide them with good jobs at good wages and to continue to assure them of fair treatment. By raising their education and economic status, we would raise the whole economy of the state."

Of Daniel's own work force of 8,800, 26% are Negroes; about 800 are skilled mechanics working alongside white workers at equal pay.

Muttering

Daniel's pursuit and capture of industrial building in and for South Carolina has been so vigorous that inevitably, there has been some resentment. There have been mutterings that he controlled the State Development Board, got inside tips. Daniel's executives snort that he is better able to give tips than receive them.

Walter W. Harper, director of the board, insists Daniel gets exactly the same treatment as any other contractor. But he adds that Daniel's bigger effort in the field naturally brings greater results.

Wider

Daniel's orbit swings a good deal wider than most contractors'. He travels widely to seek new plants and visit business friends, is a member of the Business Council, sits on the board of eight major companies, including Eastern Air Lines, Prudential Insurance Co. He gets the call for such groups as the committee formed by top businessmen last year to push a tax cut.

The center of his activities, though, is his highly efficient building organization; he has no hobbies, no children, digs his feet in at the hint of vacation. He has let much of the day-to-day business go to five hardworking executives in Greenville, especially Executive Vice-Pres. Buck Mickel, his wife's nephew. This leaves him free for the wide-ranging business-social mixing he is skilled at and enjoys.

IV. DRIVE TO BUILD

A long-time friend, Pres. Roger Milliken of Deering Milliken, Inc., hits Daniel's most obvious quality — "drive, he works seven days a week." When not traveling, he roams the office, poking into details. Every day or so he jumps in his car and drives off to look over a construction job. If he sees something that's not right, the field supervisor soon is reminded that he's working for a tough, self-made man.

One Thing and Another

This drive, plus organizing skill, won Daniel a reputation for fast, efficient building when he launched his company in 1935.

It started a process he casually calls "one thing leading to another" — as, for example, at the Chemstrand nylon plant in Pensacola, Fla., which DuPont originally built for Chemstrand. Daniel, called in on a small job eight years ago, has been "building one addition after another" until his work there comes to about $150-million,, and has built $100-million for Chemstrand elsewhere.

In all, some 70% of current work is "repeat business" like this.

Complete, Speedy

Two things especially characterize his work:

> — He lays heavy stress on offering a "complete package" — just taking over and performing "turn key" serivce: "The company just orders the plant, tells us what it wants. We do everything up to the day we turn over the key to the finished plant."
>
> — His organizing talent and drive to keep men and materials on schedule largely account for his astonishing construction speed. Says Woodside Mills' Pres. Robert S. Small: "Don't tell Charlie Daniel you want your plant before you really want it — because you'll get it."

A maker of door locks once told Daniel he couldn't meet his schedule. Daniel said all right, but he'd go ahead with the dedication, with signs on the doors saying there were no locks because X Co. failed to meet its commitment. "We got the locks," says Daniel.

Chapter 10

His Last Project

The last project in which Charlie Daniel was personally involved from conception to start-up, Milliken's Magnolia Finishing Plant, is referred to in the last paragraph of the *Business Week* magazine article in the preceding chapter. The author did not identify the project for which a maker of door locks advised Daniel he could not meet his schedule; but it was the Magnolia project, one of the most fantastic design-build achievements in the construction industry. As the article implied, makers of manufacturing equipment and building supplies performed their own miracles in keeping pace with 2,200 engineers, supervisors and craftsmen.

Roger Milliken had decided that rather than continue as the marginal greige goods supplier to other textile manufacturers who dyed and finished cloth for sale to garment customers, it would be more advantageous for his company to process the material and sell it directly to the ultimate consumer. "Thus we could better control our destiny," he explained. "And making a big change like this made us fear that we might lose some customers in the interim. Therefore, we felt it incumbent upon us that we move ahead as rapidly as possible as we entered this period of change.

"We started looking for property and talked to Charlie Daniel about doing the job on a basis where we would have to start from scratch and build our plant while making our plans as we went along. We asked him if his company wanted to enter into a really vast program of building a plant that ended up costing $13.5 million. He said that he would be interested and he would develop the full resources of his company to us."

The dyeing and finishing plant, a 383,000-square-foot complex, was scheduled for production early in September of 1963; yet the January page had already been torn off the calendar. Bradley Dewey, a consultant who had been America's chief rubber director during World War II, suggested that model makers be brought in to

81

model the plant. "So we hired these model makers," Milliken said, "and they wanted to know what the foundations would be like. We told them we did not know because we had not designed the building. Then they wanted to know how can we expect the contractor to start if he does not know how to work on the foundations." The model makers were not familiar with Daniel.

Wallace Storey, manager of Milliken Engineering, had gone to Europe in late February to see what new ideas he could pick up with the dyeing and finishing plant in mind. "I was to be over there three weeks," he said, "but I got a call after two weeks to come back because they wanted to start construction." He denied a rumor that the building was completed before the drawings were finished.

"Actually, a contractor doesn't generally do anything until he has something to show him what to do," Storey explained, "and, therefore, it's a misunderstanding to say that you build it first and design it second. What you do, of course, is minimize the drawing in many cases such as this. For example on our grading we knew that we had to go down to a certain level. So, in effect, grading was going on even without a drawing. You can frequently do things of that nature, or maybe you design things sketch-wise. We very often make little freehand sketches on the job and let someone be working from them while we are translating them into the final drawing. And that means you are saving time."

Even though the title to the property had not been cleared, ground was broken for the plant on March 25, 1963. The site, visible from Interstate 85, is near the town of Blacksburg, north of Milliken's headquarters in Spartanburg. With Daniel working from freehand sketches part of the time and applying completely coordinated client-engineer-constructor innovations in methods and materials, the completion date of September 3, 1963, was met.

This is what was accomplished in just over five months: site preparation, access roads, a bridge, a parking lot, the main plant structure, equipment installation, process piping and instrumentation, a low-level dam and pumping station, boiler plant, water treatment facilities, service buildings, a reservoir, waste disposal facilities, and a warehouse. On dedication day, the plant appeared to be at least six months old because of the esthetic touches added at the last minute. The yard was sodded and landscaped, and for the final touch artificial magnolias were attached to the magnolia trees. The facility was still a showplace 17 years later, and Daniel was building another addition to it. The first fully instrumented and controlled dyeing and finishing plant, Magnolia introduced continuous chemical process methods to the textile finishing industry.

Milliken said, "I think it probably cost more to build than if we had done it on a slower basis, but time was money in this instance. We felt that it was a very worthwhile achievement, and one which I doubt will be repeated." The normal construction time for such a process complex would be about 18 months. Everyone involved in the engineering and construction agrees that the meetings held each Saturday morning during the planning and construction period made it all possible and greatly expedited the completion.

Milliken chaired the Saturday sessions, and Daniel attended many of them along with such regular attendees as Mickel; Calmes, the project manager; and Johnson, manager of the Mechanical Department at the time. In addition to Milliken and Daniel supervisors, the meetings were attended by the subcontractors. The sessions were held in a large conference room at Milliken headquarters, and a blackboard covered most of the walls. The chairman invited everyone to comment on their specific portion of the work and present any problems they might be facing. He noted the conditions, the progress or delays, and any problems on the blackboard and followed that up with obtaining the input needed for finding the solution, making notes of who said what and the date by which the work was to be accomplished. A secretary put all that information on paper, and a copy was given to everybody in the room. A review of that week's work and what each needed to do was held the following week.

"This kept everybody on time with their plans," Milliken explained. "As a result we were able to invite a large number of our potential customers and suppliers to a special luncheon on the given date when we were to start up and walk through the plant and see all the machinery turning." The invitation, mailed weeks in advance, referred to it as the "It Can't Be Done Dedication." Storey said as soon as the invitations were received, he began getting telephone calls from subcontractors and suppliers who would say: "I've got this invitation. You're not serious, are you?" The invitation, a bit of psychology, did the trick because those subs and suppliers who had protested that "it can't be done" managed to accomplish what they were supposed to do with that added pressure.

Storey admitted to using "all of the leverage of Milliken and Daniel to get things done. For example, we had one piece of equipment that we had a hard time getting. Mr. Milliken was on the company's board of directors, and he wrote them, saying, 'We hope you get this equipment here, because if you don't there will be a sign saying this is where blank piece of equipment is supposed to be.' He got it."

The Saturday morning meetings also helped solve the problem of getting a bridge across a creek on the main entrance to the plant. The Highway Department designed the bridge as a conventional poured-in-place concrete structure. The low bidder designated February of 1964 as the completion date. Storey asked the department to redesign the bridge and use prestressed concrete to expedite construction. "They were most cooperative," he said, "and put it out for bids again. This time the completion date was November 1, 1963." Storey reiterated that the bridge must be in place months earlier and asked the Highway Department, "Can we build the bridge for you? They didn't know quite what to say, but they agreed, and said they would give us the same amount of money requested by the low bidder. So I turned to Calmes and told him that he was now a bridge builder. We finished the bridge on schedule." Daniel has never been in the bridge-building business, and that effort did not put it in that type of construction; yet a similar emergency came up several years later, and the company built its second bridge.

Just as precast concrete expedited the bridge for Milliken, it was a key factor in the record-time completion of Magnolia. Storey explained, "We used 110-foot clear-span concrete single tees, the first time they had been built; and, being architecturally inclined, we wanted to have it as clean looking inside as possible, with no conduit exposed." After hearing more it-can't-be-done excuses, Storey said, "Calmes and I decided to do it anyhow, and the results were most interesting." He explained that the electricians placed conduit in the tees at the concrete yard in Greenville; and when they found that they had some time on their hands, they decided to go ahead and pull the wire too. So prewired tees were erected in the plant, saving days of additional work and $40,000. Through those and other innovations, Magnolia is a testimony to the drive, speed and ingenuity of both the client and the constructor.

"I don't believe any other contractor in the country could have possibly marshalled the resouces, raw materials and skills of all the different trades that go into contracting in the way Charlie Daniel and his organization did," Roger Milliken has stated on more than one occasion. "It was a very exciting thing."

The project was equally exciting to Daniel personnel. Numerous prospective clients have been shown Magnolia as a prime example of the company's "total package" capabilities and construction speed. A color slide presentation, depicting weekly progress on the site from groundbreaking to the artificial magnolias has been viewed by thousands.

Charlie Daniel's illness began taking its toll on his time and energy in early 1964, and it was a struggle for him to attend the groundbreaking ceremonies on June 29 of what would have been his most interesting project of all — the 25-story Daniel Building on the 300 block of North Main Street in downtown Greenville. The event was attended by a large crowd of national, state and city officials, along with the excited public; and they could see what was to be 18 months later on the huge rendering erected high above the corner of Main and College Streets.

Daniel made a brief speech at the groundbreaking, saying, "It is my hope that Daniel Construction Company's expression of faith in a great future for Greenville, in erecting the state's tallest office structure, will cause others to join in building a dynamic 'new' city for the Carolinas.

"A minimum of $50 million expended on Greenville's business areas would be a good start toward this ultimate goal. The great cities of America, and those struggling for greatness, have people who stand unafraid to commit themselves to the future.

"Greenville possesses such people in greater numbers than any city in eastern America. I urge them to answer the call for a greater Greenville today."

Immediately after the groundbreaking, a luncheon was given in his honor at the Poinsett Hotel. Here again, the crowded banquet hall included industrial and business leaders, all personal friends, who were grateful for this opportunity to show their appreciation for what he had done for their country, states and communities. That was Charlie Daniel's last public appearance.

A plaque was presented to him at the luncheon. It read: "To Charles E. Daniel, in recognition of the invaluable contribution which you have made to the advancement of the economic, the governmental and the social well-being of the peoples of the state, region and nation by your unparalleled leadership in the field of industrial development; by your service in the halls of the nation's Congress; by your ever-fearless readiness to let your voice be heard in the consideration of local, state and national issues; and by your personal integrity of character, the people of this community, as represented on this occasion by the mayor and aldermen of the City Council of Greenville, the senator and members of the Greenville County Legislative Delegation, and the president and directors of the Greater Greenville Chamber of Commerce, hereby express their deep and abiding appreciation and their recognition of your worth to this community, to our state and to our nation and for what you have wrought for the good of all."

The plaque was signed by the city mayor, David G. Traxler; the county senator, P. Bradley Morrah, Jr.; and James M. Henderson, president of the chamber. It was dated June 29, 1964.

The construction man that he was, Daniel wanted to watch progress at the building site. Several weeks after the groundbreaking he made one of his last visits to the office, one block from the job, and asked Harry Cunningham, his personal choice as the project manager, to walk with him to the site. Excavation was still underway, and he was pleased with what he saw.

Charles Ezra Daniel died on September 13, 1964.

CHAPTER 11

Changing of the Guard

The changing of the guard within Daniel Construction Company on January 1, 1965, was only a formality, because Charlie Daniel had delegated most of the responsibility and authority a year earlier. Therefore, he had the satisfaction of knowing he would leave the business in experienced and capable hands. On that New Year's Day, Hugh Daniel became chairman and chief executive officer, retaining his treasurer's title, and Buck Mickel was placed in charge of the daily operations as president and chief operating officer.

Working closely with them at the executive level were George McDougall, Ted Johnson, Blake Moose and John Odom at corporate headquarters, and Charlie Cox at his sales manager's office in New York. Managers of the operating divisions and the various corporate functions coordinated their activities with them. Probably because of his total responsibilities in the broad areas of revenues and operations, Mickel was the one person who most closely emulated Charlie Daniel. Like the founder, he had become a workaholic; in his new role he was working 12 or more hours a day, and his workweek ran the full seven days.

As the company continued to expand in major projects, particularly in the areas of chemical, synthetic fibers, food processing and paper plants that were jobs requiring larger numbers of supervisors and craftsmen, three regional managers were appointed in mid-1965. Caldwell Englund was placed in charge of the Alabama and Louisiana divisions; L. G. Longcrier, Jr., was placed over Arkansas, Kentucky and Virginia; and E. F. Matteson became responsible for North Carolina, South Carolina and Florida. They had been division managers and were experienced in marketing and operations. Their previous positions were filled by seasoned project managers: John W. Gustafson in Alabama, T. Howard Suitt in North Carolina, and Clyde T. Green, Jr., in Virginia.

That middle management concept did not lessen Mickel's load, primarily because 1967 revenues reached a record high of $346 million. The new contracts broadened the company's geographical range in the United States and Europe; and in 1968, the top management tier was strengthened by appointment of the two general managers: Charlie Cox and George McDougall. The three regional managers were reassigned, and two vice presidents of construction were appointed: Matteson over all Regional Division work, and Johnson in charge of the larger projects assigned to the Corporate Divisions.

The creation of additional positions allowed the new executives to quickly practice Charlie Daniel's philosophy of promoting from within, as he had always insisted, with emphasis on youth. Mickel, for example, was just two weeks beyond his 39th birthday when he picked up the president's reins. Young project managers were promoted to fill the divisional management vacancies. The transfer of Cox to corporate headquarters created the opportunity for Currie B. Spivey, Jr., Southeastern sales manager, to move into the top New York sales position at age 32.

As the company entered calendar year 1969, the significant news was that Daniel's stock was being offered to the public for the first time on March 19. That milestone in the Company's history resulted in the first public announcement of earnings, because as a privately owned company Daniel declined to reveal its financial status. This was the year, too, that the company made its major move into the electric generating industry with the award of a contract to construct a coal-fired station at Cliffside, North Carolina, for Duke Power Company. In the next 10 years, Daniel grew into one of the country's leading constructors of power stations, and maintained that position after adding synfuel plants to its building capabilities in the decade of the 1980's.

In the first quarter of fiscal year 1970 (the last three months of calendar year 1969), the volume of new contracts established a company record; and in the first six months, earnings increased 51 percent over the same period the previous year. New work, coupled with existing projects, put Daniel in second place among American general building contractors, according to a survey by *Engineering News Record* magazine. During that fiscal year, net earnings were up 21 percent, and backlog had increased by 15 percent. Another highlight was the occupancy of the newly completed 20-story Daniel Building in Birmingham. It was featured on the cover of the 1970 annual report, just as the 25-story Daniel Building in Greenville, occupied in 1966, was on the cover of the first (1969) annual report.

The directors of the company at the time it went public were Mrs. Homozel Mickel Daniel, Hugh Daniel and Buck Mickel. Shareholders elected Alester G. Furman, III, president of The Furman Company in Greenville, and Harry B. Brock, Jr., president of Central Bank and Trust Company, Birmingham, to the board in 1970. A year later, the number of directors was increased to seven with the election of Vice Presidents Cox and McDougall.

It was at the February 16, 1971, annual meeting that Chairman Hugh Daniel announced a change in the corporate name to Daniel International Corporation, effective March 1. It would be the holding company, with Daniel Construction Company and other divisions and subsidiaries retaining their identities. He explained that the reasons for adopting the new name dated back to the establishment of the international construction subsidiary and the decision to make the stock available to employees and the public. He pointed out, too, that the company's international work had increased.

Officers also felt that in view of the intensive diversification program and continued emphasis on engineering and maintenance, the word construction in the company name might inadvertently disassociate the corporation from its numerous capabilities and services not normally associated with general contracting. That thinking became more pronounced over the next several months with the acquisition of the Fortis Corporation of King, North Carolina, which put Daniel in the low-cost housing business; the establishment of American Equipment Company in Greenville, a move that expanded sales and services of construction equipment to the public; the formation of Tool Service Company, which made construction and industrial tools handled by Daniel available to other firms; and the acquisition of Goldston Inc. of Eden, North Carolina, a purchase that broadened the company's earnings base into truck leasing, sales and service.

The original corporate officers of Daniel International, in addition to those also serving as directors, were the three vice presidents: Greg Rothe, finance; Robert Stirm, law; and Caldwell Englund, administration. They were listed in the 1971 annual report which noted a 39-percent increase in earnings per share over the previous fiscal year. William M. Hofacre had come aboard as corporate vice president and controller before the 1972 annual report was published. That report included these pertinent facts: the company had 30 operating profit centers and 23,000 employees providing a variety of services on four continents, and the 21-percent increase in earnings per share marked the fourth consecutive year in which Daniel exceeded its goal of increasing earnings 15 percent annually.

The company's growth continued in fiscal 1973, both in earnings and operations. Its goal was exceeded again with a 22-percent increase in earnings per share, and dividend payments were increased for the sixth consecutive year. Frank T. Bailey was added to the corporate staff as vice president in charge of development. International operational growth included expansion into Mexico, South America, France, Austria and the Netherlands. Meanwhile, regional operations were established at Dallas, Texas. A year later, a regional Power Group office was opened in Kansas City, Missouri, as the result of new work in the Midwest; 54,000 square feet were added to the Greenville Daniel Building to make room for the rapidly expanding Engineering Group, and Daniel International (Canada) Ltd. was organized. Applied Engineering began flexing its expansion muscles with the acquisition of Smith & Norrington Engineering Corporation of Boston.

Charles W. Cox was elected Daniel's fourth president in its 40-year history as result of a realignment of top management by the directors following the annual shareholders' meeting on February 19, 1974. He succeeded Buck Mickel as corporate president and chief operating officer. Mickel was elected chairman of the board, the third person to hold the chairmanship. He succeeded Hugh Daniel, who retained the dual titles of chief executive officer and treasurer.

In spite of an energy crisis and major changes in the country's economy, 1974 was another record year. The construction backlog was the largest in history, 24 percent more than in 1973; the growth goal was exceeded for the sixth consecutive year; and cash dividend payments increased for the seventh straight year. A 3-for-2 stock split was effected in March, the fifth split since the company went public. Employment increased by 6,000 during the year, including 300 college graduates for positions requiring degreed personnel. The construction projects and other activities were so widespread that Daniel personnel were paid in 10 different currencies.

The company further diversified its services and products during the mid-1970's into industries served by its construction divisions and subsidiaries. Blu-Surf, Inc., of Parma, Michigan, was purchased in 1975, moving Daniel into the design, building, testing and installation of gas-fired heat-processing equipment. In that same year, Assured Industrial Maintenance (AIM) was established to provide process equipment repair services to petroleum, chemical, industrial and utility companies. AIM opened shops in Mobile, Alabama, and Tulsa, Oklahoma. Over the next two years, Daniel entered the textile equipment business with the acquisition of the

Bond Company of Greenville in 1976 and expanded operations in the Southwest through the purchase of Skrla, a Houston-based grading and paving company, in 1977. As the corporation reassessed its strategic long-range plans in the late 1970's, it became apparent that certain operations no longer aided in accomplishing the revised objective of strengthening its full-service construction profile. As a result of that review, Daniel gradually divested itself of those companies, in many instances reverting them back to the original owners.

CHAPTER 12

Reaching the Top

Engineering News Record magazine, an international publication serving the world's engineering and construction industries, assigned a member of its New York staff to write a feature story on Daniel International in October 1974. He was to probe into the company's reorganization and continued growth during the 10-year period that saw the founder's death, a corporate name change and the sale of the company's family-owned stock to the public.

The reporter did such an excellent job that his editor selected the article for the weekly magazine's front cover on the November 7, 1974, issue. The story is reproduced on the next few pages by special permission, © 1974 by McGraw-Hill, Inc., New York. All rights reserved.

An interesting sidelight to the story is that when it was chosen as the front cover article, an urgent late afternoon call was made to Daniel for a color photograph. The film had to be airmailed to New York the next day. The editor wanted Hugh Daniel, Buck Mickel and Charlie Cox in the picture. The reporter recalled seeing a large lighted world globe in one of the Daniel executive offices. He suggested the trio be assembled behind it as a photo possibility. As luck would have it, the three men would be available the next morning. But one was missing because Cox had to leave on an important project matter. He was able to cut his trip short and returned in midafternoon by way of company jet.

Van Moore, a Greenville master photographer, had been alerted and was set up to shoot the moment Cox arrived. He shot two rolls at the editor's suggestion and air-expressed them in two separate packages to make certain at least one roll of the film would get to New York on time. Both rolls made the deadline.

The *Engineering News-Record* story, titled "Energy, Turnkey and Open Shop Help Push Daniel to the Top," follows.

ENERGY, TURNKEY AND OPEN SHOP
HELP PUSH DANIEL TO THE TOP

Daniel International Threads The Way
From Textiles to the Big Time

While the rest of the country is bogged down in a sluggish economy, the Southeast is running away with the marbles. Daniel International Corp. (DIC), Greenville, S. C., the largest construction company in the Southeast, is matching and surpassing the growth of the area and coming away with a lot more than marbles.

Company officials predict that its 1974 revenues (fiscal year runs from October through September) will be about 40% above last year's total of $595 million and profits up 20% over last year. Daniel, the nation's second largest publicly owned general contracting firm, was No. 4 on ENR's list of the Top 400 contractors in 1973 with a total of $1.88 billion. According to Charles W. Cox, Daniel Corp.'s president, the company has a backlog of $8 billion.

Daniel's growth can be attributed to a blend of salesmanship, which convinced numerous northern corporations to establish bases in the South; to a largely open shop operation, which results in lower costs to clients; to being in a geographic area that has boomed in the past 10 years; and to a diversification program that has taken the once exclusively textile-oriented company into other profitable areas.

Daniel has over 39,000 employees involved in 43 divisions and subsidiaries. DIC's largest component, Daniel Construction Co., is involved in over 200 major projects in the U. S., all east of the Rockies, and 12 foreign countries.

Full Service Umbrella

Daniel offers total engineering and construction services, including fabrication and installation of equipment and plant maintenance after construction is completed. According to Cox, "Daniel is the world's largest maintenance and millwright organization." The company's design-construct function, adds Cox, "provides Daniel with its second largest source of income."

Within its complex organization, Daniel has an equipment division that rents its 5,000 pieces of equipment solely in house, a tool service division that rents and sells both to Daniel and to the public, a fabrication division that handles prefab pipe up to 4-ft diameter. About the only capability Daniel doesn't have is nuclear powerplant design. Daniel also will not go after fixed-price contracts, preferring cost-plus arrangements.

About 90% of Daniel's profits are from construction. But, according to Cox, "in the late '60's we began to expand in non-construction fields, hoping eventually to reach a 50-50 mix. However, our construction capabilities expanded much too rapidly to achieve that."

Daniel's organization goes after business on three fronts. The first is geographic. Local Daniel divisions usually operate on a state level and concentrate on design-construct projects worth less than $6 million. With the opening of the Texas division this year, Daniel has seven geographic divisions, mostly in the Southeast. "These divisions," says Cox, "give us the pulse of labor, construction and cost conditions throughout the area."

The second thrust for Daniel is its corporate divisions: textiles and fibers, started in 1934; industrial, which handles all non-processing plants; power, which builds powerplants for utilities; chemicals, started two years ago; and the energy resources division that will provide construction services for gasification, oil shale and basic fuels projects.

All the disciplines to support these corporate divisions are located in-house at Greenville. Projects handled here are multimillion-dollar affairs, each managed by a task force with total responsibility for it.

Daniel's final thrust is an extension of the others — doing maintenance and millwright work. Cox believes that providing this service puts Daniel in the forefront in landing plant expansion contracts. "We're already there."

Enticing Northerners

The company was started in 1934 at Anderson, S. C., by Charles E. Daniel with $25,000 in borrowed funds and it expanded quickly (ENR 10/17/57 p. 339). By 1936, an Alabama division was established with R. Hugh Daniel, a younger brother, in charge. During much of Charles Daniel's 30 years with the firm, he talked hundreds of northern companies into putting up plants in the Southeast, many in South Carolina, and his company built 400 of them. When the elder Daniel died in 1964, his brother became chairman.

In convincing companies to move south, the elder Daniel helped diversify what was once a one-industry region. And Daniel moved into many of these new areas itself.

Three in Charge

Top management today consists of a compatible trio: Daniel, 68, now treasurer and chief executive officer; Buck Mickel, 48, chairman of the board; and Cox, 56, president and chief operating officer.

Daniel, on the scene for all 40 years of the company's existence, is known as the leveling influence within management. Mickel, who started with Daniel in a ditch and moved through field operations, is considered the long-range planner and an old-school salesman of the company's fine points. Cox, versed in management techniques, sparks the day-to-day operations, and is known to keep things bouncing.

Daniel began broadening its executive base in 1957 and, according to Hugh Daniel, "We lost only one executive in 14 years." "If you look at Daniel's history closely," says Mickel, "we hit a series of plateaus from which we diversified." "One organization chart can do well for three to four years," says Cox, "but then it gets to the point where it has to split into more units."

Top managesment is quick to boast that Daniel never had a loss-year in its history, never missed a dividend and has plowed back an average of $2 million per year into the company.

In breaking down where Daniel's loyalties lie, Mickel lists the people within the organization first, then the customers, and finally the corporation. Cox, who spends a good deal of his time out on projects, frequently brings employees in from the field to the main office for possible advancement.

Training Program

To move its employees along, Daniel has one of the largest training programs in the construction industry. Roy Turner, in charge of Daniel's $1-million training effort, says that during 1974, the company trained 10,500 persons and predicts that during the next fiscal year this will go up 500 persons. Daniel's craft training program generally is equally divided between upgrading employees already within the company and new employees. "During 1973 there was a big push for welders, so we produced 800," says Turner.

Daniel feels its recruiting and training efforts are among the most sophisticated in the industry. They use a careers-in-construction van that recruits high school and college students. A computer keeps track of Daniel employees, their skills and their availability. Turner says Daniel keeps ahead of labor shortages by doing a job analysis of new construction starts. "That way we know what will be needed and our computer tells us what we can gear up to avoid shortages," adds Turner. "We can't afford the luxury of a three to four-year apprenticeship program," says Bob L. Banks, vice president of personnel, "we sell people and the ability to do the job now."

Open Shop

Daniel considers itself one of the two largest open-shop contractors in the U. S. (The other is Brown & Root, Houston.) Cox estimates that Daniel operates around 75% open shop but emphasize that "we are geared to operate both open and closed." As Daniel moves out of the Southeast it is entering strong closed-shop bastions. Daniel has handled this by "becoming the leader in developing project agreements to get the job done best," says Cox. Daniel is currently working under seven project agreements involving nearly $2 billion in work. "The labor conduct of our company is the most important thing we have," says Cox.

Historically, much of the Southeast has been an open-shop area. In the late 1960s, when Daniel decided to get into the large powerplant field in a big way, most utilities were operating closed shop. "It took us a long time to break that barrier," says Howard W. McCall, vice president and head of the power division. Georgia Power Co. finally gave Daniel its first open-shop powerplant job, which was finished on schedule and under budget. "When other power companies saw what we accomplished there, the jobs began to flow in," adds McCall.

After only five years in power work, Daniel now is working on 13,000 mw of powerplants. Half of Daniel's large backlog is in power work.

Expanding Abroad

Some of Daniel's growth has occurred overseas. Moving overseas was a result of expansion of former clients into that market (Daniel estimates that 70% of its business is with repeat clients). Lloyd W. Donnelly, vice president of the chemical division, says that Daniel's greatest success outside continental U. S. has been in Puerto Rico. Since 1966, Daniel has constructed a total of 35 plants for 22 pharmaceutical companies. "When we first got there we discovered that we needed to train an entire workforce, nearly 4,000 persons. Now we are one of the top three employers on the island and the only major U. S. construction company that keeps a full engineering force in Puerto Rico."

Benefiting from all the booms in the Southeast in the past 20 years, especially the power boom since 1969, Daniel is gearing up for the area in which it expects the next surge — chemicals. A remark by Donnelly reflects Daniel's confidence: "If a refinery gets built around this country, somebody's going to have to decide not to give it to us."

CHAPTER 13

Entering the '80's

Predictions of a record fiscal 1974, as reported in the preceding *Engineering News Record* article, were substantiated by year-end statistics. Revenues were 44 percent above 1973 and four percent over the forecast, and earnings topped the predicted 20-percent increase by three. Even so, the company's always bullish officers were outdone a year later when 1975 turned out to be the best year in history. Revenues, earnings per share, cash dividends, and construction backlog increased for the eighth consecutive year.

Buck Mickel expressed the general optimistic attitude within Daniel when he spoke at the 1974 annual meeting of the Greenville Chamber of Commerce. He opened his remarks by saying, "I am extremely bullish on construction starts in 1974, particularly in the Southeast and Southwest United States." He also stated that any industry using electricity for its total energy requirements would be a prime candidate for locating in these areas, particularly in South Carolina, "which is so little dependent on foreign crude for its electrical sources." On that score, he said, "Our biggest problem is to project our energy problems and opportunities factually to the public so that there is no panic."

Mickel told the leaders, "From a purely personal point of view, I would like to talk about the philosophy of the nation. Certainly we have a shortage of fuels, we have a shortage of materials, we have inflation. All are very real problems faced across the entire land, not just in Greenville. We as a nation must put aside issues that are political and deal with issues that are meaningful. Frankly, to hell with Watergate."

Daniel's 1975 annual report recognized the economic trend of the time, yet noted that: "Although a few segments of our business felt the impact of combined recession and inflation, we were able to achieve record results through your company's main source of earnings from construction and engineering. Our broad experience enabled us to obtain a substantial volume of new contracts in such major growth industries as pharmaceuticals, pulp and paper, food processing and herbicides."

Power plant construction continued to make a significant contribution to profits, and the 16,000 megawatts of power construction then under contract represented an amount nearly equal to the electricity being generated at the time for all five New England states. One power contract alone represented capital expenditures of more than $4 billion.

Since growth in profits begets expansion, Daniel moved into additional geographical areas; new bases of operations were established in Dublin, Ireland; Jeddah, Saudi Arabia; and Houston, Texas. Construction services were also expanding. Southern Industrial Supply Company in Raleigh was acquired by American Equipment Company. Under the supervision of P. C. Gregory, III, American Equipment and its Tool Service Company affiliate were spreading out; they opened additional branches in South Carolina, North Carolina, Alabama and Texas, and later in Mississippi and Louisiana.

The move into the Middle East opened several avenues for Daniel's diversified services, including construction management, maintenance and both craft and supervisory training. Too, it resulted in the establishment of Daniel International (Saudi Arabia) Ltd. George McDougall, first president of the new company, had been a key figure in securing a construction management contract in joint venture with Saudi Arabia Parsons Ltd. for the construction of the world's largest single integrated airport complex at Jeddah. Cost of the project was estimated at "several billion dollars."

The formal contract announcement was made at a press conference at Daniel's Greenville headquarters in August 1976, by Colonel Said Amin, director of the project for the Ministry of Defence and Aviation. Another Saudi involved in the lengthy contract negotiations was Reda Nazer, president of Saudi Arabian Trading and Construction Company Ltd. Thomas W. McCormick, who became Daniel's deputy project manager of the airport in 1977, was later promoted to president of the Saudi Arabian subsidiary, and McDougall was named vice chairman. Meanwhile, Colonel Amin had been promoted to the rank of general.

To help direct the worldwide activities of the ever-expanding company, shareholders elected three new directors at the 1976 annual meeting, including Charles W. Daniel, a nephew of the founder and son of Hugh Daniel. Joining the board with him were General George M. Seignious, II, then president of The Citadel, and

James W. Foley, retired president and vice chairman of the board of directors of Texaco, Inc. Re-elected to bring the board membership to nine were Hugh Daniel, H. M. Daniel, Buck Mickel, C. W. Cox, Harry Brock and Alester Furman.

The annual report noted that fiscal 1976 was the second best year in the company's history despite the continued sluggishness in industrial capital spending. At its November meeting, the board declared a first quarter 1977 cash dividend of 20 cents per share, the 11th dividend increase since the company went public. The letter to shareholders in the 1976 report pointed out that the company had operated in an unfavorable capital spending environment since 1974, causing profits to dip after eight consecutive years of record earnings.

At the annual meeting of shareholders on February 15, 1977, Mickel announced that the corporate structure would be realigned to permit all operations to be handled by two principal divisions. The 37 construction units and subsidiaries in this country and overseas were transferred to Daniel Construction Company, Inc. The 21 nonconstruction-related activities were assigned to the newly established Daniel Industrial Services.

Mickel explained, "Our prime business today, just as it has been since the company was founded, is engineering, construction and industrial maintenance, but our long-range plans are to expand further into other services and products so that in the future these activities may account for a much larger portion of our earnings." In that vein, he alluded to the slack in 1976 construction profits due to the depressed economy and said that much of that reduction was taken up by the subsidiaries in the areas of truck leasing and real estate.

In the realigned corporate structure, Charles W. Cox was elected vice chairman of Daniel International and chairman of Daniel Construction Company. Currie Spivey was named president and chief operating officer of Daniel Construction Company. Spivey had been elected a vice president in 1970, and for two years prior to his appointment as president he had been group vice president for business development and served on the corporate Senior Management Committee.

Greg Rothe, who had helped broaden Daniel's earnings base for the past 10 years through acquisitions and internal expansion, was appointed president of Daniel Industrial Services. Prior to that assignment, he had been vice president of corporate development since 1974. Rothe continued as head of Industrial Services until his death on September 10, 1979.

On April 28, 1977, Rothe, also a corporate officer and a member of the Executive Committee, telephoned the company's public relations office early in the afternoon to say that he would shortly bring someone to that office. The person was not identified. An hour later, Rothe called back to say that he had been delayed and would be there in a half-hour or so. About 4:15 p.m., he visited the public relations director and brought with him Richard B. Humbert. Rothe said, "Dick has a story we want you to get on the Dow Jones ticker as soon as possible."

The one-paragraph story contained this dynamic message: "Fluor Corporation announced a proposal by Fluor to purchase the stock of Daniel International Corporation held by certain of the Daniel directors for $30.00 per share and a subsequent cash offer by Fluor to acquire all of the outstanding shares of Daniel at the same price. Buck Mickel, Daniel chairman, acknowledged receipt of the proposal and is calling a special meeting of the Daniel board of directors as soon as possible to consider the proposal submitted by Fluor."

On May 4, this updated story was released:

> "Daniel International Corporation and Fluor Corporation announced jointly that, after discussions between Daniel and Fluor, Fluor has revised its previous proposal to acquire Daniel and intended to make a cash tender offer for all of the outstanding shares of common stock of Daniel at $31.20 per share. J. Robert Fluor, chairman of the board and chief executive officer of Fluor, said the offer is expected to commence on Friday, May 6, 1977. Buck Mickel, chairman of the board of Daniel, stated that although the board of directors was not taking a position on the merits of the Fluor offer and felt that each stockholder should make his own decision, in order to facilitate consideration of the Fluor offer by Daniel stockholders, Daniel was furnishing its list of shareholders to Fluor. Mickel also stated that he had been advised that a majority of the Daniel board will tender their shares at the revised price."

Mickel commented in the story that "the board of directors of Daniel is pleased with the intention of Fluor to maintain the Daniel organization, headquartered in Greenville, South Carolina, which has operated so effectively during the past years in the interests of Daniel International and the shareholders."

Fluor indicated his pleasure that there would be Daniel representation on the Fluor board and stated, "The present Daniel management team will be a superb additon to the Fluor family."

That story, as expected, received big headlines in many newspapers, particularly in Greenville and Los Angeles, where the corporations were headquartered at the time. Fluor later moved into its new corporate offices in Irvine, California.

The *Los Angeles Times* expanded on the story, adding that "Daniel stock had been selling at about $20 a share on the over-the-counter market as recently as late last week. It was the most active OTC issue Thursday, gaining $4.75 a share to $30.25 on more than a million shares traded." The *Times* also reported that "based on 1976 revenues, the acquisition of Daniel would enlarge Fluor by more than one third."

The *Times* headlined the story: "Fluor Boosts Construction Firm Offer to $220 Million."

The Salomon Brothers firm, which acted as financial advisor to Daniel in the transaction, ran an advertisement in newspapers June 14, 1977, in which it stated: "Fluor Corporation has acquired, through a cash tender offer by a wholly-owned subsidiary, more than 97 percent of the outstanding stock of Daniel International Corporation."

The next day Fluor announced that Mickel and Cox had been named to its board of directors following an amendment in the corporation's by-laws to expand membership to the board from 16 to 18. Mickel was immediately elected to the Executive Committee of the Fluor board and was later named a Fluor group vice president.

At the same time that they were elected to the Fluor board, Mickel and Cox were elected chairman and vice chairman, respectively, of the Daniel board, which had been restaffed following the resignation of seven of its members after the acquisition. Mickel was also named president of Daniel International. The revamped board consisted of four members from Daniel and five from Fluor, the other two Daniel representatives being Rothe and Spivey. The Fluor members, and their positions in the parent company were as follows: J. Robert Fluor, chairman, chief executive officer and president; David S. Tappan, Jr., vice chairman; Charles N. Cannon, president of Fluor Engineers and Constructors, Inc.; Richard M. Humbert, vice president of law and tax and secretary; and George A. Mefferd, senior vice president of finance.

Mickel explained that the changes were in line with the overall plan to maintain close coordination between the two companies while ensuring that Daniel operates under its established management as a separate profit center.

Fluor's 1977 annual report featured the acquisition and carried a full color photo of a Daniel project in South Carolina on the front cover. It noted that the purchase of approximately 99 percent of the stock was effective May 31 that year, and the inclusion of Daniel's contribution for the final five months of the fiscal year (ending October 31) allowed Fluor to achieve record financial results. The purchase price was placed at approximately $218 million.

The report pointed out that "Fluor and Daniel have been much alike in management philosophy, so an excellent working relationship has quickly developed between the two companies. Daniel's clients are in the power, chemical, fibers, pulp and paper, pharmaceutical, and several other industries not traditionally served by Fluor. More than 95 percent of Fluor's current backlog consists of projects outside the United States; the reverse is true for Daniel . . . Daniel's revenues have grown from $227 million in 1969, when the company went public, to $1 billion in 1976."

The approximately 200 projects Daniel had under way at the time of the acquisition were handled by 4,500 permanent (salaried) employees and more than 40,000 craft (hourly) personnel. The job Fluor singled out for its annual report cover was the nuclear power plant being constructed at Jenkinsville, near Columbia, for South Carolina Electric & Gas Company and the South Carolina Public Service Authority. The photo showed a 284-ton nuclear reactor vessel being positioned for installation in the containment building. The adjacent pumped-storage facility was shown on an inside page in an aerial view of the site.

It was a significant year for Daniel's Power Group. Two plants were brought on line, including the first nuclear project, an 860-megawatt unit constructed in seven years for Alabama Power Company at Dothan. The other station put into commercial operation was a 600-MW coal-fired plant for Kansas City Power & Light Company and Kansas Gas and Electric Company at La Cygne, Kansas. Those two firms also awarded Daniel the contract to construct an 1,150-MW nuclear unit at Burlington, Kansas.

Fluor's 1978 annual report notified shareholders that "the Anti-Trust Division of the Department of Justice informed us that it had closed its investigation on Fluor's acquisition of Daniel. This news is welcome in view of our constant efforts to bring Fluor subsidiaries together on projects."

That allowed Daniel to further broaden its efforts in the areas of natural resources through joint venture projects with other Fluor units. As it entered the 1980's, the company had a substantial volume of work by which it was helping the United States become less dependent on foreign oil.

With gigantic synfuel plants programmed for the new decade, plus the company's continued services to traditional clients, Daniel was gearing to practically double its personnel. Coupled with the anticipated increase in business and employees would come the retirement of several top management administrators; and in keeping with Charlie Daniel's policy of maintaining a young company image, the new leaders were already being singled out at the middle management level, thus presenting challenging opportunities for those in other levels who would be in their twenties and thirties. In essence, at that point in time would come the second major changing of the guard. The original "other Charlie Daniels" would be succeeded by yet another experienced group well trained in the traditional "Daniel way." In this manner the company will continue to operate by the guidelines and philosophies set forth by the founder and will remain "Charlie's company."

CHAPTER 14

The Organization

To detail significant differences in Charlie Daniel's company more than 15 years after his death would be simply to recognize the social, economic, industrial and energy changes that have occurred over the same period. Basically, Daniel Construction Company remains the same company he managed for three decades until 1964 — just 10 times larger.

Not even the acquisition by Fluor Corporation in May 1977 brought about any change in operations and philosophies. This was assured immediately after the purchase, when J. Robert Fluor extended "a sincere welcome" to all Daniel employees into the Fluor family of companies. His letter to "Dear Fellow Employees" of Daniel included this explanation:

> "Fluor and Daniel are two successful companies in their own right. . . They are compatible with each other in reputation and business philosophy. . . . It is appropriate for Daniel to remain autonomous, functioning as a profit center under the stewardship of its current management. And, since Daniel enjoys an excellent reputation throughout its industry, it is appropriate that the company retain its name."

At the same time as the Fluor greetings, another letter went out to all Daniel employees. It was signed by Buck Mickel, chairman; C. W. Cox, vice chairman; Currie B. Spivey, president of Daniel Construction Company; and Greg W. Rothe, president of the Daniel Industrial Services Group. The letter acknowledged that the acquisition had created "a great deal of interest within the company," and it gave employees this reassurance:

> "Daniel management is confident that the joining of Daniel and Fluor will be in the best interest of our company and each of

us as individuals. Daniel will remain headquartered in Green-ville under the direction of the same management team; the Daniel name will be retained and the operations in which you are presently involved will remain unchanged. You should know that your loyalty and hard work will continue to be the foundation of our company as we continue our growth in the future."

So, just as Charlie Daniel led his company into new technolo-gies and a broader geographic range, his management team and those it has trained have likewise kept pace with the times and changing conditions. As the company entered the 1980's, that team had moved it ahead in the critical areas of natural resources and synfuels while retaining leadership in engineering, construction, contract maintenance and a large variety of construction services in the company's traditional markets. Thus the increased services and the flexibility to tailor them for each contract continue to charac-terize the company.

The intent of this chapter is to identify Daniel's construction and industrial units, all the result of the founder's visions, plans and business philosophies; and to recognize the officers, past and pres-ent, directing those activities. For clarity, the principal elements will be listed in their respective corporate divisions — Daniel Con-struction Company and the Daniel Industrial Services Group — as they appeared at the end of fiscal 1980 and within a few weeks of the company's 46th anniversary. Their combined earnings base repre-sents more than 100 separate profit centers.

The executives directing Daniel Construction Company are C. W. Cox, chairman; C. B. Spivey, president and chief operating officer; and T. C. Johnson, executive vice president of construction.

The principal elements of the Construction Division and their group vice presidents are as follows:

Corporate Construction Groups: Industrial (R. W. Dean); Chemical & Fibers (L. G. McCraw); Power (H. W. McCall, president); Engineering (L. W. Donnelly); Maintenance & Mechanical (J. A. Wood); Regional (C. T. Green, Jr.); Com-mercial (R. L. Carter); Operations Support (R. L. Ogden); International, Western Hemisphere (T. P. Townsend, Jr.); Eastern Hemisphere (G. E. McDougall); Marketing (C. R. Cox, executive vice president); Industrial Relations (B. L. Banks); and Personnel (J. J. Schroeder).

F. T. Bailey, a corporate vice president, is group vice president of the Industrial Services Group, which comprises both acquired and established subsidiaries of Daniel International. Applied Engineering Company of Orangeburg, (mentioned previously) represents the company's first acquisition (1970) and is managed by W. W. Dukes, Jr. The other Daniel-acquired subsidiary (1971) is The Fortis Corporation, of which M. D. Gentry is president. It is based in King, North Carolina, and leads the Carolinas in the construction of economical houses. Fortis also performs commercial construction and makes special wood products.

The other two principal units of the Industrial Services Group are Daniel Realty Corporation of Birmingham and American Equipment Company of Greenville, each an established subsidiary. The Goldston Transportation Group was transferred to Fluor in 1979. Daniel Realty was chartered in 1964 to manage the company's property; yet under the guidance of R. C. Englund, president, it has grown into a substantial profit center through property management for others, brokerage, land development, and equity projects.

American Equipment Company was established in 1971 under that name, yet it is an offshoot of the original Daniel Equipment Division which had its beginning shortly after World War II when equipment and tools were returned from the company's large defense projects. Its president, P. C. Gregory, III, has developed American Equipment into a major Southern dealer in construction equipment and tools.

For its historical value and to highlight the contribution to company growth by numerous managers over nearly five decades, the following table identifies 30 construction activities within Daniel, the dates the units were established and their managers.

1936 ALABAMA (South Central)

1936-1954	R. Hugh Daniel
1954-1963	Joseph A. Dentici
1964-1965	R. Caldwell Englund
1965-1971	John W. Gustafson
1971-1975	Fred C. Ayers
1975-1976	Marcus G. McCoy
1976-1979	John W. Gustafson
1980-	George P. Killorin

1946 EQUIPMENT DIVISION (American Equipment Company)

1946-1950	Earle Daniel
1951-1952	C. B. Graves
1952-1964	Wendell Williamson
1964-1969	Allen P. Sloan
1969-	P. C. Gregory, III

1946 MECHANICAL
1946-1954	Walter Houseman
1954-1955	Carl Rouse
1955-1960	T. C. Johnson
1960-1971	Wes Holcombe
1971-1972	L. W. Donnelly
1973-1975	Joel Thornton
1976-1979	Gene Cribb
1980-	Merged with M&M

1948 PERSONNEL
1948-1959	Barrington King
1959-1969	W. W. Bradley
1969-1976	Bob L. Banks
1976-1979	LeRoy R. Turner
1979-	John J. Schroeder

1954 SOUTH CAROLINA (Southeastern)
1959-1962	George E. McDougall
1962-1965	Joseph J. Stroud
1965-	Harry L. Cunningham

1954 VIRGINIA (Northeastern)
1954-1962	H. L. Longcrier, Sr.
1962-1965	H. L. Longcrier, Jr.
1965-1977	Clyde T. Green, Jr.
1977-	W. Preston Stuart, Jr.

1955 FLORIDA (Southern)
1955-1958	Harry Stellman
1959-1961	Carl G. Englund
1961-1963	R. Caldwell Englund
1963-1968	E. Warren Parker
1968	Sherman S. Watkins
1968	Clifton P. Coleman
1968-1969	Joel C. Thornton
1972-1975	E. F. Matteson
1975-	J. Ronald Howey

1958 NEW YORK SALES
1958-1968	Charles W. Cox
1968-1977	Currie B. Spivey
1977-1981	B. Kenneth Bolt
1981-	R. D. Mitchell

1960 DANIEL ENGINEERING
1960-1967	Harry J. Payne, Jr.
1968	Arthur Smith
1969-1973	R. L. Carter
1974-1979	L. W. Donnelly
1980-	C. D. Bassett

1960 GEORGIA
1960-1969	James F. Daniel, III
(Consolidated with other divisions)	

1960 NORTH CAROLINA (Mid-Atlantic)
1960-1966	E. F. Matteson
1966-1967	T. Howard Suitt
1967-1968	E. F. Matteson
1968-1972	Bobby E. Wells
1972	James B. Cashwell

1961 MAINTENANCE & MECHANICAL
1961-1964	Claud C. Calmes
1964-1966	Roger M. Scovil
1966-1969	P. C. Gregory, III
1969-	John A. Wood

1964 EUROPEAN DIVISION (Brussels)
1964-1966	Norman Smyth
1966-1974	William Kramer
1974-1976	Roger M. Scovil
1976-1977	R. L. Bradley
1977	Moved to East Kilbride, Scotland
1977-1978	Earle L. Harrison
1978-1979	Roger M. Scovil
1979-	Paul L. Wiget

1964 CARIBBEAN DIVISION (Puerto Rico)
1964-1974	Roger M. Scovil
1975-1978	J. Dan Whisenhunt
1979-1980	Ed J. Edminister
1981-	James E. Barry

1964 CHICAGO SALES
1964-1967	Clifton P. Coleman
1967-1980	Jack B. Kliesrath
1980-	James A. Merchant

1965 KENTUCKY DIVISION
1965-1968	Joseph Stroud
1968-1969	P. C. Gregory, III
1969-1974	Frank Eskridge
(Consolidated with other divisions)	

1965 LOUISIANA DIVISION
1965-1967	Thomas Sutter
1968-1969	Raymond Wise
(Consolidated with other divisions)	

1965 ARKANSAS
(West Central)
1965-1975   Marcus G. McCoy
1975-1977   Gerald E. Guy
1977   J. D. Genier (acting)
1978-1981   Peter A. Stipp

(Consolidated with other divisions)

1967 DANIEL NAVARRA S.A.
(Pamplona, Spain)
1967-1968   Claud C. Calmes
             (Inactive)

1967 UNITED KINGDOM (Scotland)
1967-1971   Monroe Durham
1972   Alan Marshall
1972-1975   Monroe Durham
1976   Harry Charnley
1977-1978   Earle Harrison
1978-1979   Walker Murray
1979-1980   Dan Clendening

1971 GERMAN BRANCH
1971-1976   Paul L. Wiget
1976-   Peter Strauss

1973 DANIEL INTERNATIONAL
SARL (Lyon)
1973-1975   Mike Gilian
1975-1979   Inactive
1979-   Mike Gilian (acting)

1974 TEXAS (Southwestern)
(Dallas)
1974-1975   Carl T. Berglund
             Gerald E. Guy
             (Co-Managers)
1975-1976   R. D. Mitchell
1976-1979   James A. Hopkins
1979-1980   Phil J. Watson
1980-   Greg R. Wilkinson

1974 KANSAS CITY (Power Group)
1974   C. E. Bradley
1975-1978   Bobby E. Wells
1978-   Leo R. Smith

1976 HOUSTON
(Western/Chemical-Fibers)
1976-1977   Carl T. Berglund
1977-1978   Richard D. Gunderson
1978-   Paul J. Varello

1976 DANIEL INTERNATIONAL
(SAUDI ARABIA) LTD.
1976-1978   George E. McDougall
1978-   Thomas W. McCormick

1978 DANIEL VIRGIN ISLANDS
1978-   Philip J. Southerland

1979 COMMERCIAL
1979-   R. L. Carter

1980 DANIEL/McCARTHY LTD.
(Dublin, Irland)
1980-   P. E. McCarthy

1980 SALT LAKE CITY
(Western/Industrial)
1980-   Ken P. Sharp

CHAPTER 15

Life with Daniel

This chapter contains short stories and amusing anecdotes featuring a number of Charlie Daniel's employees and friends.

The Daniel-Crouch Team

A. C. (Alex) Crouch, founder and for many years chairman of Piedmont Engineers, Architects and Planners, Inc., was a close business associate and personal friend of Mr. and Mrs. Charlie Daniel. He often recalled many interesting incidents of that association, one of his favorites being the $20 episode. Alex told it like this:

> "We were returning to Greenville from a site trip downstate. I was in the front seat with the chauffeur, and Mr. Daniel was in the back seat with T. Frank Watkins, an Anderson attorney. This was in the early 1950's. There was a little Chevrolet in front of us. It was going like crazy, and we were keeping up with it. A highway patrolman came up behind us and stopped both cars. He said he would have to give us a $20 speeding ticket, to which Mr. Watkins said 'Charlie, let me handle this.' He got out of the car, puffed up his chest in real courtroom manner, and lit into that poor cop. He couldn't talk him out of the ticket, so he reached into his pocket for $20. He didn't have it and asked Mr. Daniel for the money. Mr. Daniel didn't have $20 on him either. Being just a little engineer riding with those important men, I proudly said I had $20. So I paid the fine, and that's the last I ever heard of that $20."

He remembered how Daniel figured in the first WPA (federal relief public projects) job in upper South Carolina. Crouch's father was pastor of the First Presbyterian Church at Clemson, and about 1932 the church burned. "Nobody had any money back then," Alex

110

said, "so my father negotiated with Charlie Fant, an Anderson architect, to design a new church. He negotiated with Townsend Lumber Company through Charlie for the materials, and he negotiated with the government to get the project under WPA. He knew it was a private church, but he was clever enough to gear the rebuilding project to the fact that the church served Clemson College, therefore the state, and therefore it was eligible for federal aid. I remember vividly that we paid only $17,000 for the entire building materials; and I was just a kid then, but I also remember Mr. Daniel's name being mentioned frequently in connection with the construction. That was really my first brush with him."

Crouch was involved in the mechanical system, especially in the yard and garden, in the construction of the Daniel residence on Roe Ford Road in Greenville in 1959. "One thing Mr. Daniel was always meticulous about was his swimming pool," Crouch said. "Early in the game, he said there wasn't enough water pressure, so he had George Dill, his mechanical superintendent, and I put in a big booster pump station. But we misdesigned it, and the first time we turned it on we sucked the water out of everybody's house on that system. I don't know how true it is, but Charlie one time is said to have accused the superintendent of the Greenville water reservoir of letting frogs grow in it, because he found some in his swimming pool."

Alex made numerous trips with his friend Charlie, first by auto and train, and in later years in Daniel's company aircraft. They would ride the Southern Railway Crescent to New York, leaving Greenville at 4:20 in the afternoon. "Actually," Crouch said, "it was a marvelous ride. I took it several times. Charlie would take that train and arrive in New York about 8:00 the next morning. He would do a day's work, catch the Piedmont train about 6:00 or 7:00 that night and arrive back in Greenville about noon the next day. It was a brutal round trip for him, but he would take it religiously.

"The times I made the trip with him he was always doing something — working, working, working. He would walk through the coaches now and then and introduce himself to people, always looking for work. He loved people. Along those lines, he liked nothing better than to 'hear' a construction job without looking at it. He used to say if he saw material laying on the ground he would be losing money, because those materials shouldn't have been purchased before they were actually needed. He was very close to people who worked with him and to those he worked for. He really, really cared. Usually after a plant was completed, he was visiting it constantly, asking if everything was all right; and if there were any problems, he was quick to fix them."

Much of Crouch's early work with Daniel was on Milliken projects. Several of them were crash programs to get a plant in operation in time to produce a new product or to catch a changing market. "I don't know another client as faultlessly demanding as Milliken," he said. "Other people are demanding, but they are clumsy at it. Of course, Milliken wouldn't stop at an answer to a question if he was not satisfied. He would probe and keep pushing. I learned never to talk to Roger Milliken unless I had my paperwork done thoroughly. Sometimes it's hard for people to learn that. Once they learn it, they have a very exciting experience. Well, Mr. Daniel was the same way. He wouldn't tolerate an excuse, yet he was sympathetic with a problem. And he was an absolutely marvelous experience to anybody who was associated with him. He never stopped. He was going all the time, either with you or somebody else. Incidentally, the most horrible trip I ever made with Charlie Daniel, from a personal standpoint, by far the most exquisitely agonizing trip, was the one to New York in that Twin Beech when I accidentally sat on his new hat. I didn't know what to do. I jumped up and got it and told him I was sorry. He didn't say a word, but he spent the next hour trying to smooth out that hat. I never did live that down. Yes, sir, trips with him were never uneventful."

Crushed hat or not, the Daniel-Crouch friendship and business association was life-long. "As far as I am concerned," Crouch said of that relationship, "the pattern which he set down, his methods of operation, his tremendous feeling of integrity with everybody concerned — that was such an overriding obvious asset in what made his company great." Did Daniel's policies have any bearing on how Crouch set up his engineering firm? "Oh, definitely," he admitted. "You're damn right! I used to tell myself that if I can operate in the mode, with the splendor and simplicity and straightforwardness which Mr. Daniel can, I've got it made. I knew that. There's no question about it."

The Furman Association

Just as Charlie Daniel liked to be around people, he was especially fond of those who could keep up with him. And there weren't many who could. Alester G. Furman, Jr., could and did. They became close friends from the day Furman's realty company located a site on North Main Street for the first Daniel office building in Greenville and a lot on Crescent Avenue for the first Daniel residence in the county. They made many trips together and were involved in numerous business transactions. Furman knew as much about Daniel Construction Company and its founder as any man.

Furman related this account of the close relation between Daniel and his employees: "Of the many trips I made with him to job sites, one in particular is most illustrative. He asked me to go with him on a hot July day to visit the Singer project in Anderson. An 1,100-foot solid brick wall was being constructed. Charlie said to Superintendent Ed Moore: 'Ed, you told me that you were going to have that wall built by Friday, and you haven't got a chance to do it.' Moore fired back: 'Mr. Daniel, I haven't told you any such damn thing! We're laying those bricks just as fast as anybody can lay them.' Charlie said 'Ed, I know that. I just came over here to be sure that you were being supplied with all of the materials necessary to get this wall built as quick as it could be built.' Charlie turned that very attractive smile on Ed Moore, and I realized then that there was a relationship between them that couldn't be broken by anybody. That was Charlie's relationship with most of the men he worked with."

Charlie Daniel would often drive his car 200 or 250 miles to job sites or business meetings, work six or seven hours and drive back home in the evening. He was a believer in the old Chinese proverb: "The best fertilizer on a man's farm is the footprint of the owner." Furman tells of another trip with Daniel: "He called me and said he was going to Elizabethton, Tennessee, to see about building a plant there, and he wanted somebody to finance it and thought I might be able to help him. He said, 'Be at my house at 5:00 in the morning; we'll have breakfast and leave from there.' I was there at 5:00 a.m.; his wife, Mickey, was up; his cook was up; we had a delicious breakfast; we got in the car; and we arrived at the bank in Elizabethton at a quarter of nine, even before the bank president got there. We inspected the plant site, made arrangements for financing the job and drove back home late that afternoon. That's typical of trips he made, and you know to do that he had to drive pretty fast. As a matter of fact, now and then when I would be with him, I would shut my eyes sometimes to be sure I didn't see it if we hit something."

When Daniel purchased its first airplane (Twin Beechcraft) in April 1956, Richard Young and Wesley Holcombe flew it from Wichita, Kansas, the pickup point, to Birmingham. Hugh Daniel, Joe Dentici and two others joined them for the second leg of the trip to the plane's home base in Greenville. This took place on a Saturday, and Charlie Daniel was there to meet them. Knowing Charlie's reluctance to fly, Dentici bet Hugh $5 that it would be a month at least before anybody could get Charlie Daniel in his own plane. Upon landing in Greenville, Hugh asked Young and Holcombe to stay in the pilots' seats while Charlie inspected the interior of the plane. Once inside the aircraft, Hugh suggested to Charlie that they take a quick spin over the city. Surprisingly enough, he agreed. That did it. Within a few months a second plane was purchased, because Charlie and Alester were utilizing the original plane practically all the time. Never really interested in flying before that, Charlie used the plane thereafter for most of his trips of 100 or more miles.

Fore!

Daniel has never lost an employee to the pro golf circuit for the simple reason that no employee has ever had the time to play often enough to become a scratch golfer. Therefore, when clients are entertained on the links, Daniel players explain their scores as simply playing "client golf." Sometimes, however, that is difficult because clients are not always par shooters either. For instance, James F. Daniel, III, and Hugh Daniel once entertained a couple of clients from England. One of the Englishmen had problems with water hazards. They psyched him out, and he was usually guilty of looking up and topping the ball into the water. The foursome reached a hole where the tee was behind the lake. The psyched-out Englishman hit his first ball into the lake, then the second and third. He became frustrated, but would not allow frustration to overcome his determination. He exhausted his supply of balls and asked Hugh for one. That went on for three or more futile attempts, and he asked Hugh for still another. As Hugh tossed the ball to the angry man he casually mentioned, "These balls cost over a dollar apiece." That remark triggered a pointed outburst from the Englishman: "I say, old chap, if you cawn't afford the bloody game you should give it up!"

High Cuffs

Solomon Blatt, esteemed speaker emeritus of the South Carolina House of Representatives, knew Charlie Daniel well, and together they helped change laws that further enhanced the state's chances of obtaining new industry. Blatt said, "I've been in the House of Representatives for 44 years; and during that time I met a lot of outstanding business people; and Charlie Daniel was one of the finest businessmen, and the best salesman, I ever knew. I never met a man that did as much to bring industry to South Carolina and get the poor fellow off his poor farmland and into a job. I'm sure the state would not have half as much industry had it not been for him."

Having paid Daniel that tribute, Blatt smiled and said, "And speaking of Charlie, I remember how he dressed. He was a very neatly dressed fellow, but I will always remember the length of his trousers. His cuffs were always over the top of his shoes." (Physical note: Charlie Daniel was 6 feet tall and weighed around 185 pounds; he had brown hair, gray eyes, and a ruddy complexion.)

Needy Athletes

Thomas C. (Nap) Vandiver, well-known South Carolina bank executive, grew up in Anderson with the Daniel boys and went on to establish Southern Bank & Trust Company in Greenville. Like Charlie and Hugh Daniel, he attended The Citadel and is a staunch alumnus. He recalled: "General Mark Clark, then president of The Citadel, took Charlie to a football game at Clemson — even though I know Charlie was not crazy about football. They sat in the rain and watched The Citadel take a 60 to 0 beating. After the game, Charlie and Mark agreed that something had to be done about the college's football program, and that led to a large gift to The Citadel of Georgia-Pacific stock which Charlie owned. It was to establish a fund for needy boys, and you would be surprised how many good football players coming out of high school were needy."

Start of Design-Build

Harry H. Payne is the grandfather of Daniel Engineering and has a great sense of humor. The fact that he came from Elberton, Georgia, whence came Charlie Daniel, Homozel Mickel Daniel and Buck Mickel, is coincidental. He was a man with a drawing board, architectural talents and ambition. But since he is still on the payroll, let him tell the history briefly and without quotes:

Daniel entered the design and build field cautiously, hoping that no one would notice. Charlie Daniel was not enthusiastic, being reluctant to risk offending the architectural and engineering offices with which the company had to cooperate. However, Buck Mickel, then a combination estimator and project manager, foresaw the trend and risked a trial. In 1953, I was engaged to do the engineering for a small alteration contract, my charges being $173 including expenses. When the other professionals mounted no protest march, Buck became a little bolder; and the package contracts became larger and more frequent. With neither announcement nor fanfare, Daniel was in the practice.

In the beginning, warehouses were our meat. Design information was informally communicated, usually consisting of the outside dimensions and clear height. Occasionally, Buck would send me a sketch on a scrap of paper no bigger than 4 × 6 inches. Anyone who has seen one of Buck's sketches knows that it is a real design package. More often than not, the client had already been given a price, and the design was tailored to the estimate.

The grading subcontractor was always called first, then I; and I had to draw with both hands to have a foundation plan ready. I suggested the radical idea of having a site plan before commencing grading, but when Buck learned that it would require at least a day, he said: "Hell, I don't want it pretty; I want it this afternoon!"

We pioneered tilt-up construction in this area. Many textile mills were in need of cotton storage facilities, and concrete-enclosed compartments 50 feet wide and 200 feet long gave a lot of space with a low insurance rate. The drawings consisted of two sheets: a site plan on which the number of compartments was shown, and a second sheet with a typical compartment and details. Harry Cunningham made sepias of the second sheet in 1955 and used it for warehouses all over South Carolina. Someday, I am going to send him a bill.

The order of the day was speed. As Harold Thompson was to remark later, the day he came to work he was two weeks behind. To further prove the claim of "quicker, cheaper and better," it was believed that a standard building could be designed. Two versions were devised: Mickel's Minimum Mill, and Buck's Budget Building. These did not revolutionize the construction industry. . . . Work increased, and by 1957 Daniel was employing freelancers as well as at least one local architectural office. In 1958, Architect Phifer Bird was hired on a temporary basis, and he still does not know if his job is permanent.

When a package contract was signed with Burlington Industries for the James Fabric Plant, the time had come for Daniel to acquire a captive design office. Buck and I reached an agreement by telephone on Friday, April 29, 1960; and the following Monday, a Daniel truck moved my equipment to Greenville.

My first Daniel office was in a one-room apartment of the Calhoun Towers. My son, who had been my associate, came along to help until a staff could be assembled. When the staff became three, the office was too small. We were allowed to move into the "old Daniel building," but we felt like an illegitimate child that had been acknowledged by its father. Mr. Charlie was still not running a temperature about design work, and sometimes seemed to be pretending that we were not there. We loved him just the same, though.

The force had grown to six or seven, and we had a problem. Since we had no budget, there was no way for us to buy furnishings and supplies. Out of necessity, we became rustlers, resulting in our identity as "The Rat Pack." In order for us to develop into a separate organization it was essential for us to receive credit for our earnings and to assume our expenses. I called Johnny Odom for advice and assistance, and Johnny said: "I'm sorry; when I said 'Hello' I told you all I know about it." Eventually, we were fitted into an organization, reporting to George McDougall. He helped us to become a profit center, and even gave the operation its name by sending a terse memo: "Have your receptionist answer the telephone 'Harry Payne and Associates.'"

The Accounting Department coveted our space, so we returned to the Calhoun Towers, where we occupied a suite of three apartments, later taking over eight apartments scattered over two floors. We were the first tenant of the Daniel Building (winter of 1965). The eighth floor was finished, but nothing else. One elevator was operable — most of the time. The greatest handicap was the lack of heat; but being devoted to duty, the fellows were on the boards wearing overcoats, hats and gloves. By then, the force had reached 60, largely enticed from other offices, from whom you can bet we received no Christmas cards.

On January 1, 1968, HPA became Daniel Engineers under new management. Seventeen of the original group were still with Daniel Engineers 12 years later. I am still around in one capacity or another. — Harry Payne.

Rum Raisin Ice Cream

J. Mason Alexander, prominent hotel manager for many years, was managing the Poinsett Hotel in Greenville in 1947 when Charlie Daniel suggested that rum raisin ice cream be added to the menu. Mason admitted he had never heard of it, and Charlie explained that he ate it at the Waldorf Astoria just about everytime he was in New York. Alexander obtained the recipe from the pastry chef at the Waldorf and put it on the Poinsett menu as "Charlie Daniel's Rum Raisin Ice Cream." The Borden Company was reluctant to make it at first; and even though it was to have been a Poinsett exclusive, it was sold generally in about a year, and Borden couldn't make enough of it for quite a while. Alexander explained that the recipe was synthetic rum and white raisins, and otherwise it was more or less vanilla ice cream.

Always Another Job

Many of the company's employees followed in the footsteps of their grandfathers and fathers, picking up their trades early in life. There is good reason for that, and it is best explained in a comment by Superintendent Ed Moore years ago: "We were on the Gailey Mill project at Marietta, Georgia, back in 1951; and one day Mr. Daniel came on the job with a group of clients, showing them our work. After they left, a foreman asked me where we would go on our next project. That's because any time Mr. Daniel came around with a client, we knew we would have another job ready for us when our current one was finished."

Breakfast at Clemson

Ed Moore could talk all day about his Daniel experiences; like this one: "While we were lifting the face of Clemson College in 1954 we were working against time, knocking down old buildings and constructing new barracks. We had only the three months during summer vacation to tear down and rebuild the mess hall. Mr. Daniel was worried because we hadn't even got around to the mess hall, and he was afraid we wouldn't have the job completed by the time the students returned September 15. He was getting on me about it one day, and I told him: You've got a beautiful, air-conditioned office over in Greenville. You just go back over there and sit down, and come back on the 15th of September and have breakfast with the boys in their new mess hall." . . . As usual, Ed finished the job on time.

A 4' × 8' Check

Claude (Humpy) Smith, who joined the company in 1939 and worked up to superintendent, refers to himself as having been Charlie Daniel's "do-it-boy." For example, there was the time three dump trucks were purchased during grading at the Army Air Base in Greenville. "Mr. Daniel told me he wanted those trucks to haul enough dirt in 90 days to pay for them," Smith said. "I guess we did, because we kept them."

Later, on the Continental Can project in Augusta in 1960, Smith was on the kind of job that superintendents like to talk about during reminiscing sessions. He described it as fitting Daniel's description: "The impossible we do immediately; miracles take a little longer." The paper machine building was being constructed on a crash program, and one of the owner's representatives was so skeptical about Daniel making the schedule that he bet Charlie $50 the job would not come in on time. For added inspiration, a bank check in that amount was painted on a regular 4' × 8' plywood board, made out to Daniel Construction Company and placed prominently on the site. When the job was finished ahead of schedule, Smith hauled the check to the bank, cashed it, and was allowed to keep the money.

A Yank in Time

Arthur F. Magill, Greenville industrialist and staunch supporter of the city's cultural life, asked Charlie Daniel to help him locate a site for Her Majesty Industries. That was in the 1950's when the Golden Strip was being developed from Greenville to Simpsonville. Magill said: "Mr. Daniel and I went out to look at a piece of property, which I later purchased. We were standing on the bridge over the railroad, and he was looking towards Simpsonville, his back to an on-coming car. I yanked him onto the little one-foot walkway just before somebody came along and hit him. He was a bit shaken and looked at me and said, "Let's get the hell out of here.' "

Telephone, Harry

Harry Cunningham, vice president and manager of the Southeastern Region, would never verify the story, but at a luncheon observing his 30th anniversary with the company he was given an old banged-up telephone in the presence of such special guests and admirers as Mrs. Charles Daniel and Currie Spivey. The presenter explained to the group before he gave Harry the telephone, neatly wrapped in a box, what prompted the gift. This is how the story goes: There have been a few occasions when Harry could not control his temper. One day in the old (first) Daniel Greenville office, he was talking to someone on the telephone. He didn't like what he heard, and at the conclusion of the conversation he jerked the telephone off the line and threw it out the door. His office was on the second floor and the door was at the head of the stairway, so the telephone bounced down the steps. At the same time, Charlie Daniel was coming up the steps. He picked up the phone, walked into Cunningham's office, placed it on the desk and said: "Harry, I believe this is yours." Daniel said nothing more and walked out.

Mechanical Man

George Dill is one of the last of the old-timers in whom Charlie Daniel had complete confidence. He started with the company as a mechanical superintendent and retired as a mechanical project manager. He was handpicked to supervise all the mechanical (plumbing) work during construction of the Daniel residence on Roe Ford Road, and he was given similar responsibilities on the 25-story Daniel Building.

Dill first met "the boss" in September 1947 when he was repairing plumbing fixtures at the first Greenville Daniel residence on Crescent Avenue. As he was leaving the house, he said, "Mr. Daniel drove into the yard, introduced himself, and asked what I was doing. I told him, and he said, 'Well, whatever it takes to satisfy Mrs. Daniel, go ahead and do it. Just like the old saying, if she wants a gold guinea, you get her a gold giunea.' I said, Yes sir; that I will do."

Along the way, there were a few surprises and unpleasant moments for Dill. Like the day the nine-zone sprinkler system was first tested at White Oaks, Daniel's Roe Ford Road residence. This is how George tells it: "The system is controlled from inside the house. Mr. Daniel had driven up, and we didn't know it. He must have gone out to inspect the sprinklers in the main court, which covered about a quarter of an acre. So we turned on the sprinklers in that area and went out to see how they were working. It takes about 15 seconds for it to take over, and when the sprinklers are on, it's nothing but a heavy misty fog; can't see more than 40 or 50 feet in the area. We walked back to the court, the sprinklers going full blast, and Mr. Daniel was running out of there wringing wet. He was mad, and he blamed me; said it was done on purpose. I just stood there and took it; but after he went upstairs and changed clothes, he finally got a big laugh out of it."

Beautifully Embarrassing

There is another episode to George Dill's sprinkler system at the Daniel residence. In his own words, this is how it happened: "The house was completed in 1959, and we had another funny experience two years later. It was January, and it snowed. I was at the office early that morning and the telephone rang. Mrs. Daniel was calling, and she said 'George, don't you laugh; you are not going to believe what I am about to tell you, and you had still better not laugh. I just want to tell you the lawn sprinklers are on'.

"And here it is, six inches of snow on the ground, and the sprinklers are on full blast. And this is 7 o'clock in the morning." George said he told her he would be right up in his truck and turn them off. Before hanging up, he recalled, "Mr. Daniel got on the phone and he was laughing. He told me, 'Don't be in a hurry; it's very beautiful to see all the ice on the trees, snow on the ground, and the sprinklers going.' " George said the lead cable running from the controls inside the house had shorted out, "So I went to the pump-house, killed the controls, and shut off the sprinklers. But from then on, anytime I was in a meeting with clients and Mr. Daniel was there, he would have to laugh and tell them, 'If you need to install sprinklers, we've got one of the best lawn sprinkler engineers in the country.' " On the serious side, George said "Mr. Daniel was a man who had all the confidence in the world in you. He often told me, as well as his other supervisors, 'You please the client, and you please me. The client always comes first.' "

The Handshake

Daniel was constructing a Stevens textile plant near Piedmont in late 1963, and Charlie Daniel visited the site. When he parked his car, he heard someone shouting his name, and he saw a hand waving from a ditch where a pipe was being placed. He walked over, and a black pipe-layer was climbing the ladder out of the ditch. He was quickly recognized as a long-time employee. As they approached each other, the man said: "Mr. Daniel, could I ask you one favor?" "Certainly," was the reply. "I would just like to shake your hand, Mr. Daniel. Just want to let you know that I've been with you for 20-something years. If it hadn't been for Daniel Construction Company, my two sons wouldn't be in college today. I wanted to let you know how much I appreciate that opportunity, Mr. Daniel." They discussed the man's sons for a couple of minutes, and Mr. Daniel turned to meet the job superintendent who was approaching. But he stopped, called to the pipe-layer who was going back to his work, and said: "Now, can I ask one favor of you?" The man replied, "Yes, sir!" Mr. Daniel asked him, "Can I just shake your hand?"

Charles E. Daniel had observed his 41st birthday just three days before this reproduced picture was printed in the November 13, 1936 edition of The Anderson (S. C.) Record on the occasion of the dedication of the Clemson College barracks constructed by his company.

F. Keith Prevost is shown in a repr duced 1936 Anderson (S. C.) Reco photograph. As president of Townse Lumber Company, of which Charl E. Daniel was an officer and stoc holder, Prevost helped his long-tir friend and associate establish Dani Construction Company in 1934.

122

..niel Construction Company was organized in the above Townsend Lumber
..mpany office at Anderson, South Carolina, on December 11, 1934. The com-
..nies shared the first floor until mid-1936, at which time the second floor was
..ded to accommodate Daniel's growth.

..niel Construction Company moved from Anderson to its new office building at
..9 North Main Street in Greenville, South Carolina, in February, 1942. Both
..ildings on this page were sketched by Renato Moncini, the company's creative
..ordinator.

*The 25-story Daniel Building in Greenville, South Carolina, completed in 1966,
the home of Daniel International Corporation.*

The 20-story Daniel Building in Birmingham, Alabama, was completed in 1970. Its occupants include Daniel Realty Corporation, the South Central Regional Construction Division, and the South Central Maintenance & Mechanical Division.

Mrs. Charles E. Daniel unveiled a large rendering of the Daniel Building *Greenville, climaxing groundbreaking ceremonies on June 29, 1964. Photogr* *pher Henry Elrod caught the excitement of that historic event.*

Daniel Construction Company bought its first airplane on April 26, 1956, and Charles E. Daniel is shown boarding the Model 18 Twin Beechcraft that same day. Richard Young and Wesley Holcombe were the pilot and co-pilot. William Coxe, pilot-photographer, was on hand to record the occasion.

Division managers reported projects on schedule and in the money at the 1963 mid-year corporate meeting. Seated, left to right: H. L. Longcrier, Sr. (Virginia); George E. McDougall, assistant general manager; Joseph E. Stroud (South Carolina), and Joseph A. Dentici (Alabama). Standing, left to right: James F. Daniel, III (Georgia); R. Caldwell Englund (Florida/Alabama); E. F. Matteson (North Carolina), and Warren Parker (Florida).

Charles E. Daniel welcomed 400 employees and special guests to the company's all-division meeting, the first in its 29-year history, in Greenville on Friday, June 28, 1963. The officers who directed the company after his death in 1964 are shown at the table with him. Left to right: George E. McDougall, Buck Mickel, R. Hugh Daniel, and Charles W. Cox.

These original company officers and key personnel represented over 300 total years of construction experience at the 1963 corporate meeting in Greenville. Left to right: W. E. Watt, R. Hugh Daniel, C. A. Thrasher, C. G. Englund, Charles E. Daniel, Carl Thrash, J. A. Dentici, Lawrence Yeargin, and Ed Moore.

Charles E. Daniel (left), former U. S. Senator, posed with Senator Strom Thur-
mond (center) and Greenville Mayor David Traxler at the 1963 gathering of
company officers and supervisors. Thurmond and Traxler were guest speakers.
Referring to the amount of new industry being brought to South Carolina and his
county, Traxler said "we are very glad to have the Daniel Chamber of Commerce in
Greenville."

Brothers Hugh (left) and Earle Daniel shared an amusing story at company outing in Greenville in 1963.

Mrs. Mary Rubino, first secretary to Charles E. Daniel, reminisced before his photo on the occasion of her 32nd anniversary with the company October 26, 1967. The newspaper feature story picture was posed by Bennie Granger, staff photographer of the Greenville News-Piedmont. The observance of her 45th anniversary in 1980 was even more special.

131

DANIEL EMPLOYMENT 1934—1980

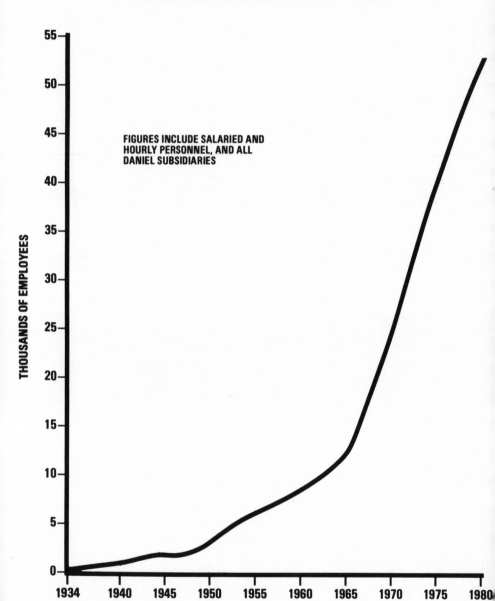

FIGURES INCLUDE SALARIED AND
HOURLY PERSONNEL, AND ALL
DANIEL SUBSIDIARIES

THOUSANDS OF EMPLOYEES

DANIEL SUMMARY OF REVENUES 1934—1980

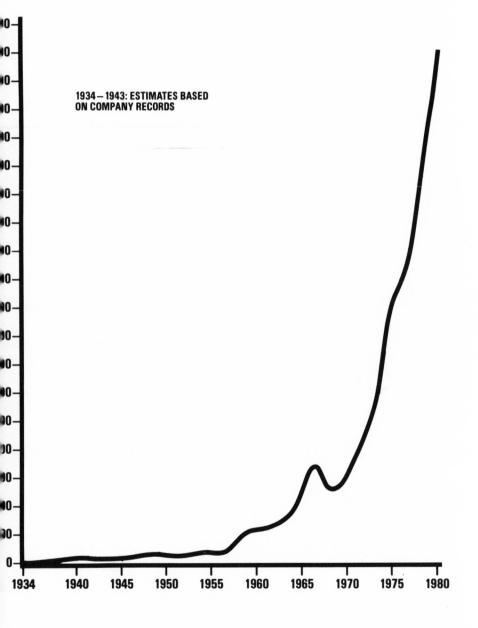

1934—1943: ESTIMATES BASED
ON COMPANY RECORDS

Daniel broke ground in November 1980 for a multi-phase project on a 106-acre s
off Haywood Road in Greenville. The first phase included a seven-story 429,00
square foot engineering center, and a 19,000-square foot conference room ar
health facility. First occupancy of Daniel's expanded corporate operations con
plex was in late 1981. Photos show (top) a rendering of the engineering buildi
and (bottom) site development plans.

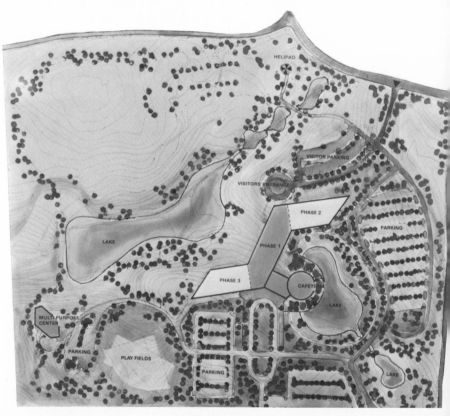

PART 2

A Constructive Citizen

CHAPTER 16

The Military Mood

Charlie Daniel's horizon, which heretofore had been necessarily limited to the vicinity of his birthplace in Elberton, Georgia, and his boyhood home in nearby Anderson, South Carolina, was broadened significantly in 1914. It was in that year that he won a scholarship to The Citadel, entering the military college in the fall as a gangling youngster without any foreknowledge of what was to be a prolonged involvement with the military.

His entry onto The Citadel scene is recalled by a classmate, Milton A. Pearlstine, later to achieve prominence as a Charleston merchant and who, years later, was to renew his contact with Daniel when both were involved with the State Ports Authority. But to revert to the early Citadel scene, these are Pearlstine's recollections of his initial meeting with Charlie Daniel:

"I think it was September of 1914 when I walked through the sally port with a lanky, stoop-shouldered recruit (we were called 'rats' at that time) from Anderson. He was attending The Citadel as a beneficiary cadet, having had a scholarship from Anderson County. He roomed on the first gallery (the second floor of the barracks); I roomed on the second gallery. We were in different companies, but at that time there were only about 280 cadets. We were in the area where we could see and recognize each other and know each other's habits and things like that.

"Charlie and I both finished the freshman year and Charlie came back a second year. . . . He was active in the corps, socially prominent; his personality was outgoing, and he acquired many, many friends."

As a freshman, it was not to be expected that his presence in the cadet corps would be prominently noted in *The Sphinx*, the college yearbook, for that year. Nevertheless, he was listed and occasionally appeared in group photographs of such campus organizations as Company C, commanded by Cadet Captain R. W. Hudgens (who was later to achieve military and civic prominence in the Greenville area), the Polytechnic Literary Society and the cadet relay team.

Incidentally, he was on The Citadel's track team the following year as well, performing sufficiently well to warrant this observation many years afterwards by Carter (Scoop) Latimer in his *Greenville News* sports column:

> "Charlie Daniel, head of the big construction company that will erect the buildings at Greenville's Army air base, was a jim-dandy, all-around athlete at The Citadel before he resigned from the military academy to volunteer for immediate service in the last war. He still follows sports whenever he has time, which is seldom because of business pressure. . . ."

When Daniel returned for his second academic year at The Citadel, his class had dwindled in number from 101 to 60. He was still assigned to Company C as a private, but *The Sphinx* for 1916 lists him as sergeant-at-arms of the Polytechnic Literary Society, a member of the track squad and a member of the Commencement Hop Committee.

One event that marked Daniel's stay at The Citadel and that was to arouse interested inquiry for years thereafter was an episode that left him with a scar that he carried, literally if lightly, the remainder of his life.

It was the custom of the cadet corps then, as for years before and after, to participate in ceremonies on Confederate Memorial Day (May 10) at Charleston's Magnolia Cemetery. Habitually, the cadets would be conveyed to the Magnolia site by trolley car. On the particular occasion involving Daniel's ill fortune, he happened to stick his head out of a window just as the trolley was passing another trolley on a curve. As a consequence, Daniel had a small part of his ear clipped off by the other vehicle, leaving him with a permanent, although not prominent, nick that provoked good-natured comment. Indeed, one of his old Citadel cronies noted the nicked ear in a photograph displayed in the press some 40 years later when Daniel's entry into the U. S. Senate as interim replacement for the late Senator Burnet R. Maybank evoked a spate of publicity. In typical — but perhaps truthful — fashion, his classmates said the ear incident stemmed from Charlie's sticking his head out of the window while waving at a female acquaintance.

Moving from the trivial to the temporal, it is pertinent to record at this juncture that Daniel's adaptation to the military life, coupled with his sense of obligation as an American citizen, prompted his decision to forego returning to The Citadel for his junior year, which would have been 1916-17, and to volunteer his services to the U. S. Army. World War I was raging in Europe, and it was obviously just a matter of time before the United States would become caught up in the conflict — as indeed it did officially in April 1917. In the meanwhile, hosts of young Americans were flocking to the colors in anticipation of America's involvement, and among them was Charles E. Daniel of Anderson.

He underwent his officer training at Fort Oglethorpe, Georgia, and was commissioned a second lieutenant on December 15, 1917. While stationed at Oglethorpe, incidentally, he underwent a serious siege of illness and was confined for some time to the hospital in nearby Chattanooga, Tennessee. Thereafter, he was assigned to the 51st Infantry Regiment; it became an element of the Sixth Division, which was sometimes referred to as the "Walking Sixth" because of its paucity of motorized equipment. In his book, *The Doughboys*, Laurence Stallings, the World War I historian and officer, includes this reference to the division in which Daniel served:

"The U. S. 6th Division, virtually without transport, animals and trucks, tried to reach the Argonne front before November 11 (of 1918), jesting as they hitched themselves to wagons like Eskimo dogs, barking and yapping, gunners serving as army mules, hee-hawing and kicking from time to time."

In any event, Daniel served in the American Expeditionary Force (AEF) from July 1918 to April 1919, being honorably discharged on May 31, 1919. Upon his discharge, the men under his command manifested their regard for his qualities as a man and as a leader by tendering him a watch on which these words were inscribed:

"Presented to Lieutenant Charles E. Daniel in grateful appreciation. Company B, 51st Infantry."

There is little on record to indicate a continuation of Daniel's contact with the military after his World War I stint, nor with The Citadel for that matter. The latter connection was reestablished in the mid-1920s, however, when he arranged for the entrance of his youngest brother, R. Hugh Daniel, as a cadet. One of the stories which has grown up about that development hinges upon the question supposedly posed to Hugh by friends: "Hugh, did Charlie think as much of The Citadel as everyone says he does?"

Hugh's answer purportedly was in this vein: "He thought enough of it to make me go there."

Their subsequent evidence of loyalty and service to The Citadel gives a ring of truth to the meaning conveyed in that reported exchange. In any event, subsequent years were to demonstrate time and again the Daniel brothers' high regard for and continuing dedication to the South Carolina military college.

Although both Charlie and Hugh Daniel were steadfast Citadel men from their cadet days, it was not until General Mark W. Clark became president of the college that their commitments and contributions took on truly substantial proportions. In many ways, the association of the three was a "mutual admiration society," with favors and visits being exchanged at frequent intervals.

One of Clark's first moves upon assuming The Citadel's presidency in January 1954 was to develop a fund to be used for scholarships for young men needing financial aid for their college education. As he surveyed the list of well-to-do alumni who might be in a position to help, the names and economic standing of Charles and Hugh Daniel loomed as likely prospects for solicitation.

But even before Clark could set in motion the machinery he hoped would bring him into close and useful contact with the Daniel brothers, he received requests for aid from both of them, albeit aid of a different type. A telephone call from Charlie Daniel brought word of the latter's desire to meet the new Citadel president and an expression of interest in having him make the keynote address for a forthcoming meeting of the Greenville Community Chest. Clark accepted the invitation, which included a cordial weekend visit with Mrs. Clark at the Daniel residence where the two couples struck up an immediate and lasting friendship.

Within a week after his Greenville speech, Clark received an invitation from Hugh Daniel to make a similar appearance before a corresponding charitable group in Birmingham. Again, General and Mrs. Clark responded affirmatively, thus laying an even broader base for the Clark-Daniel relationship to follow.

Although Citadel finances were not discussed with either of the Daniel brothers on the two occasions just mentioned, it was not long before both men and their wives were invited to Charleston as guests of the Clarks at The Citadel. On this occasion, the general took the initiative and proposed the creation of a Daniel Scholarship Fund.

When Clark suggested $50,000 as a starter, the immediate reaction was "That's a heap of money." Nevertheless, after excusing themselves for a few minutes private conversation, the Daniels asked if stock rather than cash would be acceptable. Upon being told The Citadel would be pleased to accept anything of a financial nature, the Daniels agreed to give 3,000 shares of Georgia-Pacific stock to the contemplated scholarship fund.

It was at this juncture that Charlie Daniel gave the general a bit of practical advice on safeguarding the integrity of the scholarship fund. He informed Clark, who was only then beginning his exposure to the ins and outs of state government in South Carolina, that the scholarship fund should be given a separate and legal status of its own rather than being co-mingled with revenues provided the college through normal state appropriations. If all the money went into one pool, it would be subject to the dictates of legislative action and thereby possibly lose its distinctive character as a nonappropriated fund earmarked exclusively for scholarship purposes.

Clark took the advice, set up the scholarship fund in a special category, and nurtured it carefully throughout his 11-year tenure as president of The Citadel. The fund grew with revenues realized from the original stocks and other assets subsequently contributed by the Daniel brothers. Only once was it tapped for another purpose — to provide for a brief time collateral for a loan needed for The Citadel to acquire its alumni house. When Clark ended his administration with his 1965 resignation, the Daniel Scholarship Fund had grown to more than $1 million.

The Daniel contributions to The Citadel were not limited to scholarship aid, however. As Clark assessed the college's total needs, he concluded that a major deficiency of the campus was the lack of a student union building — a place where the cadets could meet with visiting relatives and friends and where amenities such as a barber shop, post office, lunch counter and other facilities could be provided under one roof. He convinced Charlie Daniel that such a need did exist and asked that he submit the lowest possible bid for the structure. As the general recounts the episode, Daniel assumed the proper military demeanor and asked, "Is that an order, sir?"

Upon being assured that Clark was sincerely interested in obtaining such a building at the lowest possible cost, Daniel not only agreed to submit a bid but actually tendered one which was about $100,000 under that of the nearest competitor. Thus, there came into being a handsome structure, later to bear the name of Mark Clark Hall.

Another anecdote sheds light on the extent to which the Daniel brothers sought to serve their alma mater on this particular occasion. When the time came for groundbreaking, Clark invited both Charlie and Hugh to be on hand for the ceremonies. Again relying on Clark's recollections, this was Charlie's response:

> "I'm terribly sorry. I must be in New York for an important meeting at that time. I've asked Hugh, and he will be there. He's bringing with him a silver shovel with which to break the ground, and I want to assure you there's not enough profit in that building to pay for the shovel."

Thereafter, the Daniel brothers continued to favor The Citadel with gifts of much worth, but there was little further involvement in construction work on campus. Contrary to a commonly held view, the handsome Daniel Library building flanking Summerall chapel was not built by Daniel Construction Company but was named to honor the two brothers for their considerable and continuing assistance to the college. Large portraits of the two men are prominently displayed just inside the main entrance to the library.

One of the most unusual of the numerous Daniel bequests to The Citadel was a handsome bell tower erected alongside the cadet chapel on campus. Bells were imported from Holland for the carillon, which was dedicated in December of 1954 with formal ceremonies attended by both Charlie and Hugh Daniel; General Clark; the Right Reverend Albert S. Thomas, a retired Episcopal Bishop and an 1892 Citadel graduate; and Governor James F. Byrnes.

The $50,000 structure, including the bells, was named in memory of a Citadel classmate of Hugh Daniel, Major Thomas D. Howie, one of the military college's heroes of World War II. Posthumously known as "the Major of St. Lo," Howie lost his life leading his troops against the German forces holding the Normandy town of St. Lo in July 1944.

The most spectacular gift ever made to The Citadel Development Foundation — both in dimension and in drama — was a 1972 Daniel contribution. Charlie had died some eight years earlier, but it was his initiative back in 1964, the year of his death, that made possible the magnificent contribution by the Daniel Foundation to The Citadel Development Foundation.

In June of 1964, Daniel had made headline news throughout the state and much of the South by announcing his company's plans for erecting in Greenville the tallest office building in South Carolina and much of the South. In appropriate ground-breaking ceremonies attended by many notables, Daniel declared his firm's decision to build the 25-story structure "as our way of showing our appreciation" to the people of Greenville and South Carolina.

As the impressive building grew to its height of more than 300 feet, it became not only a landmark but a talking point for Greenville and the vicinity. There was nothing, however, to link the Daniel building with The Citadel other than the well-established relationship that Charlie and Hugh maintained with the college.

That personal link was transformed into a highly rewarding arrangement for The Citadel in 1972. General Clark, who had long since retired as president of The Citadel but who was on the board of the Development Foundation that he had helped create, subsequently gave this account of the 1972 episode:

"One day Hugh called me from Birmingham and asked if I would fly with him to Greenville and see Mickey (Mrs. Charles Daniel). We set a date; and he came down in his plane, and we went up to Greenville.

"We went out to Mickey's home, and there were two or three other people in the room. I had taken up with me Richard Rieger, the director of the Development Foundation, because I knew this had something to do with a gift. I sat on the couch by Mickey and Hugh sat on the chair to my left and pretty soon he said, 'Well, I've asked that we gather today in order to make a donation to your Citadel Development Foundation.'

"He handed me a big brown envelope, which sort of surprised me because it was too big just to put a check in, and I wondered just what it was. I opened it, and there alone in it was a color photograph of the Daniel Building in Greenville — a beautiful sight, probably the most magnificent building in the state if not in the South. I didn't know what to say, for I didn't know what was meant by handing me this photograph. Hugh said 'Oh, turn it over, Mark.' "

He turned the picture over and it simply noted on the back:

To: The Citadel Development Foundation. To paraphase
Ralph Edwards — this is not your life
but it is your building.
Trustees,
The Daniel Foundation
Greenville, South Carolina
December 11, 1972

As a footnote to the saga of the Daniel Building, it should be recorded that the imposing tower went back into Daniel ownership in September 1980 through purchase from The Citadel Development Foundation. This unscheduled development provided a $16 million windfall for The Citadel.

CHAPTER 17

Clemson Connections

Charlie Daniel's interest in the welfare of Clemson College was evidenced over a period of many years in numerous ways, many of which involved outright contributions to the college or to certain of its programs. This continuing and sometimes consuming interest did not stem from any personal connection, as was the case in Daniel's having attended The Citadel prior to World War I. Rather, it grew out of his personal and economic appreciation for the services rendered by Clemson to the agricultural and technological advancement of South Carolina and the South, especially in fields related to textiles. This was understandable enough, considering how deeply Daniel as an individual and Daniel Construction Company as a building firm were involved in the physical expansion of the textile industry.

Dating from the early 1940's into the 1950's, Daniel's financial assistance to Clemson exceeded $1.5 million. Some of this represented direct grants to the college for scholarships. Considerable amounts took the form of contributions for the purchase of equipment and material for college programs, $100,000 going to provide machinery for training purposes in the new Clemson Textile School. Other sums represented savings to the institution made possible by Daniel's assumption of interest and bonding costs, which facilitated uninterrupted progress on major building programs such as the Clemson Housing project.

As a result of these continuing manifestations of concern for Clemson's development, coupled with his readiness to advise and consult on matters affecting the college, Daniel was a logical choice to fill the vacancy left on the Clemson board of trustees by the death in 1948 of W. W. Bradley of Columbia, one of the college's seven life trustees. The other six life trustees were Christie Benet of Columbia; James F. Byrnes, then of Spartanburg; Robert M. Cooper of Wisacky; Paul Sanders of Ritter; T. B. Young of Florence; and State Senator Edgar A. Brown of Barnwell.

145

In keeping with the provisions of the Clemson will, the life trustees comprise a self-perpetuating board, and it was the group just named that chose Charlie Daniel to succeed Bradley. As they did so, however, they realized that they had to reckon with this Clemson by-law:

"Section 141. No member of the board of trustees, official or employee of the college who is in a position either to influence the award of a contract, or to cause purchases to be made, shall be interested in any firm, company or corporation doing business with the college."

Later in the year, it became necessary to deal in specifics, for there was pending a Daniel Construction Company bid for a Clemson contract even as the head of the company was becoming a life trustee of the institution. Facing up to the situation, the board of trustees agreed that the by-law in question would stand in the way of acceptance of a Daniel bid.

In this same general time frame, however, the interpretation of the by-law was modified so as not to impair Daniel's privilege of bidding on Clemson projects where the bidding was competitive and properly supervised. On the strength of an opinion by the attorney general, Daniel assumed his position as a life trustee; and his company bid on many Clemson projects in the ensuing years.

The question continued to receive consideration several years later, resulting in varying opinions in early 1953 and mid-1957. Tiring of the controversy, Daniel decided to resign from the Clemson board in 1957; yet his fellow life trustees declined to accept his resignation. Even so, Daniel limited his active participation on the board, and one of his major acts as a trustee was to help bring Robert C. Edwards to the college as vice president in charge of development, a position that eventually led to his election as presi-dent of Clemson.

From the time Daniel submitted his unaccepted resignation, his company has not been involved in on-campus construction at Clemson; yet the firm, its executives and The Daniel Foundation have continued his generosity to the college and various of its endeavors, and Buck Mickel has been elected a life trustee on the board.

Daniel's resignation from the Clemson board drew from the Greenville *Piedmont* an editorial observation that "Clemson has had no greater friend than Mr. Daniel. He has served that institution long and well, and it is only just that he be allowed release from some of his outside responsibilities." Later in the month, after the Clemson board had detailed Daniel's many financial and personal contributions to the school, the *Piedmont* added, "it is a pity that his counsel will no longer be heard at board meetings. There is not a college in South Carolina that would fail to benefit from having on its board a man like Mr. Daniel."

In the meanwhile, as cited in the paragraph above, the Clemson trustees had themselves issued a statement through Cooper, praising Daniel's numerous contributions to the welfare and advancement of the college.

Salient sentences of the trustees' statement, released in mid-August of 1957 by Board President Cooper, follow:

> "Charlie Daniel's contributions to Clemson College, financial as well as unreserved gift of his personal time, are fully understood and appreciated by his colleagues on the board. Through the firm which he heads, Daniel Construction Company, Mr. Daniel has made major financial contributions to Clemson College in the form of low competitive bids on major building projects. He has made other significant financial contributions as direct gifts, and by saving the college large sums of money in interest charges. While his financial contributions have been extremely important to the college, Mr. Daniel's personal services, as a life member of the board of trustees, have been of even greater value in that Clemson College has benefited from his vision, his foresight and his aggressive determination to enable the institution to better serve the needs of the people of South Carolina and the nation. . . . For more than 20 years, Daniel Construction Company has consistently been the low bidder on new buildings erected at Clemson College."

Continuing developments nearly a quarter of a century after that statement prompted Dean Harlan McClure of the College of Architecture to remark that "the very fundamental role Mr. Daniel played in the academic development of Clemson is not generally known. This facet of his accomplishment may be surprising to some, but he was a man of uncommon wisdom and although he would not presume to consider himself an educator, he was above all a person with natural qualities that made him an outstanding administrator with an extraordinary sense of organization."

McClure had arrived on the Clemson campus in the mid-1950's to direct the Architecture Department at the time the South

Carolina Chapter of the American Institute of Architects (SCAIA) was spearheading efforts to improve and strengthen the department. It received Charlie Daniel's moral and financial support; and soon architecture was separated from the School of Engineering, and the Clemson Architectural Foundation (CAF) was established. Some 20 years later, the CAF helped establish the Charles E. Daniel Center for Building Research and Urban Study in Genoa, Italy, "in honor of his great interest and early progressive educational concerns."

The Daniel Center in Genoa provides a new dimension to the College of Architecture, which was being served by four departments by the early 1970's. Since almost one-third of the students were studying at graduate professional levels, an overseas center was envisioned in a historic European city. The CAF gave its full support to McClure, as did the SCAIA; and in 1977 funds were raised to defray the costs of acquiring and converting a historic Genoa villa into a modern study center.

At the end of the academic year 1981, more than 350 graduate students of the College of Architecture had resided at the Daniel center, including building scientists and managers, architects, planners and visual designers. Fourteen Clemson faculty members had served periods of residence there, and scores of foreign professionals and faculty members had contributed to its studies. A reordering of the environs of the ancient port of Genoa involved them in myriad problems in historic research as well as unique creative design, structural and planning efforts.

Dean McClure noted that "the changes that have occurred in students' awareness, method and motivation are notable." He added that "there are many collegiate overseas programs, most of which are grand tours without real roots; while the actual essence of the Clemson/CAF program at the Daniel Center is an involvement in the place, deeply and fully appreciating the rich past while approaching contemporary problems needing solution with respect and sensitivity. The results come home with dividends."

CHAPTER 18

The Postwar Period

Daniel Construction Company was moving steadily ahead in the years immediately following World War II, but a combination of two postwar developments ushered in a period that saw Charlie Daniel really come into his own as a procurer of new industry for South Carolina and the South in general. One of these was the creation of the South Carolina Department of Research, Planning and Development, established by a 1945 act of the General Assembly. The other was the election in 1946 of J. Strom Thurmond as governor of South Carolina, an occurrence that gave political influence and personal commitment to fulfillment of the same goals pursued by the newly formed board.

The broad mission of the Research, Planning and Development Board, as spelled out in the South Carolina Legislative Manual of 1946, clearly established the commonality of interest of the board, the new governor and Charlie Daniel in promoting industrial development and with it a stronger economic base for the state.

Thurmond's outstanding contribution to the attainment of those goals was his willingness to apply not only his political personality but the prestige of his office to the task at hand. For example, when corporate executives who were openly or potentially interested in establishing plants in South Carolina visited the state, they found themselves invited to luncheon or dinner at the governor's mansion. That in itself reflected an official interest in the prospect of their becoming a part of the state's growing industrial complex.

Even more persuasive, however, was Thurmond's willingness — indeed, eagerness — to visit the corporate headquarters of prospective new industries and make a personal solicitation as South Carolina's chief executive for the establishment of plants in the Palmetto State. This was a most unusual practice back in the 1940's, although it subsequently came to be emulated by the governors and other high-ranking officials of many states, especially those of the South.

Ralph M. Horton, Jr., who was chief of research for the Development Board in those days, recalls the impact of one such incident when South Carolina was seeking to persuade the Du Pont Company to establish a fibers plant at Camden. At the instigation and with the collaboration of Robert M. Cooper, then director of the board, and with Charlie Daniel playing a leading role in the drama, an appointment was arranged for Thurmond to meet with Du Pont executives at the company's home office in Wilmington, Delaware. There, the South Carolinians were greeted by the officers and directors of the company, one of whom, according to Horton's account, said: "In the history of the Du Pont organization, this is the first time a governor has ever seen fit to call on us."

Although not addicted to light talk or quipping, Thurmond himself may have put the directors in a receptive frame of mind with his opening remarks, which were to this effect: "As I look down over this table and look into the intelligent faces here today, I believe we've got more brains around this table than Truman has in his cabinet."

Whether that visit or the combined sales pitches of Thurmond, Cooper and Daniel turned the tide is a matter of conjecture, but the net result was a decision by Du Pont to locate its new plant in Camden — and in later years to add a second plant there and a large facility near Charleston. It is significant to note that Daniel lent his best efforts toward persuading Du Pont to make the decision, even though he knew that Du Pont at that time carried out its own construction projects. Du Pont has since become a major Daniel client at many sites throughout the South.

Thurmond rated Daniel as "a super salesman." Looking back over the years when the two of them pursued the common goal of promoting industrial expansion in South Carolina, Thurmond gave this estimate of "the best salesman I ever saw":

> "He had a lot of common sense, he knew what people were looking for, and he knew how to approach them. He was polite and diplomatic and not arrogant, even though he represented one of the biggest construction companies in the United States. He had a knack of conveying to people his desire to help them accomplish what they wanted to. Instead of appearing to be looking for something, he gave the impression that his main purpose was to help the individual he was talking to, and this had a tremendous impact. . . .

"I've never known a man who understood human nature better than Charlie Daniel, and a salesman has to understand human nature. I've never known a man who knew when to move in and when to go slow or to move fast better than Charlie. He was a master strategist and, although he wasn't a doctor of psychology, he deserved to have an honorary degree in psychology, as he really knew how to handle people."

Thurmond likewise gave full credit to the industrial salesmanship demonstrated by Planning Board Director Bob Cooper and by his successor, Louis W. Bishop, who held the director's office during the latter years of the Thurmond administration. Without belittling the efforts or the accomplishments of other agencies and individuals, it seems safe to say that the weight of contemporary testimony concerning industrial development of that time gives chief credit to the three-way working relationship of Thurmond, the Research, Planning and Development Board and Charlie Daniel himself.

The cooperation between Daniel and the board, as expressed by Horton, represented "a common intertwining" of aims and a "cross-pollination of prospects." According to Horton, not only did Daniel play an active role in seeking out and "selling" prospects, but "his devotion to South Carolina was such that he went the second mile to be sure that the building would be in South Carolina. . . ."

Years later, after Thurmond had been elected to the U. S. Senate, he continued to use the prestige of his political position to further the cause of South Carolina's industrial expansion, substituting the senate dining room for the governor's mansion as the locale for entertaining prospects.

In the meantime, the three-way working relationship of the governor's office, the Development Board and Charlie Daniel that had evolved during the Thurmond administration continued to prove highly effective during the four-year term of Governor James F. Byrnes. In this particular time frame (1951 through 1954), the personal involvement of the governor was enhanced by the national, indeed international, reputation that had been established by Byrnes during a half-century of public service in local, state, national and world affairs. The mention of his name often provided an entree that otherwise might have been difficult to obtain because captains of industry, no less than public officials, generally took pleasure in being identified — whether by mere conversation or meaningful negotiation — with someone of Byrnes' prominence.

One spin-off of the Byrnes-Daniel teamwork was the development of a mutual esteem and friendship that linked the two men (and their wives) in a cordiality that was evident socially as well as politically and industrially.

Typical of Daniel's constant maintenance of cordial relations with the host of industrialists, bankers, public officials and personal friends with whom he had regular or intermittent dealings was his wide-ranging goodwill gesture that stemmed from the publication of James F. Byrnes' second book, *All In One Lifetime.*

Upon learning in the late summer of 1958 that the Byrnes book was due for early release, Daniel promptly initiated a widespread effort through which he personally ordered more than 150 copies and arranged to have them mailed after being appropriately autographed by Byrnes. Recipients of the books ranged from President Eisenhower and Vice President Nixon through a wide spectrum of industrial and financial leaders to the personal ranks of old friends in South Carolina and his hometown of Elberton, Georgia. Notes of appreciation flowed back to him from individuals to whom he sent books.

For years, the Byrnes and the Daniels made periodic visits to one another's homes. One such instance occurred in May of 1961, when former Vice President Richard M. Nixon flew to Greenville to attend a private dinner party given by the Daniels in honor of Mr. and Mrs. Byrnes. (May 2 was a special day for the Byrnes in two respects, for it marked not only Mr. Byrnes' birthday but their wedding anniversary.) On this particular occasion, the Daniels commemorated the Byrnes' 55th wedding anniversary with a "purely social" affair.

An anecdote involving the Byrnes-Daniel combination was embodied in a letter in which a Clemson Experiment Station economist, James F. Miles, lauded both men. Writing to Daniel in April of 1963, Miles said:

> "South Carolina has produced many illustrious sons. Some, like John C. Calhoun, achieved national prominence as United States senator, secretary of state, secretary of war, and vice president of the United States. There has not been an equal to Calhoun in our long history, but our own James F. Byrnes comes close. As governor, senator, secretary of state and war mobilizer, James F. Byrnes ranks at the very top.
>
> "I feel that you rank among South Carolina's great — not because of your public office as United States senator, but because you have been South Carolina's greatest builder. You have done more to industrialize South Carolina — to create more wealth and more jobs — than any other person in the long history of our state. I do not know of anybody who has meant more to South Carolina than you."

There was an unusual and unintended twist in the delivery of that letter, for initially it was mistakenly forwarded to Byrnes, who in turn sent it along to Daniel with this accompanying note:

> "The enclosed letter addressed to you was inadvertently sent to me. While I do not know the writer, he is a man of good judgment. Certainly I agree with the fine statements he makes as to your record, and I am not going to deny the complimentary statements made about me."

CHAPTER 19

Senatorial Interlude

Throughout most of his business career, Charlie Daniel operated on the fringes of politics — a practice well suited to his personal interest in better government and to his understanding of the impact of political considerations upon industrial decisions. That "behind the scenes" role changed abruptly, however, in the fall of 1954 when Daniel found himself plunged directly into politics at a lofty level.

The event that triggered this sudden change was the unexpected death on September 1 of South Carolina's senior senator, Burnet R. Maybank, at his summer residence in Flat Rock, North Carolina. The former two-term mayor of Charleston and governor of the state had been elected to the U. S. Senate in October of 1941 to fill the unexpired term of Senator James F. Byrnes, who had been appointed to the U. S. Supreme Court by President Franklin D. Roosevelt. Maybank subsequently was elected for a full six-year senatorial term in 1942 and again in 1948. As he neared the end of that term in 1954, he was a "shoo-in" for yet another term, being unopposed in the Democratic primary and seemingly destined to become the first U. S. senator from South Carolina to win reelection without opposition since 1906, when Benjamin R. (Pitchfork Ben) Tillman gained a third term.

Assuming, as the populace generally did, that a special Democratic primary would be called to fill the Maybank vacancy, Byrnes let it be known that he would appoint the winner of that primary to serve the remaining few months of Maybank's term. However, when the Democratic Executive Committee decided that there was insufficient time for a primary, the governor reassessed the situation.

Under normal circumstances, the U. S. Senate would not have been in session as the calendar year drew to a close, lessening the need for a prompt replacement for Maybank. In 1954, however, there seemed every likelihood that the Senate would be called back

154

into special session to consider the censure resolutions brought by a special committee against Senator Joseph R. McCarthy. The Wisconsin senator was charged with abusing senatorial powers in his vigorous and vitriolic attacks against Communist influences in and out of government and with falsely accusing innocent persons of Communist activities or sympathies.

Irrespective of the prospect of a special session, Byrnes determined that the wisest course would be to designate an interim senator. Noting that there would be no primary election, the governor concluded, "There is no reason why I should delay making my appointment as provided by law. . . . A senator can serve his state while the Senate is not in session as well as during a session. South Carolina is entitled to two senators in the Congress."

Suiting his action to his words, the governor announced on September 6 that he was appointing Charles E. Daniel to the unexpired Maybank term:

> "I have appointed Mr. Daniel because of his splendid qualities and in recognition of the outstanding service he has rendered in bringing into the state new industries that have given employment to thousands of South Carolinians."

Daniel, who already had informed Byrnes that he had no intention of running for a full term in the forthcoming November general election, had this to say to the press upon the announcement of his appointment:

> "I realize full well the magnitude of the responsibilities that must be borne by a U. S. senator in these days of international crisis, even when Congress is not in session. I am glad to have the opportunity of rendering this service to my state.
>
> "To Governor Byrnes and the people of South Carolina I pledge my utmost to perform the duties of U. S. senator in a manner that will reflect credit at all times on the great state of South Carolina."

Despite the eminence of his new appointment, Daniel evinced little inclination to hasten off to Washington. Indeed, Byrnes himself had to prod the industrialist to "get on up to Washington" and take on the responsibility that went with the job. Byrnes' impetus was provided after he had received a number of calls from the nation's capital inquiring as to the new senator's probable course of action in voting on pending questions and individuals. One such call came from Senator Lyndon Johnson, who had met Daniel and thought highly of him.

Thus, in mid-September, Daniel boarded the train for Washington (this being at that time of his life when he tended to avoid air travel). Upon arrival in Washington, he was met at the station by Dresden Smith, who had been Maybank's administrative assistant, and by Bobby Baker, the young Pickens County protégé of Johnson. Recalling the Daniel arrival in the nation's capital, Baker said, "He was the first man off the train, carrying his own suitcase."

In short order, Senator Daniel engaged in familiarizing himself with members of the Maybank staff and orienting himself to the unfamiliar political surroundings of Capitol Hill. And, as was to be expected, the new senator promptly found himself subjected to that customary Washington ordeal — the press conference.

Prior experience in dealing with the press, coupled with his native good humor and self-possession, stood him in good stead. As a result, according to the September 19 account published in *The Greenville News*, he emerged unscathed from the episode, dubbed by the irreverent reporters, "Daniel in the lions' den."

For one thing, he refused to be trapped into an endorsement of either of the two men competing for the Maybank seat in the November general election — Strom Thurmond and Edgar Brown. "Both men," Daniel said in response to a direct question, "are close friends of mine and exceedingly able men . . . either one would ably represent the state of South Carolina in Washington." On another hot political topic, however, he did not equivocate. Praising the administration of President Eisenhower, he frankly stated that he would support the President for reelection against any Democratic opposition.

In about six weeks, as had been expected, the Senate was called into special session to consider some action with respect to Senator McCarthy. Had it not been for this extraordinary McCarthy Session, Daniel might not have been privileged to participate at all in actual Senate proceedings since the regular session (opening in January) presumably would have recognized Strom Thurmond, who won the November election.

A special session, however, was formally convened on November 8, at which time Daniel was sworn into office amid public and private observances, which made the event memorable for the entire Daniel family and a large coterie of friends on hand for the occasion. Notably and deliberately absent were Governor Byrnes and incoming Senator Thurmond. Both had been invited but refrained from attending so that the occasion would be entirely "Charlie Daniel's Day."

The scene in the Senate chamber as the body convened was one to be remembered. When Vice President Nixon called the Senate to order, the new member from South Carolina sat unflustered with a group of distinguished Southern senators, including Walter F. George and Richard B. Russell of Georgia, Harry F. Byrd of Virginia, and Lyndon B. Johnson of Texas, leader of the Democratic minority in the Senate. North Carolina Senators Alton A. Lennon and Sam J. Ervin were absent, officially excused to attend funeral services at Durham for North Carolina Governor William B. Umstead.

Shortly after the opening gavel had been rapped at noon, the new senators, five in all, assembled at the rear of the chamber, each accompanied by the senior senator of the affected state. With Senator Daniel was South Carolina's Senator Olin D. Johnston, whose role on November 8 included the tendering of a resolution of regret over the death of Senator Maybank. The formal swearing-in ceremony commenced with the five new senators being escorted down the center aisle by their home-state colleagues, with Daniel and Johnston leading the procession. The oath of office was administered by Vice President Nixon to the newcomers. In addition to Daniel, Senators Ernest Brown of Nevada, Norris Cotton of New Hampshire and Roman Hruska and Mrs. George Abel, both of Nebraska, were also sworn in. Daniel was the only Democrat of the lot.

Observing the proceedings from the galleries were several members of the Daniel family, including his wife; brothers James F. Daniel, Jr., R. Hugh Daniel and son Robert; and Mr. and Mrs. Buck Mickel. Mickel, a nephew of Mrs. Daniel, who was later to assume much of the corporate leadership role exercised by Daniel prior to his death in 1964. Also among the observers were such Daniel friends as Secretary of the Army Robert T. Stevens, a textile executive for whom Daniel had built several plants; Arthur O. Wellman of Boston and Albert Prouvost of France, wool industry magnates then beginning operations in South Carolina with Daniel's help; two Southern Railway vice presidents, W. Mason King and F. C. Toal; and a number of other dignitaries from the worlds of industry and government, including several general officers from the military. These and others, most of them accompanied by their wives, attended not only the swearing-in ceremony but a subsequent luncheon honoring the new senator.

From Greenville, there were such friends and associates as Mr. and Mrs. Alester G. Furman, Jr., Mr. and Mrs. J. Mason Alexander, Judge and Mrs. Clement F. Haynsworth, Jr., Mr. and Mrs. Langdon Cheves, Mr. and Mrs. Harold Turner, and Mr. and Mrs. Alden Simpson. The Simpsons' 10-year-old son David provided the quote of the day after sitting through the day's brief senate dabate on the McCarthy censure resolution: "They sounded like a bunch of old women."

Also present for the day's events were William G. Lyles and Louis Wolff of the Columbia architectural firm bearing their names; Marine Lieutenant General W. Oscar Brice, who had been at The Citadel with Daniel; Robert J. Saunders, a Laurinburg, North Carolina, textile executive; Edgar Morris of Pickens and Washington; and Carter L. Burgess, newly appointed Assistant Secretary of Defense for Manpower and Personnel. On December 2, by the way, Daniel entered into the *Congressional Record* this brief endorsement of Burgess' appointment:

"I want to recommend highly the nomination of Mr. Carter Burgess as Assistant Secretary of Defense in charge of personnel. Mr. Burgess is a man of great integrity, of tremendous ability, and with a background of wonderful experience. I know that he will render outstanding service to the Department of Defense and our government. It gives me pleasure to recommend Mr. Burgess without reservation."

Confirming nominations and discharging other legislative functions consumed much of the Senate's time during the special session, but the real justification for its having been convened was to discharge its responsibilities in the McCarthy situation. A special six-member committee, headed by Senator Arthur V. Watkins (Republican-Utah) had filed in late September a report differentiating the various charges against McCarthy into five counts. Out of the technicalities involved in the various counts, there ultimately evolved a resolution calling for the senator from Wisconsion to be "condemned" rather than censured for "conduct contrary to senatorial traditions."

When that proposition finally reached a vote on December 2, it was adopted 67 to 22, with six senators not voting and one (McCarthy) voting "present." Daniel was among the 67 voting for the resolution of condemnation.

As the special session drew to a close immediately thereafter, it was evident that South Carolina's interim senator had made a favorable impression upon his colleagues. From Johnson came this observation concerning Daniel:

"Because of his brief service, I have not had the opportunity for extended association with the junior senator from South Carolina. He has sat in the front row with me. I have never formed a deeper affection for any man in such a short time as I have formed for the distinguished senator from South Carolina. . . . I have always considered service in the Senate of the United States the highest honor that can befall any man. To my mind, those who are leaving this year carry with them all that distinction and all that honor and also bear my deep respect and affection!"

Similar sentiments were expressed by Senator William F. Knowland of California, who at that particular point occupied the position of majority leader during the Republicans' brief and marginal ascendancy in the Senate. Here are Knowland's remarks:

"The distinguished senator from South Carolina has been with us for only a short time; but although we on this side of the aisle have not had the opportunity to get so well acquainted with him as senators on the other side of the aisle have had, I did have the opportunity to get to know him some time ago in his own state. I hope that he, too, will carry away from this chamber the recollection of the spirit which recognizes no center aisle and the knowledge that while we may sometimes, under some considerable emotional stress, differ with each other, when the day is over and the Senate has adjourned, we can meet and greet each other as friends and discuss the many problems in which we have a common interest."

That mutual admiration note had been sounded the day before by Daniel himself in conversation with correspondent van der Linden:

"I have tremendously enjoyed this job and have been greatly impressed with the thoroughness with which all senators have treated the task at hand. This is a wonderful bunch to work with."

On December 2, the closing day of the session and the occasion for the Johnson and Knowland remarks just quoted, Daniel took the floor of the Senate for the first and last time. In his brief "hail and farewell" speech, duly recorded in the *Congressional Record* of that date, the South Carolinian gratified his fellow senators and surprised many of his constituents back home by advocating a pay hike for members of Congress and other officials of the federal government:

"Mr. President, I should like to take this opportunity to thank the majority leader and the minority leader for their kind observations about the junior senator from South Carolina. I am appreciative to all members of the Senate for the many courtesies they have extended to me since I have been a member of this great body. I leave the Senate tremendously impressed with the vast amount of work accomplished and with the burdensome load which is carried by the leaders of the two great political parties of our country.

"I am indeed sorry, for one particular reason, that I shall not be here in January, because the first order of business for me would be to urge the Senate to drastically increase salaries for all members of the Senate, the House of Representatives, the judiciary, and employees of the federal government. The people of South Carolina want to pay adequate salaries to those who serve them so well in the Congress, the judiciary, and the government of the United States. In my opinion, the Senate is the most underpaid organization in America today. If we are to continue having the best brains in this country represent this great country in Congress and the judiciary, I think that the 84th Congress should make pay increases the first order of business. Businessmen, taxpayers and citizens of South Carolina would give their full support to such a program as a matter of justice."

As the senator himself must have realized, his prediction of "full support" for such a proposition was hardly to be expected of all South Carolinians back home. Editorial reaction in the state's press was mixed.

Daniel's brief stay in the Senate was made even shorter by his decision to resign prior to the convening of the 1955 session. In doing so, he made it possible for his successor, Strom Thurmond, to acquire a few days' seniority over other new senators who had emerged victorious from the November general elections. In Thurmond's case, his election was truly historic, marking the first time that anyone had ever been elected to the United States Senate by write-in vote. The Thurmond victory was all the more extraordinary in that his opponent was one of South Carolina's most powerful and best-known politicians, State Senator Edgar A. Brown of Barnwell.

It was not at all unexpected when Daniel stepped down in advance of the new Congress' convening so that Thurmond would gain a few days' seniority over the incoming newcomers. Here is how Daniel expressed that view in a letter to Governor Byrnes:

> "My reason for submitting to you my formal resignation as a U. S. Senator from South Carolina is due to my desire to benefit our state by making it possible for the Honorable Strom Thurmond to have the advantage of seniority."

The Daniel resignation thus cleared the way for Byrnes to make another interim appointment, that of Strom Thurmond, for the very brief — but very critical — period between December 24, 1954, and January 5, 1955.

The appointment gave Thurmond preference over the other newly elected senators and allowed him to outrank them in conference committee appointments, which is what Daniel had in mind when he resigned. The resignation brought almost uniformly favorable editorial reaction throughout the state, with Charleston's *News and Courier* describing Daniel's action as being "in keeping with what we have come to expect from Mr. Daniel (who) seldom hesitated when confronted with a situation which can benefit his state."

CHAPTER 20

Southern Accent

Both explicit and implicit in the *Fortune* magazine article of October 1954 and in virtually every written or oral description of Charlie Daniel was his status as a dyed-in-the-wool Southerner. In all truth, Daniel was a Southerner not only by circumstance, having been born in Georgia and reared in South Carolina, but by conviction as well.

He saw the South as a region whose people were endowed with special character and characteristics. And whenever the opportunity presented itself or could be created, he was on hand with his 20th-Century version of the Rebel yell. But in his case and in his works, his was not the voice of the proverbial "unreconstructed Rebel," but quite literally that of a latter-day Southerner devoted to the rebuilding of Dixieland.

Whether his approach is regarded as one of construction or of reconstruction, the theme was the same. By way of illustration, the following quote is from an address to the Chamber of Commerce of his old home town and birthplace, Elberton, Georgia, on the subject of "Southern Industrial Development."

"Go back for a moment to 100 years ago, when some areas of the South ranked second only to the flourishing northeastern states in commerce, business and agriculture. Then came the holocaust of the War Between the States. The system on which the South's economy was based came to an abrupt and crushing end. The South was left completely desolate; more so than other people have ever realized — left, not with any friendly Marshall Plan, mutual aid or other sympathetic treatment such as we bestow upon the conquered Germans, Japanese and others.

"I dwell on this . . . to make a point . . . that the people of the South are different in many respects from those in other parts of the nation. They are different because our misfortune did not end with Appomattox . . . did not really end from the economic viewpoint until now, when we are beginning to get our foot in the door of the productive opportunities and prosperity of this great nation.

"The differences in our people grew out of hardship and necessity. And they grew strongly, like a slow-growing tree into a durable and unbending hardwood. The philosophers through the ages have agreed that from suffering and misfortune rise sturdy and determined people.

"Now we are eager to produce; eager to give a fair day's work for a fair day's pay because few of us, white or Negro, ever had the real opportunity before to produce and earn fair wages. Our working people do their own thinking. Consequently, it is no accident that the 11 states of the old Confederacy have all passed right-to-work laws — laws fundamental to the Southern philosophy that, while a man may join a union if he wishes, there is no power on earth that should force him to do so before he can get a job, or hold a job, and make a living for himself and his family. To do so is to destroy freedom, and the South is a great believer in freedom of choice.

"Through basic training and necessity, we became strong believers in economical government and, more important, government which serves, not masters, the people. As a result, we have today two priceless assets that represent the South's major attractions for new and increased industrial development: our people and their government. With these assets, the progress of the South moves along relatively faster than that of any other section. . . .

"I am encouraged to conclude we will develop even faster because industrialists who will not submit to compulsory unionism and radical political domination recognize that the one great haven of individual freedom still remaining in the United States is in the South."

Daniel's appraisal of Southern virtues was not merely an exercise in regional pride, it was an essential ingredient of his sales pitch to non-Southerners contemplating construction of new plants. And in typical Daniel fashion, the message was delivered straight from the shoulder. In one particular instance, about a year prior to his "home folks" talk at Elberton, Daniel expounded his thesis to a Yankee audience, the Hudson Valley Chapter of the Society for the Advancement of Management, entitling his remarks, "Why Your Competition is Moving South."

He opened his presentation with a brief and rather low-keyed enumeration of such pro-Southern factors as climate, water, transportation facilities, ports, abundance of raw materials, plentiful electric power and steadily growing markets. Then, just as he was to do later at Elberton, he launched into an exposition of those intangibles to which he attributed the South's true appeal to business and industry:

> "The South has far more to contribute to the political, social, cultural, spiritual, and — yes — the economic welfare of the nation than many non-Southerners realize or are willing to accept. The South has been aptly called the last citadel of true and enlightened conservatism in the United States. Statesmen and journalists, alarmed by the national trends, have said that this conservatism is the best hope of the nation to avoid the debilitation of socialism and the soul-searing black pit of the welfare state.
>
> "Non-Southerners are beginning to believe us when we say that the transcending issue in America today is the preservation of constitutional government among a people who have never hesitated to fight for their right of self-government and who have a genius for economic and social self-determination."

At that juncture, Daniel injected a prophetic note — this taking place in 1958 — that was fulfilled by racial developments of the 1960's and 1970's:

> "I venture the prediction that the South will solve its most touchy sociological problem long before most of the large metropolitan centers will do so."

Then, with more specific reference to the central theme of his talk, Daniel made these points by way of explanation — at least in part — of "Why Your Competition Is Moving South."

> "The South continues to respect the integrity of the individual, the sovereignty of the states. It refuses to be regimented, and it abides by the principles of the pure Americanism which were so soundly laid down for us by the founding fathers. More than 98 percent of the industrial workers in South Carolina are native-born, most of them with roots reaching back for generations. They came mostly from the farms, where their fathers and grandfathers taught them that a man had to

go all the way — to plow the soil, plant the seeds and harvest the crops . . . to make a living.

"From personal experience, developed through helping locate in the South more than 100 major industries and through the construction and equipment installation periods of same, I know full well of the eagerness of our people for industrial jobs and their determination to help new plants succeed through complete cooperation and good workmanship.

"We do not believe, however, in forgiving corporations their proper share of taxes. If there are those who hope to escape fair taxes, they had better not consider South Carolina — nor other Southern states."

Predictably, Daniel dwelt at some length on the existence of right-to-work laws in South Carolina and throughout the South, and he summed up his presentation with these words:

"I say that the strongest single answer to the South's progress is the fact that we have strong, deep-rooted American individuals who make up our population. . . . The South, my state in particular, welcomes new industry from any part of the country, so long as it is solvent, solid and responsible.

"We offer the hearty hand of friendship, assistance and the opportunity to operate industries under pleasant and profitable conditions. . . .

"Finally, I emphasize that people — people with respect for the true values of life — are responsible for the progress and productivity of the New South."

CHAPTER 21

The Timmerman Era

Consistent with the support given to George Bell Timmerman, Jr., during his 1954 campaign for governor after serving two terms as lieutenant governor, Daniel welcomed the new administration with the same sort of helpful gestures that he had extended to Timmerman's predecessors, Governors Strom Thurmond and James F. Byrnes. One notable event in this category was a New York dinner arranged with active Daniel backing by his textile compatriot, Roger Milliken. There, the new governor met with a group of industrial and financial leaders carefully selected by Milliken and Daniel as prospects for investment — or further investment — in South Carolina.

By way of preparation for the trip, Daniel went out of his way to offer a four-page letter of suggestions to be included by Timmerman in the informative presentation being compiled for him by Sloan W. Gable, acting director of the State Development Board.

It was this sort of imaginative and influential cooperation that made Daniel so valuable to a succession of South Carolina governors as they worked for the continuing economic development of the Palmetto State. But such rapport sometimes could turn sour, as it did in the closing years of the Timmerman administration.

Of the several factors that seem to have contributed to the rift, one probable cause was Timmerman's refusal to make a "show of force" during the course of a labor dispute at Rock Hill. In the summer of 1956, Daniel and several textile leaders sought to have the governor dispatch a considerable police force to suppress the demonstrations of striking textile workers; there was even some mention of calling out the National Guard. Such a step seemed unnecessary to Timmerman, as he subsequently reported to the legislature.

Timmerman associated that episode with subsequent criticism of South Carolina government, censure embodying allegations of "foot-dragging" and "unsound and punitive tax policies." It was

166

about this time too that Daniel's periodic statements and speeches became increasingly critical of what he considered to be shortcomings or inertia on the state's part.

Daniel's acceptance speech upon receiving a management award in Greenville in late September 1957 provides a case in point. In calling upon South Carolinians to work together to correct what he perceived as disadvantages, he said, "Some of my friends wonder why I keep sticking my neck out to emphasize unpleasant facts when it would be so easy to go along with the tide.

"There is but one answer — my concern for the future of this community, state and nation. To me they are worth fighting for, and I hope you will realize with me that this is the responsible obligation of all our people. . . . I am confident we will overcome our temporary handicaps by the complete fullfilment of our obligations as citizens of South Carolina."

Such statements from Daniel and perhaps others who voiced similar sentiments during this period brought no direct rebuttal from Timmerman at the time, but there is no escaping the fact that they were the target of this segment of the governor's fourth annual message to the General Assembly, delivered on January 15, 1958:

"For more than a year, our state has been accused of 'dragging its feet.' Even its good attitude toward sound industry has been questioned; and you have been branded with 'unsound and punitive tax policies.' " He then presented a chapter-and-verse accounting of South Carolina's industrial development during the first three years of his administration, drawing a favorable comparison with accomplishments during prior administrations.

Later in 1958, however, Timmerman sought Daniel's cooperation on a special project aimed at enhancing the state's industrial development. Daniel was requested to serve as a member of a Governor's Industrial Development Committee, a major function of which was to endorse a special rotogravure section in *The New York Times* stressing the economic opportunities afforded by South Carolina to firms locating in the state.

Daniel declined to serve, however, and pointed out in a letter to the governor that his personal experience and his close observation of similar promotional projects in other states gave him no assurance that such an advertising program could be justified. "It is my best judgment," he concluded, "that we would profit to a much greater extent if we would utilize the efforts and costs involved to employ one or more experienced salesmen to start pounding the sidewalks and ringing doorbells in behalf of South Carolina."

Timmerman had some misgivings then as to the true value of the program, and he expressed in a letter to the sponsoring Development Board that Daniel's opinion should not be treated lightly in view of his extensive experience in industrial advertising. But Director Robert M. Cooper and others on the board would not be swayed, and the projected 32-page special supplement was compiled and published as a section of *The New York Times'* Sunday edition on February 15, 1959.

CHAPTER 22

Seaports — Airports

Another dimension was added in 1956 to Daniel's already multi-faceted involvement with South Carolina's economic growth. It was in that year that he was named to a committee charged with stimulating the flow of trade through the state's ports at Charleston, Georgetown and Beaufort-Port Royal. Along with a number of like-minded businessmen, Daniel was distressed that South Carolina was falling so far short of its potential for export-import commerce. True, there existed a State Ports Authority, which was striving to improve the situation; but it was hampered by aging and inadequate facilities at all three ports.

The Authority itself had been created by the General Assembly in 1942 with the passage of legislation introduced the year before by Senator Cotesworth P. Means of Charleston. That hard-driving individual subsequently became vice chairman and next chairman of the Ports Authority and set out to restore Charleston and its sister ports to the eminence they enjoyed with the indigo, and rice and cotton commerce of colonial and postcolonial days. Following a long decline after the Civil War, the ports had experienced a degree of increased shipping activity during and after World War I, only to reach another low ebb prior to World War II.

During the war, the ports — especially the Army's port terminal facilities at North Charleston — were geared to the war effort and operated under U. S. control. Thereafter, negotiations were begun with the view toward restoring the facilities for commercial use.

One major step in that direction came in February of 1947, when President Truman released most of the North Charleston terminals to the City of Charleston, the original owner of the installations when they were taken over by the Army. The city promptly turned the properties over to the State Ports Authority without charge. Furthermore, and in short order, the city gave to the Ports Authority the downtown waterfront facilities, even going to the

169

extent of assuming an outstanding bonded indebtedness of $1,750,000, which occurred in 1922 when Charleston floated a bond issue to develop port terminals in the Columbus Street vicinity.

Thus, the year 1947 marked a turning point for the ports of South Carolina; but it was only a starting point. Not until a decade later, as the Ports Authority itself acknowledges, could the ports of Charleston, Georgetown and Beaufort-Port Royal be said to have entered "modern history."

It was at this juncture that Charlie Daniel began his brief but noteworthy contribution to port development in a quasi-official capacity. When the General Assembly created the State Ports Planning Committee by Joint Resolution 929 of 1956, the dual factors of Daniel's avowed interest in trade expansion and his reputation in business and governmental circles made him a logical choice for committee membership. That choice was exercised by Governor George Bell Timmerman, Jr., who named Daniel chairman of the three-man committee.

Equal discernment was shown in the designation of the other two members of the Planning Committee. Lieutenant Governor Ernest F. Hollings appointed E. Hugh Agnew of Starr, then president of the South Carolina Farm Bureau Federation. Speaker of the House Solomon Blatt named the third member, John K. Cauthen of Columbia, executive vice president of the South Carolina Textile Manufacturers' Association. Thus was formed a committee of individuals with broad knowledge and productive experience in three economic areas vital to the continued growth of the state — the construction industry, agriculture and textiles.

Reaction to the appointments was favorable throughout the state. This was especially true in Charleston, where the April 4 edition of *The Evening Post* editorialized, "Governor Timmerman did a good day's work for South Carolina when he appointed Charles E. Daniel chairman."

The committee was vested with the authority to retain consultants as necessary and to recommend "such needs, ways and means of raising revenue" to finance port maintenance and construction. Its role was extended a year later to advise on building design and construction.

Cresap, McCormick and Paget, a national consulting firm, was engaged to evaluate the ports; and out of that study came specific recommendations bolstering the major proposal the committee made to the General Assembly in 1956: the initiation of a $21 million expansion and improvement program to be financed by bonds that would be retired through state port revenues and legislative appropriations. The program was approved without dissenting vote.

Even so, the consensus that marked the committee's financial proposals did not carry over into administration. The group had urged that the Ports Authority's policymaking and administrative functions be separated; but the Authority moved in the opposite direction by giving its chairman full managerial responsibility for the operation of the state dock system through its traffic operations, accounting and engineering departments.

That development, apparently more than any other factor, led to the resignation of the entire Planning Committee in 1957. Despite those differences, however, there developed throughout the state a greater understanding that interior as well as coastal interests were served by commerce through the ports.

Within a short while after ending his personal participation in the development of South Carolina seaports (reference here being to the resignation of the State Ports Planning Committee), Daniel became just as actively involved in the promotion of another aspect of trade and transportation — this time in the realm of air travel.

In 1957, Daniel initiated discussions with community leaders in Greenville and Spartanburg, looking to the possibility of establishing a major airport in the Piedmont area of the state. From the very beginning, he had the enthusiastic cooperation of Roger Milliken, the Spartanburg textile magnate who habitually relied upon Daniel to build almost all of his firm's projects. Both men were convinced that the region was missing opportunities for industrial development due to the lack of a modern and adequate airport of sufficient size and facilities to generate as well as sustain air travel.

Accordingly, the two of them formed unofficial ad hoc committees of prominent citizens of Greenville and Spartanburg to consider the problem and to recommend a solution. Included in the group were such persons as Alester G. Furman, Jr., of Greenville and Walter J. Brown and Walter Montgomery of Spartanburg — all of whom helped to stimulate their local committees and communities into a joint effort. Some interest was shown then and later in Anderson and elsewhere; but the project soon developed essentially into a Greenville-Spartanburg endeavor. Mayors J. Kenneth Cass of Greenville and Neville Holcombe of Spartanburg added their endorsements and encouragement, agreeing with the Daniel-Milliken committees that they should avoid excessive publicity until the project was closer to fruition.

As the idea gained acceptance, Daniel and Milliken initiated and largely financed a series of studies by experts in the field of airport design and construction. Meanwhile, a very promising site had been located between Greer and Pelham, lying astride the county line and about equidistant from the cities of Greenville and Spartanburg. The choice of that site makes an interesting story in itself, as recalled by Alex C. Crouch, the Greenville engineer whose firm had done considerable work for both Daniel and Milliken in the industrial field. In this particular instance, however, Crouch had not been briefed on the pending proposition, as is clearly reflected by his account of the site selection process:

"I got a call from Mr. Daniel one morning just before lunch, and he said: 'Be out front with some maps and information on Greenville and Spartanburg counties; Roger and I are going to pick you up. We're going to look at something.'

"I gathered up all my quadrangle sheets and topographic maps and everything I imagined I would need. The Daniel limousine arrived with Mr. Milliken and Mr. Daniel in the front seat. I got in the back, all covered with those maps.

"Roger turned around and said, 'Alex, where can we put a new airport to serve Greenville and Spartanburg?'

"I gulped and said, 'What's that again?'

"He said, 'Look at the maps and tell us where we can put a new airport.'

"Well, you don't select an airport site just like that; but while they were riding up toward the county line, I was frantically looking at quad sheets. The route for Interstate 85 had just been put on the quad sheets, and construction was not really underway. You couldn't get to the site by I-85, of course; but I found a place that looked very promising.

"It really turned out to be the only place you could have an airport site on the county line, half of it in Spartanburg and reasonably close to utilities. It was hard by the Interstate, and it was a nice, lovely view for a piece of high terrain. It had a spine running in a northeast-southwest direction, which is the right direction for a runway.

"So, amidst a flurry of maps, I guided them to this place and we got out and looked around. That's exactly the site that the airport went. As it turned out, it took about 45 minutes to select the site and about two months to confirm it."

The studies and discussions continued into 1958; and late that year a "master plan" was unveiled, based on reports by Crouch's firm and Skidmore, Owings and Merrill, a New York airport architectural company. With their facts in hand, Daniel and Milliken met with community leaders, ad hoc committee members and state legislators of both counties. The proposed area airport plans were presented on November 11 and were greeted by headlines in Greenville and Spartanburg newspapers.

A joint committee representing both counties was selected by the legislative delegations; and as a result of their deliberations, legislation was passed in the ensuing session of the General Assembly. Act No. 90, which became law on March 25, 1959, created a joint Greenville-Spartanburg Airport District as a political unit comprising the two counties. The governing body included three members from each county: Milliken, L. A. Odom and S. J. Workman representing Spartanburg; and William T. Adams, Hugh Aiken and John Ratteree serving Greenville. Both Adams and Milliken were still on the commission 20 years later; and the airport, which opened October 15, 1962, greatly exceeds theirs and Daniel's earlier expectations.

In contrast with many other public facilities that he helped initiate, Daniel was not appointed to the commission; nor was his company involved in the construction of the airport. However, recognition of his role in bringing the airport into being was ensured by the subsequent installation of a handsome 140-foot diameter pool with a 50-foot fountain. Made possible through gifts from "Deering Milliken and other friends" in February 1970 ceremonies, the pool was dedicated with these remarks by Roger Milliken, the one individual who better than anyone else had reason to know the vital part Daniel played in making the airport a reality:

"This seems to be a time when we all hear a lot from and about those who would seem to want to tear down institutions and traditions that have been so laboriously created over the years. So it is with a special enthusiasm and sense of gratitude that we will turn on this fountain in honor of a man who was a builder and not a 'tearer downer.'

"The many, many plants scattered all over South Carolina and elsewhere in the South are the true lasting monuments to Charles Ezra Daniel and the big vision he had for this area and its people. Therefore it is fitting, I think, that this special memorial to him be created by his friends and associates at this gateway port to the great Piedmont area — an area for which he did so much that was creative and which was also full of beauty as is this airport of which he was a founder."

Had Daniel himself been present, it is probable that he would have been gratified not only by the plaque unveiled in his honor by

Senator Strom Thurmond but by the concurrent ceremonies that officially inaugurated the airport as an inland customs port operated by the South Carolina State Ports Authority. Here, in what had been his own immediate "stomping grounds", was an extension and final culmination of the efforts he had expended almost a quarter-century earlier to expand South Carolina's export-import trade.

CHAPTER 23

The Hollings Era

The 1958 election, which elevated Lieutenant Governor Ernest F. (Fritz) Hollings to the governor's office, ushered in another period of close cooperation between the state's chief executive and the state's top industrial developer. The affinity was natural, considering the fact that Charlie Daniel had helped provide financial backing as well as personal influence for Hollings' election. One unusual manifestation of Daniel's support took the form of a pair of new hats for the new governor — a Panama and a Homburg — purchased from a fancy New York hat shop at the expense of one of Daniel's Greenville friends "who used poor judgment in connection with the recent election."

In one sense, the joint industrial efforts that found Hollings and Daniel working in double harness represented a continuation of the teamwork that had begun between the two while Hollings was lieutenant governor. But even as Hollings moved into a post of increased influence and eminence, Daniel did not hesitate to make recommendations as well as to offer assistance.

Before Hollings took office, Daniel wrote him a lengthy letter in which he blamed "some of the State House Gang" for failure of the Planning Board to be given "adequate quarters, properly equipped and furnished in an attractive manner." He expressed the belief that the new governor would not perpetuate "the lack of aggressiveness, overall planning and progress that exists in South Carolina today." Hollings had been in office less than a month before be received another letter from Daniel. This time the industrialist proposed alternatives to Hollings' budget-balancing proposals. Daniel opposed a proposed tax on electric power and an increase in personal income tax. Instead, he suggested a one-cent soft drink tax and an income tax witholding system.

One anathema to Daniel was the "kickback" system, long prevalent in South Carolina, whereby certain state-collected revenues were returned to counties or municipalities according to predeter-

175

mined formulas — often based on population. As a matter of principle, he was steadfastly opposed to kickbacks. Here is a characteristic attack on the practice, incorporated in a May 1959 letter to Hollings:

> "We need millions of dollars for the proper development of state hospitals, the further development of our ports and multitudinous other essential state functions. Every kickback that takes away from the state the opportunity to provide these necessary essentials will only add to our difficulty in developing industry and in getting South Carolina out of the rut as the third lowest income state in the union.
>
> "Counties and municipalities that cannot pay their own way are not entitled to be subdivisions. They should be merged into stronger units and efforts should be put forth to further merge city and county governments. If the legislature of South Carolina had the necessary courage to vote funds for a resurvey and reevaluation of all property in South Carolina, a substantial amount of the kickbacks could remain in the State Treasury, and we would be in much better position to present a picture of honesty and fairness to management of industry seeking new locations. . . ."

In the meanwhile, as he had done for previous governors, Daniel helped arrange conferences in New York, Wilmington and elsewhere at which Hollings could discuss the state's industrial potential with top executives in the manufacturing field. Somewhat interestingly, Daniel by now had concluded that brief personal visitations to selected industrial leaders would prove more advantageous to the governor's prospects than would the usual luncheons or dinners to which numerous individuals were invited. Also interesting was Daniel's frequent inclusion of the following paragraph or its equivalent in the numerous letters of invitation and introduction he dispatched to longtime friends, clients and business associates in anticipation of a Hollings visit:

> "Here in South Carolina we have a new governor, the Honorable Ernest F. (Fritz) Hollings, 37 years old. He is a strong advocate of economy in government, maintenance of our Right to Work Law and a good friend of business.
>
> "We believe he is going to develop into a real statesman and we expect to send him to the United States Senate four years from now in order to broaden his opportunities and strengthen the weak spot we have there."

The close working relationship that developed between Hollings and Daniel in 1959 continued unabated into 1960. If anything, there was even greater interplay of effort as Daniel sought constantly to have the governor participate in conferences, luncheons, business meetings and social events attended by industrial executives who had plants or who might be persuaded to locate plants in South Carolina. There was a continuing flow of correspondence and personal calls between the two, seemingly with results that were gratifying to both and helpful to South Carolina.

At the same time, however, there also were frank exchanges of views in which Daniel severely criticized several of the state's governmental practices, chiefly in the field of taxation, to which Hollings responded with citations of facts and figures dealing with the particular practices under attack.

A characteristic Daniel epistle to the governor — this one dated April 14, 1960 — voiced a comprehensive lament that included these specifics:

"I think all of us interested in the future development of South Carolina hope that enough statesmanship would be generated in the legislature this year, under the more favorable conditions existing, to cut back the heavy increases in personal taxes. In lieu of that, there has actually been another increase because of the change in exemptions. It may be good county politics to handle the situation this way, but it is decidedly detrimental to the best interest of our state.

"Your best friends resent the failure of the legislature to recognize this situation, and they are doubly critical now because the legislature and you, as governor, have recommended a further kickback of approximately $3.5 million to the counties, making a total of approximately $20 million, primarily to take care of petty county politicians.

"There are hundreds of worthy things that we desperately need to do for the future good of our state but I will only emphasize a few, either of which could have been accomplished with the additional kickbacks."

To make his point, Daniel mentioned what he perceived to be critical items and offered suggestions: improving state hospitals; building a new penitentiary on farmlands owned by the state; developing and equipping trade schools; providing adequate salaries for schoolteachers and college faculties; completing a property survey of all land and buildings and reevaluating commercial buildings and industrial plants; requiring certification by architects and constructors of the full value of every new project; and requiring that every sale of property be indicated at the transfer price.

Having identified those areas needing attention, Daniel's letter to the governor continued: "Apparently, nothing is being done about any of these important things so necessary to our future. . . . I understand a tax manual may be approved and will probably be as valuable as a Sears Roebuck catalogue and, certainly, will not be used as often."

Criticizing the lack of industrial development efforts by state officials and county delegations, Daniel wrote, "I, along with many thousands of others, am disgusted with the entire situation and the ineffective approach of our legislature".

The intensity as well as the content of such letters and personal conversations reflected one aspect of the Daniel personality that often brought despair, sometimes desperation, to his many acquaintances in government. By word and deed, Daniel revealed his conviction that politicians who accepted his assistance, whether in funds or influence, should likewise accept his advice.

That attitude of course, precipitated some drastic splits between Daniel and political figures with whom he was more often than not in general agreement. One such parting of the ways came in 1960, when the presidential race broke up what generally had seemed to be a Daniel-Hollings honeymoon in their joint efforts to further industrialize and develop South Carolina.

This particular rift grew out of Hollings' support of the Kennedy-Johnson Democratic ticket in opposition to the Nixon-Lodge slate put up by the Republicans. Here again, the personalities involved took precedence over partisan identification. Daniel, who had developed a friendship with Texas Senator Lyndon B. Johnson back in 1954 when Daniel served as an interim U. S. senator from South Carolina, was hopeful that the Texan would gain his party's nomination at the national convention to be held in Los Angeles in July of 1960. This hope was all the more intense because the alternative seemed to be the nomination of Massachusetts Senator John F. Kennedy.

As the convention got under way, Daniel was highly gratified at the efforts of the South Carolina delegation, led by Hollings, on behalf of Johnson. Indeed, as press reports portrayed the South Carolinians' firm and undiluted backing for Johnson, Daniel dispatched this glowing telegram of approbation to Hollings as head of the Palmetto State delegation:

"You and your associates acquitted yourselves with courage, dignity, and honor at all times during the convention and the people of our state are extremely pleased with the action of their delegation. No white people and few colored people can stomach the approved platform. Hurry home and we will start all over again.

"With warm personal regards.
Charlie Daniel"

The "starting over," however, was not at all to Daniel's liking. Hollings, as the Democratic governor of South Carolina and as chairman of the state's delegation to the national Democratic convention, obviously felt himself bound to support the decisions reached by the party at the Los Angeles convention. And this, of course, meant that he would back the presidential candidacy of Kennedy — an individual whose political position and platform policies were totally out of line with Daniel's thinking.

So strong were Daniel's convictions that he promptly set about wielding all the influence he could muster on behalf of the Republican ticket headed by Richard M. Nixon, whom he had come to know during the latter's service as vice president during Dwight Eisenhower's two terms in the White House. The upshot of this situation was virtually a complete rupture of relations between Daniel and Hollings, precipitated by the polarity of their opposing positions with respect to the presidential contest. And it was at this juncture that Daniel began a series of speaking engagements, supplemented from time to time with newspaper advertisements, warning South Carolinians and Southerners against the adverse impact upon regional development to be expected from implementation of what seemed to Daniel the ultraliberal platform adopted by the Democratic party.

Despite the political differences that ultimately alienated Daniel and Hollings, the two men nevertheless contributed greatly to the state's industrial growth. One factor in this regard was the advent of Walter W. Harper on the scene as replacement for R. M. (Bob) Cooper, then stepping down as Development Board director after two separate stints in that capacity.

As had some of his predecessors in office, Harper found that working with Charlie Daniel could be a ticklish business on occasion, somewhat akin to handling a two-edged sword. For example, he had to contend with the impression generated over a period of years that Daniel, as Harper put it, "had the State Development Board in his hip pocket." Nevertheless, Daniel gradually seemed to realize the board's position and its problems, thereafter becoming much more cooperative and constructive in his relationships with the state agency.

Speaking of changed attitudes, Harper himself revised his own assessment of Daniel during his seven-year tenure as Development Board director. Here's how he describes the transition, which was one of degree more than depth:

> "I felt when I arrived in South Carolina during the summer of 1959 that Mr. Daniel had been one of the most important forces in the industrial development of the state and that he had gained a considerable national reputation in the development field. My tour of duty with the state confirmed and expanded these impressions.
>
> "By the time I left the board early in 1967, I had decided that his most important contribution to the state may not have been the many industrial plants he had helped locate in South Carolina, even though they were very important. More beneficial, I believe, was the great influence he had had on good government, constructive industrial legislation, general acceptance of the free enterprise system, positive race relations and many other important factors affecting economic development and the overall welfare of the state."

Contrary to Harper's opinion that the contractor encouraged local development programs to remain relatively weak, preferring to utilize their services, sites and facilities for new industries, Daniel did indeed promote local boards. In only one instance, he told the Abbeville County Development Board in August of 1956:

> "Our State Development Board has rendered exceptional service, and we are finding that the various county boards are in turn rendering meritorious service and splendid cooperation to the State Board. . . . A strong county board can also render tremendous service in protecting existing industries, which is, of course, our first obligation."

A year later he gave somewhat similar advice to Charlestonians, deploring their failure to make the industrial progress achieved by other parts of the state. He urged the Charleston Development Board to begin working closely with the State Development Board.

Any discussion of Daniel's relationships with local development agencies would be incomplete without reference to continuing and effective efforts made by the Greenwood Chamber of Commerce through its Industrial Development Committee to anticipate and meet the requirements of potential builders. The effectiveness of such teamwork paid off more than once for Greenwood and for Daniel as major industries chose that area for the location and/or expansion of their plants.

Greenwood's gratitude for Daniel's involvement was demonstrated in April of 1963 when the Chamber of Commerce sponsored a well-attended "Appreciation Day" for Daniel's contributions to the region's growth. Plaudits were heaped upon the industrialist by speakers of local and statewide stature, prompting a suitable and grateful response on his part.

It was on that occasion, by the way, that Daniel made one of his most specific recommendations for reducing, through merger, the number of counties in the state. This was one of his constant themes, but at Greenwood he proposed that South Carolina's 46 counties be reduced to 17 or 18:

> "We can't afford not to consolidate. . . . This is inevitable among all states. Therefore, the first state to begin consolidating will be that far ahead of the others."

His reiteration of that theme at Greenwood was no more productive of results than similar expressions he had made elsewhere, but at least he had the knowledge that he was speaking to South Carolinians who valued his services and observations. But even as he spoke, he tacitly acknowledged the political difficulties confronting consolidation and added wryly: "I'm sure you all can see I'm not running for anything."

CHAPTER 24

Black and White

When Charlie Daniel was convinced in his own mind that a particular course of action was correct, he let his convictions be known without biting his tongue or tailoring his remarks to an audience's probable reaction. An outstanding example of this propensity toward plain talk occurred on July 1, 1961, as he delivered the principal address at the Hampton Watermelon Festival.

The topic of his speech was "South Carolina's Economic Challenge," and in it he called for forceful and enlightened leadership on both the political and economic fronts, spelling out what he considered to be the state's most pressing needs. But he did not content himself with generalities; rather, he got down to specifics, some of which would have deterred an ordinary individual.

Sensitivity over the race issue, then a hot topic of sociological and educational controversy in South Carolina, would have persuaded most speakers to avoid the topic, especially at a festive occasion in a predominantly black area of the state. But despite the attending circumstances — or perhaps because of them — Daniel spoke his mind, capturing attention locally and regionally.

Daniel sought to convince his listeners that any progress of substance would necessarily involve blacks as well as whites. There was his usual plea for good government and against compulsory unionism of the work force, but the real news in his speech was embodied in his challenge to South Carolinians to "foresake some of our ways." Citing the general proposition that "we have large numbers of white and Negro citizens whose productivity and earnings must be substantially and rapidly increased," he bolstered that contention with this line of reasoning:

"The desegregation issue cannot continue to be hidden behind the door. This situation cannot satisfactorily be settled at the lunch counter and bus station levels. We must handle this

182

ourselves, more realistically than heretofore; or it will be forced upon us in the harshest way. Either we act on our own terms, or we forfeit the right to act.

"Key employees of new plants considering South Carolina are disturbed about school conditions for their children. Most major industries have contract relations with the federal government, subject to antidiscrimination laws; so management is concerned about conditions which could develop within their plants. They want the good will of the communities. They want to accept and respect reasonable local customs and traditions; yet they must obey the law.

"The Negro population represents a large working force in South Carolina, relatively untrained. It is an important potential to industry. We have a definite obligation to increase the productivity of our Negro citizens, to provide them with good jobs at good wages, and to continue to assure them of fair treatment. By raising their educational and economic status, we would raise the whole economy of the state.

"With a tremendous feeling of pride and confidence, I say that we can continue to manage our own affairs in South Carolina far more effectively and satisfactorily than can the confused, impractical powers in command of the federal government in Washington.

"However, with all the sincere devotion I have for South Carolina, I emphasize that we cannot successfully manage our own affairs under the same pattern of inaction we have followed in the past."

As subsequent events were to prove, Daniel did not approach the Watermelon Festival with the intent of expressing a few platitudes and generalities. As early as May 1, in responding to the invitation extended by First District Congressman L. Mendel Rivers, he had this to say:

"You are fully aware of the fact that I am no speaker. In addition, it is customary on occasions like this to make a glowing chamber of commerce speech and I would be absolutely no good in that direction.

"If you and the committee would like to have me attempt a speech enumerating the outstanding needs of South Carolina and indicating a concrete program for development of same, I will be very glad to try."

He was assured by Rivers that he could speak on "any subject you like"; and the congressman appended this specific reaction to the Daniel proposal, "The lower state is quite interested in development since very little has come to our part of the world."

Reaction to the Hampton speech undoubtedly exceeded Daniel's fondest expectations. News coverage of the event, coupled with Daniel's having provided a number of newspapers with an advance account of the gist of his proposed remarks, aroused continuing interest not only in the Lowcountry but throughout the state and the South, with an appreciable carry-over into the rest of the nation as the Hampton message spread. In many instances, newspapers, trade publications and other print media printed excerpts from the address, some, as did the *America's Textile Reporter*, going to the extent of republishing the entire speech. Although tempered by some doubt and criticism from a few quarters at the outset, editorial comment was generally favorable both with respect to the general tenor of his economic challenge and his specific advice to upgrade the industrial and educational opportunities of Negroes. And as time and circumstance brought added contemplation, reaction to the speech became all the more favorable.

On the local scene, Tom O'Connor, editor-publisher of both the *Hampton County Guardian* and the *Allendale County Citizen*, wrote: "He advanced sound suggestions . . . (and) noted the foolishness of having a citizenry, half at work and the other half unproductive, because jobs, training for jobs, are not available. . . . Mr. Daniel's talk deserves wider hearing. . . . If it takes a political race for that, more power to Mr. Daniel."

The Charleston News and Courier praised Daniel for having spoken "with the voice of a statesman . . . (He) has helped enlighten the people. . . . We hope that his statesmanlike comments will be heard again in the months ahead." The same line of reasoning characterized the editorial reaction of *The Augusta Chronicle:* "This is the time for those in office to think of the next generation rather than the next election. . . . We are glad Mr. Daniel said as much in South Carolina. We wish someone in high places would say it in Georgia, too." *The Columbia Record* called the address "among the most important delivered in the state in the past ten years." *The Record* also cited figures reflecting the state's poor showing in school retention of blacks.

The Greenville News editorialized, "It is not a matter of one man's taking another man's job, or it should not be. It is a matter of creating more jobs for both whites and Negroes and training the people to fill the jobs. . . . In that direction lies the hope for the future of the South." *The Greenville Piedmont* tended toward the same position, but with a note of pessimism: "It takes a lot of time for social and economic patterns to change, and South Carolina has never been much of an example of a state where patterns are changed quickly. . . . Mr. Daniel has dared to point out a route which might well be followed if the state is to make the advances of which it is capable."

Such editorial response to the Hampton address did not fade away with the passage of time, as might be expected under most circumstances. In this instance, the content of the message coupled with the stature of the person who delivered it provoked continuing appraisals for years to come. Meanwhile, another form of immediate reaction was manifested in the congratulatory and appreciative letters that flowed in to Daniel. They came for the most part from persons who subscribed to the point of view he enunciated at Hampton and who were delighted to have it so forcefully expressed by a man of his stature.

The letters were written by a cross-section of the state's citizenry, industrial, business, religious and educational leaders; many came from ordinary people who totally subscribed to Daniel's opinions and philosophy. They expressed the hope that something would be done to improve the economic and educational standards of all of the state's people because "South Carolina has no choice in the matters you discussed and advocated."

Ranking politicians from both major parties also had something to say about the "Watermelon Speech." J. Drake Edens, Jr., an active Republican from Columbia, wrote: "There is tremendous support for your thinking . . . many of us hope, and almost pray, that you might even consider making this race on the Republican ticket in '62. Whether that be possible or not, your remarks will always fall on attentive ears in South Carolina."

And from longtime state senator and former South Carolina governor, Richard M. Jefferies of Walterboro, this counsel came to Daniel, "If you would just return to the Party of your fathers, you could be of great help in restoring it to leadership in the conservative cause."

Before the year was out, Daniel was repeating the same message on December 11, 1961, to the Executive Club of Rock Hill. In October of the following year, addressing a select group of some 300 business leaders from throughout the state, assembled in Columbia at a luncheon honoring soon-to-be Governor Donald S. Russell, Daniel sounded the same theme but in a more optimistic context: "We are finding solutions to the problems among our Negro citizens.

. . . Our Negro population is becoming an increasingly necessary productive force in the state's economy. This is as it should be."

Meanwhile, the composition of the Daniel work force continued to validate the biracial hiring policies repeatedly enunciated by Daniel. At dedication ceremonies for the impressive Magnolia Finishing Plant, a Deering Milliken facility located at Blacksburg, Daniel took a crack at Northern critics of Southern customs and gave some figures to show that the actual facts presented a different story:

> "Only free American labor on an open-shop basis, regulating their own right-to-work laws, could have accomplished this remarkable project [put on the line in 134 working days]. The politicians in Washington never give anyone in the South credit, but there is no discrimination among our construction employees." He pointed out that 26 percent of Daniel's total work force was black.

Reminders such as that continued to attract public notice long after the initial reaction to Daniel's Hampton speech had subsided. Thus was attention periodically focused on Daniel's own industrial operations in what, perhaps unintentionally, developed into a comparison of promise and performance with respect to the advancement of the Negro's economic opportunities.

One such evaluation took the form of a lead editorial in the Sunday, September 15, 1963, edition of *The State*, South Carolina's largest newspaper:

> "Charlie Daniel is no 'do-gooder'," obsessed with the cause of integration. Nor is he a politician catering to minority bloc votes. He is a builder by inclination and occupation. If there be any 'social consciousness' in his scheme of operations, it is the consciousness that his people need good jobs at good pay — and are willing to produce in such jobs."
>
> "Fortunately for Daniel, and for his thousands of employees, he is not hog-tied by restrictive labor union practices, including those of racial discrimination. Skilled workers, white or colored, get skilled jobs with Daniel. . . . No one is telling Charlie Daniel he must hire these people."

Although Daniel was not in the least obsessed by the race question, he was deeply concerned lest its difficulties be aggravated either by well-intentioned "do-gooders" or by power-hungry politicians and labor leaders. Sometimes his remarks caused eyebrows to lift and brows to furrow, as must have been the case at the 1961 Hampton Watermelon Festival. But he sounded that same message elsewhere, even in such unlikely and lavish surroundings as those of the Waldorf-Astoria Hotel in New York City. There, accepting an award as the 1963 Industrialist of the Year from the Society of Industrial Realtors, he included these comments in response to the presentation made by Richard M. Nixon:

"To review the serious problems of integration, won't you please visit with us in the South. . . . Without equivocation, I report that the responsible people, your kind of people, have taken the upper hand in most places in the racial plight which came upon us. We are rapidly surmounting the hump with confidence and increasing indications of reasonable solutions to our problems.

"The white and colored races have lived, worked and developed our Southern area together for so long. We need each other. Our Negro friends are entitled to and do vote freely in South Carolina on the same basis as white people. They are entitled to full educational opportunities, and in our state we have made tremendous strides toward providing them with these opportunities. . . . We have approximately 7,000 Negro teachers in our schools. Can you name any state in the East, North or West with a better record?

"Our Negro friends are well-deserving of full economic opportunities. They are being employed in our industrial plants as fast as they can qualify. Our economy needs and welcomes them. They are being accepted.

"Construction companies in neither New York City nor any other major cities have anywhere near as many Negro employees as our company. Why? Because the dominating union bosses refuse to take them as members. In the places where they have control, they openly and deliberately deny them these opportunities. The discrimination which they practice is of the rankest sort. Their exploitation of these people is a national disgrace.

"In South Carolina and in the 11 states of the old Confederacy, all with strong state right-to-work laws, the Negro construction workers can find equality of opportunity. This is certainly not true in other areas."

Daniel's forthright championing of the rights of Negroes to adequate training and jobs may have been a factor in his subsequent appointment by President Johnson in 1964 to the National Citizens Committee for Community Relations. The committee scheduled its first meeting for mid-August at the White House, but Daniel's illness was so far advanced by that time that he could not attend. Had he been able to participate in that and subsequent meetings of the committee, the sessions might have been quite lively for Daniel remained until the very end of his life a champion of states' rights.

How he would have reacted to discussions and proposals voiced at the August 1964 meeting of the National Citizens Committee is open to speculation since he died within weeks after that event. But the waves he had set in motion back in 1961 at the Hampton Watermelon Festival were still attracting attention as late as 1966. On June 13 of that year, South Carolina's Third District Congressman, W. J. Bryan Dorn, inserted the following into the *Congressional Record* under the heading, "Senator Charles E. Daniel Looked Ahead":

"Mr. Speaker, many solutions have been offered to the civil rights problems confronting our beloved Southland and the nation in recent years. Some have stood in the schoolhouse door. Others have suggested nullification, interposition and massive resistance. Still others have sought a solution to this problem through street demonstrations and disrespect for law and order.

"The late U. S. Senator, Charles E. Daniel, offered a positive solution to the people of South Carolina and to the people of the South. South Carolina's industrialists, educators and men of good will at the local level largely followed Senator Daniel's advice, creating job opportunity and educational opportunity for all of our people."

Following these introductory remarks in the *Record*, Dorn then inserted excerpts from Daniel's Hampton speech of July 1, 1961, noting that the fifth anniversary of that date was imminent.

And as recently as 1979, the Hampton speech was evoking such memories as these, voiced by South Carolina's Comptroller General Earle E. Morris, Jr. He recalled that such an address "was not the most popular speech to make, but it was the correct and statesmanlike speech to make. Charlie was a man of foresight and vision. He said that we could not ignore the large segment of our population who have been undereducated and underfed, underhoused and underutilized. He was talking about the black people in South Carolina, at that time about 40 percent of the state's population. He said they must be utilized in better-paying opportunities. Charlie never minced words."

The consistency of Daniel's attitude on race relations was reflected once again in 1963 in his role as a life trustee of Clemson College. When the college was faced with the decision of admitting its first black student, Harvey B. Gantt of Charleston, Daniel recorded himself as favoring that precedent-setting step.

Although the issue arose during that period when Daniel was habitually absent from trustee meetings (having tendered his resignation, which was not accepted), he nevertheless stated his position in a formal letter to the board, declaring himself to be "in full favor of the recommendations of the Clemson administration and in favor of admitting Mr. Harvey B. Gantt."

CHAPTER 25

The Labor Front

The nature of his work kept Charlie Daniel constantly in contact with the workers who comprised his construction crews, maintenance forces and other units identified with Daniel Construction Company. Furthermore, the nature of the man himself kept him alert to the best interests not only of his industrial enterprises but those of the individuals who labored with him to make the name Daniel synonymous with sustained growth and fair wages.

As a rugged individual, Daniel was ever on guard against what might seem to him to be unwarranted governmental intervention in economic affairs. However, Daniel found in South Carolina's right-to-work law an almost exact reflection of his personal attitude on labor relations. That law, enacted in 1954 during the administration of Governor James F. Byrnes, wrote into the state's Code of Laws this statement, which almost perfectly portrayed Charlie Daniel's oft-expressed concept of equity in employment:

> "It is hereby declared to be the public policy of this state that the right of persons to work shall not be denied or abridged on account of membership or nonmembership in any labor union or labor organization.
>
> "Any agreement or combination between any employer and any labor organization whereby persons not members of such labor organizations shall be denied the right to work for such employer or whereby such membership is made a condition of employment, or of continuance of employment by such employer, or whereby any such union or organization acquires an employment monopoly in any enterprise, is hereby declared to be against public policy, unlawful and an illegal combination or conspiracy."

Time and again, Daniel embodied that credo in his personal remarks and public pronouncements. His emphasis, or at least that

190

accorded him by the news media, was upon the right of persons to gain work without having to join a union. But Daniel was insistent also that a worker should have the right to join a union if he chose to do so — a statement that was often overshadowed by his warnings against the actual and potential harm wrought by unscrupulous and "power-mad" labor bosses, a number of whom he would identify by name and reputation.

The following excerpts from a Daniel address in June of 1956 to the South Carolina Textile Manufacturers' Association typify the theme that surfaced time and again in his speeches and that was aimed at arousing public concern over what Daniel termed "America's greatest menace . . . compulsory unionism:"

"I believe in the dignity of labor, whether with head or hand. I believe that the world owes no man a living, but that it owes every man an opportunity to make a living.

"I recognize the right of men and women to join a union and am willing to fight with them to maintain that privilege. This right of association has been upheld many times by the Supreme Court of the United States.

"I believe equally in the right not to join, for without this right there is no such thing as a right to join and membership becomes servitude. . . .

"There can be no doubt that compulsory unionism is the biggest issue of all on the labor front. Left-wing radical leaders of the labor unions, supported by unprincipled politicians, are now the greatest enemy of the American way of life. . . .

"Where unions are in power, there is no longer in this country freedom of contract with respect to union membership or with respect to employment. Individuals are relegated to the status of pawns, and an employer is forbidden to contract with his own employees. . . .

"The intent of the existing labor conspiracy and monopoly is plainly aimed for the establishment of a labor government with strong socialistic and communistic influences. The union leaders are plainly seeking supreme political power as well as supreme economic power. . . ."

That sort of warning, accompanied by a challenge for American businessmen and citizens generally to join in opposition to union "bossism," was incorporated in numerous Daniel speeches throughout the decade between his brief stint as a U. S. Senator in 1954 and his death in 1964.

Daniel had a few face-to-face confrontations with organized labor; and when he did there were no holds barred, as, for example, when his firm was targeted for unionization at its Greenville home base in 1961 by representatives of the Plumbing and Pipefitting affiliate of the AFL-CIO. The National Labor Relations Board (NLRB) set an election in mid-November and made an unprecedented ruling that not only was the current mechanical work force of Daniel entitled to vote, but also former employees who had worked for as much as 30 days in the calendar year preceding the election or for 45 days in the two-year period before the election.

Although he could do nothing about the NLRB ruling, Daniel fought vigorously against the union through his personal efforts and public statements. One such statement took the form of a full-page advertisement that appeared in many newspapers of the region in mid-November just prior to the election. The ad, which bore Daniel's signature, carried a banner headline declaring, "The South is threatened again!"; the ad also specifically predicted the industrial and economic consequences of voting for or against the union.

At the same time as the placement of the newspaper ads, on November 13, 1961, Daniel dispatched a four-page letter to each of the company's mechanical employees, in which he plainly stated his open-shop philosophy.

There is no way of knowing just what impact the letter or the newspaper advertisements had upon the voting of eligible Daniel workers, both past and present; but when all the results were in, the union had taken a rather bad beating. In round numbers, subject to minor changes depending upon the state of the counting and challenging process, the anti-union vote was about three to one; some 520 workers voted against union representation, while only 174 favored the union. A number of votes, pro and con, were challenged after the election; but the results remained substantially the same.

Daniel greeted the outcome with a statement that said in part, "The labor board and the power-mad, money-grabbing union bosses now have their answer from our loyal employees. . . . We congratulate our people and again promise our continued efforts on their behalf and that of the South."

Despite the lopsided nature of the vote against the union effort to gain bargaining rights at the Daniel company, the issue was not settled by the 1961 election; however, the National Labor Relations Board did confirm the company's victory after reviewing all ballots cast. Thereafter, union officials lodged a protest with the NLRB, alleging unfair labor practices on Daniel Construction Company's part. They received a sympathetic hearing; and in February of 1964, more than two years after the election, the NLRB set aside the election results and ordered that another vote be held.

The dispute then moved from the NLRB into the courts; and Daniel suffered another adverse ruling in January 1965 when the Fourth Circuit Court of Appeals, in a two-to-one decision, ruled that the company had been in violation of fair labor practices. The dissent in this case, filed by Judge Albert B. Bryan, observed, "We have indeed come to a servile economic state when it is unlawful for an employer to explain to his employees his reasons for opposing a union."

Ultimately, another election was scheduled to be held in 1969; but by the time the vote drew near, the union itself withdrew its petition; and the matter finally died on the vine, at least with respect to that particular effort at organization.

Those experiences, relating to a specific instance of attempted labor organization affecting the Daniel company, reinforced the recurring statements and observations made by Daniel himself on the subject of labor relations and gave further substance to the company philosophy that accorded top priority to the individual worker. It was a major element in developing the concept that Daniel Construction Company was a people-oriented organization where the interests of the individual would not be subordinated to the dictates of any person, clique or organization outside the company. To this day, Daniel executives — and most of all, Buck Mickel — seek not only to perpetuate that attitude but to emphasize it in their dealings with workers, whether employees or prospective employees.

Here Buck Mickel interprets that basic philosophy concerning labor relations and the frame of mind that Charlie Daniel himself built into company thinking:

"He was never anti-union, but 100 percent open shop. That was something he stressed over and over, and we stress it today. Some of the best jobs that Daniel ever had — even today — are union jobs. His philosophy was that no man or woman has to pay somebody for the right to work.

"Every man or woman should be free to choose if they want to belong to a union. His whole basic philosophy in life was wrapped up in that — the right of the individual and the independence of the individual. He believed in that, I believe in that, and we work at it. I think our people believe in it.

"We have many people in Daniel today that have union cards, and they work where they want to. To them, that is a means of making a living. What we try to do on our union projects is to have the union belong to the men, so therefore our job still has got the esprit de corps and the drive.

"If we can get the individual to understand that through his personal pride and his own personal ambition there is no limit as to what he can do in this company, then with that comes his loyalty to the company and to the job on which he is working. We never have any question in our mind whether he belongs to a union or not. That's a decision he reaches."

CHAPTER 26

The Local Scene

Charlie Daniel left many imprints, both tangible and intangible, upon his hometown of Greenville; but looming over all in both the figurative and literal senses is the handsome 25-story office building that dominates the city's skyline. Daniel himself acknowledged the symbolic aspect of the skyscraper, the tallest in South Carolina at the time of its construction, at the groundbreaking ceremonies held on June 29, 1964.

Speaking for himself and for Mrs. Daniel, who was on hand to unveil an artist's rendition of the completed structure, Daniel said:

"For 20 years or more, South Carolina has been good to us. This prestige building is our way of showing our appreciation. It will, we hope, inspire downtown business and become a center of industry.

"This is a momentous occasion for all of us who have been making plans for many months for this day, and I am humbly grateful to all of our friends who are taking part in this event."

Those friends included U. S. Senator Strom Thurmond, who called Daniel one of the greatest South Carolinians and Americans of his time, a man who "has done more to alleviate poverty than any other man in the South or South Carolina"; Governor Donald Russell, who "came to pay personal tribute to a man who has contributed more to the industrial growth of the South than anyone else"; and James F. Byrnes, who cited Daniel's "passion for the development of industry, which has created thousands of jobs at good wages."

In a similar vein, *The Greenville News* tipped its journalistic hat to the projected skyscraper with an editorial entitled "Erecting More Than a Building." It pointed out that "the Daniel Building is expected to do something for downtown Greenville that it long has needed. It will stand as a sparkling example of what can be done to revitalize the central city and we hope it will mark the beginning of a general movement in that direction."

The newspaper's comments turned out to be not only appropriate but prophetic, because less than four years after the Daniel Building groundbreaking on North Main Street, the publishing firm contracted with Daniel Construction Company to construct a handsome new building of its own at the southern end of the central business district.

Those major additions on opposite ends of downtown Greenville were the forerunners of a general redevelopment program that was still progressing in the 1980's, a program passionately championed by Charlie Daniel. He did not live to see the results of his oft-repeated encouragement for Greenville to "do something." But he prodded the city into action as long as he was able to make a speech. On one such occasion he told the Downtown Greenville Association that the city was "unclean and neither attractive nor competitive with comparable progressive cities." He proposed renovating and rebuilding "on a block basis."

Along with those criticisms at various gatherings, Daniel renewed his constant complaint against inequitable tax assessments and repeated his persistent call for consolidating city and county governments. The target was not only Greenville but other cities and communities in the state as well; yet he created additional hometown conversation in a 1961 address to the Greenville Woman's Club in a speech titled "Greenville — Ghost Town or Metropolis?"

He told the wives of the city's business leaders that "the tragedy of Greenville is not just that it is ugly, but that so few people seem to care." He cited numerous examples of why the city had let itself get into such a condition, relating them to reasons for "the dozens of vacant buildings and the progress we are making in becoming a ghost town."

He saw much of what he proposed as being attainable through intelligent planning, coordination and cooperation. As for the cost, he visualized a $60 million capital improvement program "to move the community forward to its deserved status as the ideal city and a great metropolis."

There was support in the community for much of what he proposed, and *The Greenville Piedmont* predicted that "perhaps in time, the prophet will be honored — even in his own town."

Max Heller, a former Greenville mayor who did not serve in that capacity during Daniel's time, was asked why there was limited reaction to Daniel's oft-repeated challenges to the city. "I think basically it would be because much of what he said was true, perhaps all of it," Heller replied. "He put it out on the table where it belonged . . . that's the kind of person he was and that's why he got things done. He had a tremendous amount of common sense. He could relate to everybody, because he made everybody feel like they were important. He was more than a great salesman. He was a doer."

No recitation of Charlie Daniel's various involvements with his home town of Greenville would be complete without a mention of two ironic situations that developed out of his antipathy to the Kennedy clan of Massachusetts.

In 1959, a year before he turned the full force of his political and personal opposition against the nomination and subsequent presidential candidacy of John F. Kennedy, Daniel found himself sharing a public platform in his own hometown with Robert F. Kennedy, brother of the president-to-be.

The occasion was a meeting of the Greenville Chamber of Commerce's Buttonhole Club, at which Daniel was to receive the 1959 Distinguished Service Award, having been selected for that honor by the Southern Association of Science and Industry. The principal speaker for the event was none other than Robert F. Kennedy.

The setting for the next ironic situation grew out of the John F. Kennedy presidency — ushered in by the 1960 election during which Daniel fought tooth-and-nail against the Kennedy clan and its policies. Thereafter came the overblown journalistic references that likened Washington during the Kennedy administration to the Arthurian community of Camelot.

As luck would have it, when the time arrived in 1967 to dedicate the new Charles E. Daniel Theatre (made possible through Daniel gifts exceeding $100,000 to the Greenville Little Theatre), the very first play presented in the new structure was "Camelot."

There was yet another unusual note to that event, for U. S. Senator Ernest F. Hollings was on hand for the dedication with laudatory remarks about the late Mr. Daniel, with whom he had differed strongly during the campaign that had put Jack Kennedy in the White House.

CHAPTER 27

Advocate of Good Government

Daniel's brief interlude as a member of the U. S. Senate did not result in his being "bitten by the political bug," but it did heighten his interest and involvement as a concerned citizen in public affairs. It also refueled the recurring rumors that he might become a candidate for public office. Indeed, he had been petitioned by friends and admirers over a number of years to enter politics — generally with the governorship in mind.

Such sporadic agitation took on added intensity as Governor James F. Byrnes neared the end of his term (1951-54), prompting Daniel to talk personally with Byrnes about the matter. Byrnes' advice, as recalled by Alester G. Furman, Jr., a mutual friend of both men, was in this vein:

> "Charlie, you are a businessman, not a politician. You approach things so differently from a politician, and you're so anxious to get everything done now that politicians can't follow that course. And I would advise you not to run."

An appropriate sequel to that story occurred in September of 1955 when Daniel was invited to address the Pickens County Goodwill Club at its regular gathering at Rocky Bottom, a rustic retreat in the upper part of the county. Again, Byrnes, Daniel and Furman were together, this time accompanied by Greenville businessman J. P. Williamson. En route to Rocky Bottom, Williamson sought to persuade Daniel to seek the governorship. Daniel's response was to this effect:

> "I have no political ambitions, and besides, my wife wouldn't let me run."

The real punch line of that story, however, was reserved for the return trip, when Governor Byrnes wryly observed:

"Charlie, on the way over there, you said you had no political ambitions. After hearing you make that speech, I think you proved it to those who heard it, because no politician could say the things you said, that needed to be said, to those people tonight."

Actually, the speech contained much material that would have been considered appropriate by any politician for such an occasion. But when Daniel began detailing the needs and calling for the initiative to meet those needs, he moved into areas where cautious politicians were not likely to tread. Not many would have called for an outlay of more than two-and-one-half billion dollars in capital expenditures over the next 10 years, even though most of it ($1.4 billion) was proposed for private enterprise.

Addressing the twin subjects of industrialization and capitalization on numerous occasions, he advised that "money goes where it can make a profit." He firmly believed that South Carolina was an ideal place in which to invest, and he strove constantly to make it even more attractive to new industry and to encourage the expansion of established facilities in the state.

Good government, in the Daniel view, was the sum total of good men with good motives in public office, adherence to constitutional principles, equitable policies of taxation, and widespread citizen involvement. Had he been running for office, that could well have been described as his "platform." And since his views often were sought either as private counsel or public testimony by officeholders as well as the citizenry, it seems reasonable to ascribe to him some measure of influence in bringing about a number of changes for the better, especially in the realm of taxation.

Speculation that Daniel might be persuaded to run for governor picked up in 1957 after his resignations from the State Ports Planning Committee and the Clemson Board. Four years later, some speculated that he might be a candidate for the seat held by U. S. Senator Olin D. Johnson. On each occasion he disavowed any intention of running, yet he did say that the state and nation needed public officials "who don't give a damn whether they are reelected." His senate experience and constant pleading for good government generated the rumors; and simultaneously, the number of requests for speeches grew to the point that he received far more invitations than he could accept. For instance, on November 19, 1958, he crowded speeches into his day's schedule at Spartanburg and Greenville, telling each group that "the most imperative need for the triumph of good government — of vast economic development — is for good citizens to get busy and act like good citizens."

The Spartanburg Journal editorialized that "Mr. Daniel's frank appraisal of current conditions is timely. The state, counties and cities almost without exception are in financial difficulties. If more people of Mr. Daniel's experience and proven business ability urge modernization of government as the alternative to higher taxes at this time, the chances are good that something constructive can be accomplished along this line."

Daniel did not just go about the state saying what he perceived to be wrong. He followed up his criticisms with recommendations for improvement, pointing out a better way. Here, in summarized form, is a synopsis of his recommendations for improving the performance of government in South Carolina and its political subdivisions. These proposals, made for the most part over the 10-year span from 1954 through 1963, were put before groups as diverse as the South Carolina Tax Study Commission and the Pickens County Goodwill Club.

In general, the following presentation reflects Daniel's own phraseology; and where paraphrasing is employed, the sense of the Daniel proposals is preserved.

— The Constitution was excellent when adopted in 1895; but now with more than 300 amendments, it is out of date and should be revised.
— The 60-odd divisions within the state government should be consolidated into six or eight, each with well-paid and experienced leadership.
— There should be a three-member policymaking tax commission, with each commissioner being familiar with federal tax laws and the tax laws of other states.
— Cities and counties should collect such taxes as are needed for their services; the state should collect only those taxes required for state purposes.
— The property tax system should be changed, which permits 12 to 15 percent of all property to escape taxation and allows unbelievable variances in assessments.
— All property should be revalued every five years.
— A permanent committee should be established to study state-owned property with the authority to dispose of surplus properties.
— The feasibility of placing all roads in the state under the South Carolina Highway Department should be considered.
— An economic development board should be established in each county, organized into congressional district group-

ings; and each district should be represented on the State Planning Board.
— At least four major commercial airports should be built with full state cooperation.
— With more than 600 different taxing divisions, it would be sensible to merge many counties into larger, self-supporting units and to consolidate many cities and counties.

Daniel also proposed revision of labor laws, making them equally applicable to business and labor organizations. He urged the strenghtening of Worker's Compensation laws and the placement of their administration on a sound business basis. Vitally interested in public schools and public and private colleges, he said that frills and progressive promotion in public schools should be eliminated and replaced by new emphasis on fundamentals and common sense. He felt that pupils must be made to realize that their promotions will depend upon passing grades, not sociological sympathy; that the school year should be lengthened; and that unnecessary functions should be eliminated.

State colleges, Daniel believed, should be brought into a university system supervised by a board of regents; and tuition at those colleges should be reasonable and should not constitute an unfair subsidy detrimental to the continued development of private colleges. He felt that overlapping facilities should be eliminated and that strong entrance requirements should be maintained, along with definite standards of performance. He further believed that public education at all levels, including the technical, could be expanded through the state's educational television.

Along with his admonitions for improvements that would enhance his state's progress, Daniel stressed the need for both long- and short-range planning with the realization that change takes time. The goal he portrayed was a stable and productive economy in which agriculture was balanced with industry. Without such a balance, he said, South Carolina conceivably could undergo the economic trauma that befell much of New England when scores of textile mills closed or moved South, leaving thousands of persons unemployed during the late 1940's and early 1950's. At that juncture of his speeches, Daniel could have justifiably laid claim to a major personal achievement in developing an agricultural-industrial mix in South Carolina, because he was successful in persuading industrialists to locate new plants in rural areas so that farm folk could augment their sometimes-meager income with factory wages. Thus they could maintain the sense of security and independence that went with the ownership — and tillage — of their small farms.

CHAPTER 28

Textile Teamwork

From the beginning to the end of Charlie Daniel's career, he was closely associated with the textile industry, not only as a builder of textile plants but as a confidante of textile magnates and often as a member of textile boards of directors. Then, too, there was a personal relationship between Daniel and many leaders or spokesmen for the industry.

No small credit for his continuing and constructive output of speeches and statements pertaining to public affairs — whether economic or governmental — may be justifiably attributed to his close working relationship with John K. Cauthen, for many years executive vice president of the South Carolina Textile Manufacturers' Association. In that capacity, Cauthen rubbed shoulders with, exchanged ideas with, and exercised influence upon many of the state, regional, and national industrialists who were so much a part of Charlie Daniel's world. More importantly, he and Daniel shared many common viewpoints as to the challenges faced by South Carolina across a broad spectrum of problems, especially those in the fields of finance and taxation.

Time and again, the two would consult with each other — by telephone, through correspondence, or in person — on "things that need to be said." In this connection, Cauthen's background as a veteran newsman, former executive secretary to two South Carolina governors (J. Emile Harley and Richard M. Jefferies) and member of several state boards and commissions stood him in good stead as a Daniel conferee. Not only was he almost always thinking in the same terms as Daniel, but he had the writing and working experience to convert their joint thinking into effective and often persuasive terminology.

In the late 1950's particularly, Cauthen and Daniel collaborated in their speech writing, with first one and then the other taking the initiative in formulating addresses. Upon request, Cauthen would suggest a specific approach to a given audience. Alternatively,

202

Daniel would pull his own thoughts together in a rough draft and then submit it to Cauthen for such refinement or revision as the pair might find desirable. But always, whatever the procedure, the end product was a presentation expressing those value judgments and personal suggestions characteristic of Charlie Daniel.

The following excerpts from a letter to Cauthen prior to Daniel's addressing the Batesburg-Leesville Chamber of Commerce in 1958 reflect not only Daniel's thinking but his collaboration with the Textile Manufacturers' Association executive:

"It seems to me an excellent opportunity to point out briefly, but emphatically, the inequalities in the method of assessing property throughout the state, the unfairness of the existing system, as well as the difficulties presented by same in our efforts to secure new industry.

"There are those who say we should not emphasize this fact, which is a detriment to our statement; but if we confined our comments only to favorable things, we would never correct inequalities.

"Our good legislature has done an excellent job with tax reforms, and the Supreme Court has acted quickly in denying unfavorable directives as to Workmen's Compensation. This leaves the matter of tax equalization as being an important problem in South Carolina yet to be resolved.

"The State Constitution very clearly states . . . that property should be valued on an equal basis. We have not had the executive leadership with the courage to enforce the Constitution and, through such action, help our state.

"Could we determine, without too much difficulty, the number of counties that are presently receiving more kickbacks in various forms from the state and federal governments than they are paying in local taxation?

"Can we point out some of the glaring inequalities that exist throughout the state, emphasizing that simple justice and honesty only cause concern to those who are chiseling under the present setup?

"The state is now carrying entirely too much of a load for various counties and municipalities, with the result that major state functions are suffering and lagging desperately behind similar activities of other states with which we must compete for industry.

"I want to be as nice as possible about the entire situation, but I do not believe that we can correct our problems by hiding inequalities; and changes can only be made after presenting the facts to our people who have shown time and time again that they want to be fair.

"These troubles are not the problem of our legislature alone; they belong to all of our people; and correction can only come through people throughout the state by devoting at least 10 percent of our time to the affairs of our government in all its stages.

"You will know much better than I do how to prepare this address and of the necessity of congratulating the people of the area on their strenuous efforts to improve their economical conditions and the prospects of the future . . ."

Another major factor contributing to the close working relationship and continuing communication between Daniel and Cauthen was the fact that the economic and governmental goals of their respective organizations — the South Carolina Textile Manufacturers' Association and Daniel Construction Company — were almost always on the same wavelength.

Both advocated tax laws and procedures, at both state and local levels, that would be fair to industry. They favored economy and efficiency in government. And they sought to offset or minimize the political and economic power so avidly coveted by organized labor. Furthermore, Daniel's continuing and comprehensive involvement in the construction, expansion, and maintenance of textile plants throughout the state and the South naturally put him in league with that industry in most of its programs and policies.

Their collaboration, however, extended beyond matters that had a direct dollars-and-cents impact upon their respective trades. They sought, to cite only a few examples, to bring about an up-to-date revision of the state's antiquated Constitution of 1895, to promote the modernization and expansion of the State House at Columbia, and to provide better working quarters for such agencies as the State Development Board.

CHAPTER 29

Presidential Politics

A political phenomenon that characterized hosts of South Carolinians — including Charlie Daniel — from the late 1940's into the mid-1960's was the pattern of voting Democratic at the local and state level but otherwise in presidential contests. As time passed, more and more Palmetto State citizens demonstrated their willingness to vote openly as Republicans in national elections; but for many years, hosts of Carolinians avoided voting a Republican ticket by casting their ballots, often for Republican presidential nominees, through third-party mechanisms.

Thus, Daniel had considerable company in 1952 when he supported General Dwight Eisenhower for president — not by way of the Republican ticket but through the third-party effort designated as "South Carolinians for Eisenhower." He met the general during the latter's campaign visit to the state and maintained a cordial relationship with him in succeeding years. During and following his own brief stay in Washington as interim U. S. senator, Daniel was high in his praise of Eisenhower and was predicting in December of 1954 that the Republican president would "get excellent cooperation from the Democratic Party (in South Carolina), certainly on all matters for the good of the country."

In 1956, however, Daniel's high regard for Eisenhower did not prompt him to support the president's bid for reelection. Instead, Daniel renewed his affiliation with the independent faction, which in 1952 had been designated as "South Carolinians for Eisenhower," but which in 1956 termed itself "South Carolinians for Independent Electors." There is little in the record to indicate that Daniel had fallen out with the president although there were a number of South Carolinians who had become disenchanted with some of the administration's farm policies. Rather, all indications — and the recollections of some of Daniel's political associates — led to the conclusion that the independents felt that most South Carolinians were not yet prepared to vote the Republican ticket even in a presidential election.

When the ballots were tabulated, the independents had around 88,500 votes; but the real significance of the 1956 election lay in the fact that more than 75,000 South Carolinians did vote the straight Republican ticket. The Democrats, with 136,372 votes, would have lost had the opposition votes been combined. This may have spurred Daniel to greater activity in presidential politics in 1960. As the election loomed on the horizon, he devoted much time and money to "South Carolina Democrats for Nixon and Lodge" in opposition to the Democratic party and its candidate, John F. Kennedy. Richard M. Nixon was Eisenhower's vice president; and characteristically, Daniel supplemented his fund-raising efforts with periodic notes to Nixon, suggesting campaign strategy and urging him to visit the state, which the vice president did on November 3. On that day a full-page ad appeared in a Greenville weekly with the headline, "The Impact of the National Election on Southern Industrial Development." The ad prominently bore the name of Charles E. Daniel.

Strong supporters sometimes come under fire themselves, just as do the candidates. During the last few hectic days preceding the election, reports were circulated in Democratic circles that someone was putting money into television and other programs aimed at converting Kennedy's Catholicism into a political liability among the state's Protestant Democrats. The reports were vague and undocumented for the most part; yet Daniel's name did come up, probably due to his strong and open support of Nixon. He promptly denied any connection, saying, "I would be the last man in South Carolina to take part in any activity for or against any candidate on the basis of his religion."

One contributing factor to his enthusiastic involvement in the Nixon-Lodge campaign may have been his personal acquaintance with the vice president, developed during the Eisenhower years in the White House. Daniel's occasional letters to Nixon usually elicited acknowledgements addressed "Dear Charlie" and signed "Dick."

In July of 1960, Daniel drafted a letter offering to the vice president an assessment of the political climate in South Carolina, explaining: "The people here consider the Democratic platform atrocious . . . Our people want a return to sanity, to freedom of choice and opportunity for all without having to pay tribute for the privilege of working. They believe in competition but realize we are on the way to national distress and bankruptcy unless the tremendous flood of imports from low-wage countries is promptly curbed. . . ."

As the November 8 election date neared, Daniel and other Nixon-Lodge supporters were optimistic that South Carolinians were willing to break with tradition and put the state in the Republican column for the first time since Reconstruction days. They came close to realizing their expectations, but not close enough. However, they did witness the spectacle of more South Carolinians voting a Republican ticket than ever before. When all the votes were in, the Kennedy-Johnson ticket had won the day by fewer than 10,000 votes out of a total of almost 387,000.

The Democrats carried 25 counties, earning a razor-thin edge of 51 percent of the statewide vote. The Nixon-Lodge total of some 188,500 votes represented the largest straight Republican tally yet recorded in the Palmetto State, surpassing the total chalked up in 1952 by the combined vote of the Republicans and the South Carolinians for Eisenhower.

Had Daniel lived to see the results of the 1964 presidential election, he would have witnessed South Carolina going Republican (with 59 percent of the vote) for another of his personal friends in GOP ranks, U. S. Senator Barry Goldwater of Arizona. Thereafter, he would have seen Nixon bounce back by winning the state in a three-way contest with Democrat Hubert Humphrey and Independent George Wallace in 1968. And, four years after that, running against the Democratic Senator George McGovern, then President Nixon swept to an unprecedented Republican victory in South Carolina by carrying all 46 counties and amassing 73 percent of the vote.

For whatever small consolation it might have been worth in the wake of the Democratic victory of 1960, Daniel was able to point to some of the consequences to the South and say, "I told you so."

A major chance to toss a few barbs at the Kennedy administration was provided Daniel in November of 1963, coincidental with his 68th birthday on November 11. The occasion was a dinner at the Waldorf-Astoria in New York at which he was recognized as Industrialist of the Year. He was introduced by Richard M. Nixon. The event provided a platform from which Daniel could ask: "Will America Be Great Again?" In providing his own answers to that challenging question, he had this to say:

"There is deep apprehension in the business world because the economic system of America, developed on the principle of free choice by individuals in a free market, is being throttled and killed by government manipulation, interference and domination. The administration is giving us daily a convincing demonstration of its lack of economic understanding, of its inadequate knowledge or appreciation of our American system. Those men who are directing the economic and fiscal policies of our government have no faith in the very system of free enterprise which brought us to the abundant life and to the position of opportunity for world leadership. So far, the system has survived in spite of these people, not because of them. They are an indulgence which we can no longer afford to risk."

Drawing a bead on power-hungry labor bosses, pseudo-intellectuals and "educated beatniks," Daniel said, "The people must face up to the predicament and again take charge of their government and their affairs. . . . Good Americans everywhere must join in the fight to eliminate the wildly theoretical excursions into the land of dreams, the incompetent and irresponsible economic planning, the erosions of American principles and convictions (and) the insidious perversion of power for personal gain and prestige if we want to make America great again."

There was more in a similar vein, and he recommended some specific courses of action; but the total thrust of his message was a vote of no confidence in the Democratic administration then in power.

CHAPTER 30

Sharing the Wealth

It would have been out of character for either Charlie Daniel or his wife to portray themselves as philanthropists; but the extent and the regularity of their charitable gifts reflected that benevolent concern for others that is the essence of true philanthropy. With the growth of Daniel Construction Company, so grew the magnitude of their contributions to institutions, individuals, organizations and causes that they considered worthy of aid.

By the early 1940's, their donations, coupled with those of Charlie's brother Hugh (most of which were concentrated in Alabama, where he headed Daniel operations) were quite substantial. The level of giving increased also with the establishment of the Daniel Foundation in September 1947. The Foundation's initial assets, totalling only $44,700, consisted of $12,500 in cash from Charlie Daniel and stock totalling $32,200.

From that modest beginning, the Foundation grew in financial resources to the point where its charitable grants, from 1948 through 1979, exceeded $28.5 million.

The record of Daniel donations over the years does not disclose any fixed philosophy or pattern of giving. Rather, it reflects a diversity of altruistic interests ranging across racial, religious, educational and occupational lines of endeavor. The record also discloses varied responses from the Daniel family as they dealt individually or jointly with the ever-increasing flow of requests for assistance from persons, institutions, agencies and organizations.

As the years went by, the largest proportion of Daniel Foundation gifts went into the field of higher education, reflecting an evident determination to apply funds where they were likely to accomplish the greatest good for the greatest number over an extended period of time. It should be noted that the following financial data reflects only those contributions of $500 or more made by Daniel personally or by the Daniel Foundation between January 1942 and December 1963. No one will ever know the amount of

209

money and the number of recipients who were helped in time of need with a few hundred dollars — more or less — by Charlie Daniel or his wife.

During the 22-year time span just cited, more than half of the contributions went to institutions of learning, chiefly The Citadel, Clemson University and Furman University. But there were then, as later, appreciable gifts earmarked for the University of South Carolina, Bob Jones University and other South Carolina colleges, notably Wofford, Erskine and Converse. The spectrum was broad, however, and included Allen University, Anderson College, Coker College, Columbia College, Limestone College, Newberry College, Presbyterian College, South Carolina State College and Winthrop College.

Other recipients of gifts in the field of education included the special school operated at Tamassee, South Carolina, by the Daughters of the American Revolution and the South Carolina Opportunity School near Columbia, an institution dedicated to providing an educational alternative for persons whose regular education has been disrupted or interrupted.

Also included among the beneficiaries of Daniel aid to education were more than a dozen institutions in other states ranging from Virginia to Puerto Rico. Daniel Foundation funds were generally channeled to recipients recommended by Daniel executives directing operations in the affected regions. Most of the schools and institutions, however, were located in Alabama, reflecting the interest of Hugh Daniel and the Daniel Construction activities there.

A substantial portion of the Foundation's grants in the field of education went then, as now, to provide scholarship aid to deserving students. But Daniel funds also provided resources for buildings and other capital improvements, management surveys, studies and other needs, whether academic or administrative.

Among the educational institutions benefiting from Daniel grants were several in the field of medical training: the Medical University of South Carolina at Charleston, Howard University School of Medicine, Meharry Medical College, and the University of Alabama Medical College.

More direct medical aid took the form of grants to hospitals, grants that ranged from $500 up to a peak for the 1942-63 period of $103,000 to the County Hospital at Anderson, where Daniel had spent most of his youth.

Also remembered was his birthplace, for a $10,000 contribution went from the Foundation to the hospital at Elberton, Georgia. Five hospitals in Alabama were recipients of grants, as was a New

England institution concerned with the treatment of arthritis and rheumatism.

Further reflecting a Daniel concern with medical matters, one of the most consistent recipients of Daniel Foundation funding and of direct contributions from Charles and/or Hugh Daniel was the Southern Research Institute, located in Birmingham. Its locale, in the same city as Daniel Realty Corporation and the Alabama headquarters of Daniel Construction Company, may have played a contributing role in stimulating the constant flow of Daniel grants to the institution. But another factor seemed to have been far more instrumental in establishing the continuing relationship: the personal friendship of Hugh Daniel with Thomas W. Martin, long-time head of the Alabama Power Company and a moving spirit behind the Research Institute.

The oft-expressed gratitude of the Institute for the Daniel donations and personal involvement (Hugh Daniel was a trustee and subsequently vice chairman of the board during the period from 1964 until his resignation in 1980) took concrete form in November 1965. On the first day of that month, an impressive ceremony was held at which a new and important addition to the Institute was formally designated the "Daniel Laboratory." The marker placed on the new structure was unveiled by C. W. (Bill) Daniel. It bore a full-face bas-relief likeness of Charlie Daniel along with this inscription:

DANIEL LABORATORY
DEDICATED TO THE EMPLOYEES
AND ASSOCIATES
OF
CHARLES E. DANIEL
A MAN OF VISION
WHOSE MONUMENT IS HUNDREDS
OF INDUSTRIAL, INSTITUTIONAL,
AND COMMERCIAL BUILDINGS THAT
ARE THE LANDMARKS
OF TWO CONTINENTS
1965

As fully impressive as the building itself was the panel of participants in the dedicatory exercises. The printed program attested to the caliber of the individuals who were assembled by special invitation for the occasion. Among them was long-time family friend Owen R. Cheatham, founder of Georgia-Pacific, of which Daniel was elected a director in 1957.

During the course of the program, much enlightenment and considerable hope was voiced concerning man's unceasing battle to conquer cancer. But that was only one phase of the proceedings, the other being a succession of eulogies for the late industrialist in whose honor the building was named. Excerpts from some of those laudatory remarks follow:

> Senator Thurmond: "Charlie Daniel's story of success is typical of the opportunity available in America to the man who will not be satisfied with the common, the average, the ordinary. He was an extraordinary personality. Those who knew him admired and respected him because of his character, his integrity, and his great courage. . . . This institution can be proud of having the interest of such a great American, for he always had a keen desire for the progress of mankind. He was ever in the forefront of those efforts to genuinely contribute to the public welfare."

> Mr. Byrnes: "Without fear of contradiction, I say that Charlie Daniel brought more industry to the southeastern states than any man in private or public life. . . . He dreamed big dreams. He was also a man of action and he slaved to have his dreams come true. He was a philanthropist and his generous gifts to charitable causes warmed the hearts of many. Certainly one of his greatest achievements is the fact that he recruited and trained a corps of young men and molded them into a team that has already proved its ability to carry on and perpetuate his high ideals. I say in all sincerity, seriously, that in a rather long journey along the highway of life, I have met many men who have enriched my life but no one to a greater degree than my friend, Charlie Daniel, after whom this laboratory is named."

> General Clark: "All those who work in this building, I'm sure, will receive the inspiration from the name of an all-American . . . a dedicated courageous one who stood up for the principles he held dear; and I'm sure there will be great progress toward the solution of many of these diseases and problems that have bedeviled mankind for so long. I know when you do make that progress, no one in the world will be happier than that great American, Charlie Daniel."

But to turn to the cause of education rather than that of research, Daniel's interest was not limited to his association with The Citadel, where he had been a cadet for two years prior to World War I, nor to Clemson College, where he served a number of years as a member of the Board of Trustees. He maintained a lively and generous interest in the private colleges and universities of South Carolina, not only as a private citizen but as a moving spirit of the South Carolina Foundation of Independent Colleges. He was one of the original trustees of the Foundation when it began functioning in 1954, serving continuously from that time until his death 10 years later. His personal and corporate gifts to the Foundation were substantial, as indicated in a February 22, 1962, letter to him from Dr. Charles F. Marsh, then president of Wofford College.

Dr. Marsh wrote: "I can't resist adding a personal note to inform you how many visitors to the Mickel Memorial Chapel in our new Main Building express their appreciation of what you and your wife have done to make this lovely little chapel possible." His reference was to the chapel named in honor of Mrs. Daniel's mother, Viola Alston Carter Mickel, a native of Hartwell, Georgia.

At the time of his active association with the Foundation as a member of its board of trustees, the organization consisted of these South Carolina colleges: Coker, Columbia, Converse, Erskine, Furman, Limestone, Newberry, Presbyterian and Wofford. The presidents of those nine institutions served as Foundation trustees, along with Daniel, former Governor James F. Byrnes and B. M. Edwards of Columbia, F. E. Grier of Greenwood, Hugh Lane of Charleston, Roger Milliken and Walter S. Montgomery of Spartanburg, and Roger C. Peace of Greenville.

It should be noted here that the absence of predominantly black schools from the Foundation of Independent Colleges is not due to any racial policy on the foundation's part but to the fact that most black schools in South Carolina have found it to their advantage to affiliate with the United Negro College Fund, which prohibits membership in other fund-raising groups.

During the period from January 1942 through December 1963, significant contributions were made to the Independent College Foundation by Daniel or by the Daniel Foundation. Later, in 1967 (several years after Daniel's death), the Daniel Foundation made a $422,873 grant to the college group for that one year alone.

In the 1942-1963 period, the outlay to the Foundation of Independent Colleges was in addition to a total of $72,500 in direct grants to eight of the member institutions. The ninth school, Furman University, was in a somewhat separate category by virtue of being a hometown institution in which both Mr. and Mrs. Daniel took great pride and interest. During the period just cited, Furman benefited from the Daniels as individuals and as trustees of the Daniel Foundation to the extent of $450,000. That included cash contributions for scholarships, donations of stock and the transfer of ownership of the Daniels' Crescent Avenue residence and furnishings. That handsome property later was acquired from Furman by U. S. Judge Clement Haynsworth, a longtime friend of Daniel; deeded back to Furman and; still later, purchased by Buck Mickel, then the head of Daniel International.

Another indication of the Daniels' growing involvement with Furman was Daniel Construction Company's role in building virtually all the handsome structures that comprise the spacious Furman campus on the northern outskirts of Greenville. The university's appreciation of Daniel's contributions to the institution — both in grants and in quality construction at reasonable cost — prompted the naming of the dining hall in his honor. According to Dr. Francis Bonner, a Furman vice president, that decision stemmed not from any particular connection of Daniel with the dining hall itself, but because "it's such a beautiful building. . . . It seemed more fitting to name that building for him than a classroom building."

That gesture of gratitude was overshadowed in 1975 when Furman named its impressive new music building in honor of Mrs. Daniel. Made possible through a $4,365,000 grant from the Daniel Foundation, the largest such gift in Furman history, the building was dedicated on November 25, 1975, with ceremonies permanently documented in a souvenir program that carried this appropriate evaluation of Mrs. Daniel:

> "A native of Georgia, Homozel Mickel Daniel has achieved distinction in her adopted state of South Carolina in the diverse worlds of business and the fine arts. She serves as vice president and secretary and as a director of the Daniel International Corporation, the great international industrial complex founded by her late husband, Senator Charles E. Daniel. As a trustee of the Daniel Foundation, she guides the fund's religious, charitable, scientific, literary and educational philanthropies. She has contributed greatly to the cultural life of Greenville, especially to the Little Theatre and the Greenville Symphony Orchestra. Mrs. Daniel, who is a near neighbor of Furman, has been closely associated with the present campus from its beginnings. Through her interest in and generosity to the Furman program in the fine arts, music in particular, she has enriched the lives of thousands of students and other lovers of the arts."

Although most Daniel contributions were made in areas such as health, education, religion and charity in general, Daniel occasionally would earmark rather sizable sums for endeavors quite out of the ordinary.

There was, for example, an instance in February 1962 when Daniel responded to the tune of $1,000 to an appeal aimed at enhancing the preservation of wildlife in Africa. The explanation of that particular grant lay in the fact that it stemmed from a "Dear Charlie" letter from an old friend, Royal Little, head of the giant Textron Corporation. As he prepared for a three-week African safari, Little wrote Daniel (along with others of a small but select group) that the Tanganyikan government needed funds to develop its system of national parks. The Daniel check, funnelled through the New York Zoological Society, presumably helped the attainment of that goal.

One of the last fund-raising drives in which Daniel became involved was that of generating support for the Winston Churchill Memorial and Library proposed to be built on the grounds of Westminster College at Fulton, Missouri.

The person selected to head the financing effort in the United States was Charles Allen Thomas, board chairman of the Monsanto Company and a friend of Charlie Daniel. It was he who enlisted Daniel in the endeavor, correctly expecting the South Carolinian to prevail upon business and personal acquaintances for donations.

In a somewhat similar but earlier undertaking, Daniel had served as state director for a national committee raising funds in 1959 for the Eisenhower Presidential Library in Abilene, Kansas. Not only did Daniel pledge a personal contribution of $5,000 to the library fund, but his personal solicitations from South Carolinians and other friends elsewhere resulted in the Palmetto State's appreciably exceeding its $26,000 quota.

Meanwhile, in the more conventional realm of fine arts — and here was evidenced the cultural influence of Mrs. Daniel — there were such contributions as $25,000 for the Atlanta Arts Alliance in 1964. Other sums went to such similar organizations and institutions as the Gibbes Art Gallery of Charleston, the Birmingham Art Museum, and the Birmingham Civic Symphony Association. In the years following Daniel's death, there were even larger and more widespread gifts in the arts field.

At the University of South Carolina, the initial and continuing Daniel contributions are recognized by the designation of the eighth floor of the College of Business Administration as the Daniel Management Center.

Chapter 31

The Last Rites

Although 1964 opened on a note that brought additional recognition and praise to Daniel, chiefly through the January issue of *Business Week*, the year was to prove not only fateful but fatal for the industrialist. Weakened by what he called "a particularly exhausting year" (1963), Daniel had developed a serious case of influenza as the Christmas season approached. Worried by X-rays that disclosed lung trouble, he hastened to New York for treatment by a team of medical specialists. By mid-February, he was back home in Greenville, somewhat encouraged by what he interpreted as prognoses of complete recovery.

Even so, he took occasion in many of his acknowledging compliments on the *Business Week* article to comment on his uncharacteristic ill health. No longer was he readily available for public appearances and group gatherings. One of his last involvements in what might be termed a "media event" was his attendance on February 20 at a luncheon sponsored by the Abbeville County Development Board.

There, he introduced Governor Donald S. Russell, who made the unparalleled announcement that two international firms were establishing million-dollar plants at Abbeville. To no one's surprise, the announcement included the information that both plants — one for the Flexible Tubing Corporation of Guilford, Connecticut, and the other for General Cable Corporation of New York City — were to be built by Daniel Construction Company.

Daniel's next, and what were destined to be his last, public appearances were at the June 29 Daniel Building groundbreaking and at a Greenville Chamber of Commerce meeting at which he was honored. Tragically, within three months, ground was broken almost directly across Main Street from the building site for Daniel's place of interment in Springwood Cemetery. The cancer that had reduced him to a virtual invalid during the last weeks of his life

216

finally took its toll on Sunday, September 13, at his home on Roe Ford Road. He was 68 years old.

Burial services were private; but funeral services at the Mackey Mortuary, then situated adjacent to the cemetery and directly across Main Street from the Daniel Building site, drew an overflowing throng of Daniel friends and admirers from the city, the state, and points far removed. Included in their number were the governor and former governors of South Carolina, along with past and present U. S. senators.

The funeral oration, delivered by the Reverend Dr. L. D. Johnson, pastor of Greenville's First Baptist Church, was noteworthy not only as an expression of religious faith but as an eloquent recitation of familiar — and not-so-familiar — quotations from the past. Most appropriate was his reference to the inscription that marks the tomb of England's famed 17th century architect, Sir Christopher Wren. That noted builder had been laid to rest in London's St. Paul's Cathedral, a structure often described as the crowning achievement of his architectural genius. These words are etched in his tombstone:

"If you would see his monument, look around."

That inscription, cited pertinently by the Reverend Dr. Johnson, preceded this contemporary observation of his own:

"Those words might appropriately be spoken of Charles E. Daniel anywhere in South Carolina, or for that matter, across the land. No tribute of ours could burnish the record of this fabulous man's career, or write his name in larger letters across the progress of this nation than he has himself already written with his life."

A considerable portion of the Johnson eulogy was reprinted in the *Congressional Record* as an extension of remarks from South Carolina's Third District Congressman, Representative W. J. Bryan Dorn, long a co-worker with Daniel on industrial and governmental affairs.

An even longer entry into the *Congressional Record* was initiated by Senator Strom Thurmond. With the unanimous consent of the Senate, he entered into the *Record* a voluminous reprinting of news accounts and editorials stemming from Daniel's death. One notable feature of the Thurmond insert was its inclusion of the names and remarks of prominent individuals — including former Vice President Richard Nixon — concerning Daniel's life and death.

Subsequently, industrial and other trade publications across the country likewise extolled the personal and professional achievements which had become part and parcel of the Daniel saga.

But yet to come were two other noteworthy observances — one via radio and television, the other by magazine.

South Carolina Magazine devoted virtually its entire March 1965 issue to Daniel and his accomplishments, not only in editorial and reported copy but in a majority of the advertisements that appeared in the memorial edition. Many companies, most of them headquartered in the Palmetto State but some from outside, forsook the usual advertising message in favor of expressions of appreciation for the life and regrets upon the death of Charlie Daniel.

The feature article was a lengthy account of "Charles Ezra Daniel — the Life of the Great Southern Builder," edited by the magazine's associate editor, William M. Taylor. In addition, there were reprints of the *Fortune* magazine article that had appeared in the October 1954 issue; a statement by Daniel himself, which had been published in April of 1964 by *The American Banker*, entitled "Money Goes Where It Can Make a Profit"; and a rather devastating editorial from *The Anderson Free Press* in which that outspoken publication rallied strongly to Daniel's defense after the contractor had been subjected by another newspaper to a rather sneering attack entitled "Along Came Charlie." The thrust of *The Free Press* editorial, written by H. G. Anderson, was to the effect that not only the communities in and around Anderson but the entire state benefited every time "Charlie came along."

The other tribute occurred in January 1965 when Columbia's leading broadcast media, WIS television and WIS radio, announced that Charlie Daniel had been chosen as the WIS "South Carolinian of the Year" for 1964. That selection was well documented by appropriate radio and television presentations to audiences in South Carolina and beyond. Additionally, it was formalized at a luncheon program held on January 22 at Columbia's Palmetto Club, where WIS executives G. Richard Shafto, Charles A. Batson and W. Frank Harden participated in the presentation of a plaque accepted in Daniel's name by his brother, R. Hugh Daniel, and by Buck Mickel. The luncheon program also included a viewing of the television production that substantiated Daniel's right to acclaim as "South Carolinian of the Year."

WIS News Director Bob Hickman set the stage for viewing the program by reporting such information as this:

"The more than $281 million dollars in industrial expansion in the state in 1964 represents new buildings and additions to existing plants at 179 different locations in South Carolina. Charlie Daniel's construction company was working on 75 of those jobs. Put that with the schools, office buildings and churches built by Daniel, pinpoint them on a map and we get a picture of Daniel Construction Company activity in South Carolina in 1964. Altogether, Daniel Construction started or finished 90 projects in 45 different cities and towns in the state, ranging from a $40-million synthetic fiber plant to a $269 door-relocation job."

At that juncture in the televised program, Daniel was praised by the then chairman of the State Development Board, J. Bratton Davis of Columbia, for working closely with development groups, local citizens, legislative delegations and others:

"The industrial firms have responded to this super-salesmanship of Senator Daniel; and as a result, wherever one goes in South Carolina, they will find Daniel plants located."

An additional insight into the Daniel approach was cited by Alester G. Furman, Jr., Greenville compatriot and financial associate of Daniel:

"We decided that in South Carolina we had the greatest potential for industry through our wonderful local, native people who wanted to work and that if we could get industry in here, we would furnish jobs which in the long run would help the economy of this state. . . .

"He did work from daylight to night every day, traveled all over the country, went to see the prospects of industry that were developing, kept a very wide acquaintance which he made through financial institutions in the East. . . .

"I don't think he had any hobby but work. He loved people, though, and he would go to every kind of meeting that was ever around. . . . But if you'd go to a meeting, you'd nearly always find him over in a corner talking to somebody about a job that might be available. . . ."

Former Governor James F. Byrnes, another of the honored guests at the WIS luncheon, offered this observation:

"Charlie seldom talked with me that he did not speak of the industrial plants he was then striving to bring to our state. However, he never spoke in terms of the amount of money to be invested in the state by an industry. He spoke only of the number of jobs that would be created and the greater opportunities that would be offered for the employment of young people."

Then, referring to a Daniel trait that fascinated observers within and without the construction industry, Byrnes said:

"His word was as good as his bond. No better evidence could be asked of this than the fact that he constructed for the Milliken company a number of textile plants, costing millions of dollars, without any written contract or agreement. Roger Milliken, president of that company, has advised me that there was not even a letter setting forth the terms of their agreement: there was a verbal understanding only. In a time when there are frequently lawsuits between the signers of written contracts, this statement is a great tribute to the integrity and the understanding of these two men."

Alester Furman appended a footnote to that subject:

"I one time saw Charlie sign a contract with a man at the Southern Railroad station in Greenville, on an express truck, on a piece of paper in which he agreed to build a plant for a flat number of dollars. The man said, 'What's your fee?' and he (Daniel) said, 'Well, when we get through building the building, I'll tell you what your fee is. We'll negotiate it then.' "

The balance of the WIS program was devoted in large measure to a discussion of the company's internal relationship with its employees, with much personal testimony as to the impact Charlie Daniel had upon the firm's work ethic and the maintenance of its reputation in the construction field. Mickel struck the keynote in this line of discussion by stressing the utter reliance of Daniel the man and Daniel the company upon its people:

"The people make any organization tick. We're completely dependent upon the men in the field, the men who make our organization, the men who carry out and live up to the promises we make . . . because we have always made it our policy to do anything we promised."

Other executives described the company's stress on safety, a concern that won for it widespread recognition throughout the nation.

But the main thrust of the occasion was recognition of Daniel the individual and acclaim of his achievements. These three concluding quotations typify the sentiments expressed by virtually every person who was accorded an opportunity to speak:

> Byrnes: "I'm satisfied that Charlie Daniel is responsible for bringing more industry to South Carolina than any other man either in public or private life."

> Russell: "I think the contributions that Charlie Daniel made to South Carolina are incalculable. All of us feel a very special debt of gratitude to Charlie Daniel and shall carry always fondly in our hearts a memory of what he has done and did do for South Carolina."

> Davis: "I think that when the future historians are writing the history of economics in South Carolina, they will always of necessity give a very important role to Charlie Daniel because it was he who had the vision and the foresight, the thought, the energy and the ambition to realize what South Carolina had to offer and what industry required. As a result, we are now in a great period of industrial expansion and development in South Carolina, the like of which this state has never known before and all of which promises to be much greater in the future. . . .

> "In summary, when I think of Senator Daniel, I'm reminded of a quotation from Abraham Lincoln which, I think epitomizes the senator:

> > " 'It is good to find a man who is proud of the place in which he lives and who so conducts himself that his place is proud of him.' "

Index

A

Abbeville County Development Board, 180
Abel, Mrs. George, 157
Adams, William T., 173
Agnew, E. Hugh, 170
A. H. Guion & Co., 30
Aiken, Hugh, 173
Akzona Corp., 13
Alabama Power Co., 103, 211
Alexander, J. Mason, 13, 117, 157
Allen, Eddie, 38
Allendale County Citizen, 184
Allied Chemical, 64
All In One Lifetime, by James F. Byrnes, 152
The American Banker, 218
American Chatillon Corp., 9, 10, 59
American Enka Corp., 13, 77
American Equipment Co., 89, 99, 107
America's Textile Reporter, 184
American Woolen Co., 61
Amin, Said, 99
Anderson Free Press, 218
Anderson, H. G., 218
Anderson Independent, 14
Anderson, S. C., 3, 6, 8, 17, 19, 33, 36, 38, 58, 94, 115, 132, 137
Appleton Mill, 33
Applied Engineering Co., 73, 107
Assured Industrial Maintenance, 90
Atlanta Arts Alliance, 215
Atlanta Constitution, 36
Augusta Chronicle, 184
Ayers, Fred C., 107
Ayers, Thomas L., 41

B

Bailey, Frank T., 90, 107
Baker, Bobby, 156
Balsam, D. M. 10, 11
Banks, Bob L., 96, 106, 108
Barker & Turoff Eng., 33
Barry, James E., 109
Bassett, C. D., 108
Batson, C. A., 219
Beacon Mfg. Co., 33, 34

Benet, Christie, 145
Bergen, Cletus W., 30
Berglund, Carl T., 109
Bird, Phifer, 116
Birmingham, Ala., 19, 22, 24, 33, 34, 60, 64, 68, 71, 88, 107, 113, 140, 143
Birmingham Art Museum, 215
Birmingham Civic Symphony, 215
Bishop, Louis W., 151
Blackwell, W. P., 17
Blatt, Solomon, 114, 170
Blu-Surf, Inc., 90
Bob Jones Univ., 36, 69
Bolt, Albert, 38
Bolt, B. Kenneth, 108
Bond Co., 91
Bonner, Francis, 214
Borden Co., 117
Bowater, 64, 65
Bradley, C. E., 109
Bradley, R. L., 108
Bradley, W. W., 108, 145
Brazell, Jimmy, 39
Brice, W. O., 158
Brock, Harry B., Jr., 89, 100
Brown, Edgar A., 145, 156, 160
Brown, Ernest, 157
Brown, I. R., 38
Brown & Root, 96
Brown, Walter, 171
Brownlee, Frank, 9, 14, 15
Bryan, Albert B., 193
Bryant-Davis Electric Co., 40
Bryant, Hubert, 40
Bureau of Yards & Docks, 29
Burgess, Carter L., 158
Burlington, 61, 116
Burris, John T. & Son, 20
Business Council, 79
Business Week, 74, 75, 81, 216
Byrd, Harry F., 157
Byrnes, James F., 14, 52, 56, 58, 77, 78, 142, 145, 151, 152, 154, 156, 161, 166, 190, 195, 198, 199, 212, 213, 219, 220

223

C

Calhoun, Andrew, 38
Calhoun, John C., 152
Calhoun Towers, 116, 117
Calmes, Claud, 39, 70, 71, 83, 84, 108
Cambron, Harry, 38
Cannon, Charles N., 102
Carolina Power & Light Co., 72
Carolinas-Virginia Nuclear Power Asso.,
    Inc., 72
Carter, R. L., 106, 108, 109
Cass, J. Kenneth, 171
Case, Herman, 32
Cashwell, James B., 108
Cathcart, J. M. 38
Cauthen, John K., 170, 202, 204
Celanese Corp., 9, 40, 58
Central Bank & Trust Co., 89
Charleston News and Courier, 161, 184
Charlotte Observer, 74
Charnley, Harry, 109
Cheatham, Owen R., 211
Chemical Bank, 5
Chemstrand (Monsanto), 64, 80
Cheves, C. Langdon, 25, 39, 43, 47, 48, 49,
    169
The Citadel, 8, 52, 59, 99, 115, 137-144, 145,
    158, 210, 212
The Citadel Development Foundation, 142,
    143, 144
Civil War, 162, 169
Clark, Mark, 115, 140, 141, 142, 143, 144, 212
Clemson University, 19, 20, 21, 22, 25, 28,
    49, 53, 59, 62, 63, 69, 110, 115, 118,
    145-148, 152, 189, 199, 210, 212
Clendenin, John, 39
Clendening, Dan, 109
Coker College, 213
Coker, James, 38
Coleman, Clifton P., 71, 108, 109
Coleman Engineering, 33
Columbia College, 213
Columbia Record, 184
Congressional Record, 159, 188, 217, 218
Continental Can, 65, 118
Converse College, 213
Cooper, Robert M., 145, 147, 150, 151, 168,
    179
Coosa River Newsprint, 40, 41
Cotton, Norris, 157
Cox, C. R., 71, 106
Cox, Charles W.
    Chairman, 100, 106
    Director, 89
    Fluor director, 102
    General manager, 88
    Joined company, 65
    New York sales, 67, 108

Photograph, 128
President, chief operating officer, 90, 94
Vice-chairman, 100, 102
Vice-president, 66
Coxe, William, 127
Craig, James, Sr., 39
Cresap, McCormick & Paget, 170
Cribb, Gene, 108
Crouch, Alex, C., 110, 111, 172
Cunningham, Harry L., Jr., 71, 72, 86, 108,
    116, 119, 120

D

Daniel Building, Birmingham, 88, 125
Daniel Building, Greenville, 37, 85, 86, 124,
    142-144, 195, 196, 216
Daniel, Charles E.
    Birth, 8
    Corporate boards, 5
    Death, 86, 216-221
    Distinguished Service Award, 197
    Downtown Greenville, 196, 197
    Elberton speech, 162, 163
    Establishing company, 3, 15, 18, 59, 94
    Genoa, Italy, Center, 148
    Hampton speech, 75, 78, 79, 182-189
    Improving government, 199-201
    Industrialist of the Year, 76, 187, 207, 208
    Marriage, 9
    Photographs, 122, 127, 128, 129, 130
    Recognition plaque, 86
    South Carolinian of the Year, 218
    U. S. Senate, 37, 63, 74, 78, 138, 155,
        156-161, 188
    World War I, 8, 139
Daniel, Charles W., 99, 211
Daniel Construction Company
    Acquisition by Fluor Corp., 18, 101-104
    Aviation Department, 68, 69
    Company slogans, 43, 70
    Corporate construction groups, 71, 88, 106
    Divisions, departments, managers, 107,
        108, 109
    Engineering, 70, 90, 106, 108, 115-117, 134
    Equipment, 39, 93, 94, 107, 108
    Established, 15-18
    Industrial Services, 73, 100, 101, 107
    International, 65-67, 70-71, 99, 106, 108,
        109
    Maintenance-Mechanical, 21, 39, 106, 108
    Marketing, 36, 44, 65, 66, 82, 124, 126-127
    Move to Greenville, 30-33, 123
    Regional Group, 88, 106, 107-109
    Sale of stock, 72, 88, 89
    Subsidiaries, 73, 89, 90, 91
Daniel, Earle W., 8, 39, 107, 131
Daniel Foundation, 142, 209-215
Daniel, Fred A., 8

Daniel, Homozel Mickel
  Daniel Foundation, 143, 209-214
  Daniel Music Building, 69
  Director, 28, 89, 100
  Executive secretary, 37
  Marriage, 9
  Photograph, 126
Daniel International Corp., 89, 90, 93-96,
  100, 101
  (also see Daniel Construction Co.)
Daniel, James Fleming, 9
Daniel, James F., Jr., 7, 157
Daniel, James F. III, 70, 108, 114, 127
Daniel Laboratory, 211-216
Daniel, Leila Mildred Adams, 9
Daniel Library, 142
Daniel Realty Corp., 71, 107, 211
Daniel, R. Hugh
  Chairman and CEO, 87
  Chief executive and treasurer, 90, 94
  Daniel Foundation, 143, 144, 209-211
  Director, 18
  Established Alabama Division, 19
  Graduate, The Citadel, 13
  Photographs, 128, 129, 131
  President and treasurer, 28, 65
  Sale of stock, 72
  Scholarship Fund, The Citadel, 140, 141
  Townsend Lumber Co., 13
  World War II, 7, 34
Daniel, Robert H., 157
Davis, E. R., 38
Davis Electrical Constructors, Inc., 40, 41
Davis, Fred, 64
Davis, J. Bratton, 219
Davis Mechanical Contractors, 40
Davis, Wesley, 39
Dean, Richard, 72, 106
Deering-Milliken, 27, 36, 53, 60, 61, 79,
  81-84, 186
Dentici, Joe, 39, 107, 113, 127, 129
Dewey, Bradley, 81
Dill, George, 111, 120, 121
Donaldson Air Force Base, 30, 60
Donnelly, L. W., 71, 96, 106, 108
Dorn, W. J. Bryan, 188, 217
Downtown Greenville Asso., 196
"DuBrik," 11
Duke Power Co., 72, 88
Dukes, W. W., Jr., 73, 107
Dunean Mill, 36, 37
Dunham, Charles F., 18, 21
DuPont, 57, 78, 80, 150
Durham, Monroe, 71, 109
Duvall, Sam, 71

E
Eastern Airlines, 5, 80
Edens, J. Drake, Jr., 185
Edminister, Ed J., 108
Edwards, B. M., 213
Edwards, Ralph, 143
Edwards, Robert C., 146
Eisenhower, Dwight D., 56, 152, 156, 179,
  205, 207
Eisenhower Presidential Library, 215
Elberton, Ga., 9, 58, 59, 115, 137, 152, 162,
  163, 164
Elliott, J. K., 38
Ellis, Max, 38
Elrod, Henry, 126
Emory, G. H., 38
Employment chart, 132
Engineering News Record, 88, 92-98
Englund, Carl, 19, 22, 23, 24, 30, 39, 64, 66,
  108, 129
Englund, R. Caldwell, 71, 87, 89, 107, 127
Erskine College, 213
Ervin, Sam J., 157
Eskridge, Frank, 108
Evening Post, 170

F
Fairless, Benjamin F., 76
Fant, Charlie, 111
Fant, Ray, 32
First National, Birmingham, 33
First National, Greenville, 5
First Presbyterian Church, Clemson, 110
Firth Carpet project, 66
Flexible Tubing, 216
Fluor Corp., 18, 101-105
Fluor, J. Robert, 101, 102, 105
Foley, James W., 100
Fort Oglethorpe, 139
Fortis Corp., 107
Fortune Magazine, 51-63, 162, 218
Furman, Alester G., Jr., 112, 113, 157, 171,
  198, 246, 248
Furman, Alester G., III, 89, 100
Furman Co., 89
Furman University, 69, 210, 213, 214

G
Gable, Sloan W., 166
Gadsden Airbase, 34
Gailey Mills, 118
Gambrell, E. Smythe, 47
Gantt, Harvey B., 189
Garland, H. H., 38
General Cable, 216
Genier, J. D., 109
Georgia-Pacific, 5, 77, 115, 141

Georgia Power, 96
Gentry, M. D., 107
George, Walter F., 157
Gerli, Paolino, 42
Gibbs Art Gallery, 215
Gibson, Charles, 38
Gilbert, J. H. 38
Gillespie, Harold, 41
Gillian, Mike, 109
Goldston Inc., 89
Goldwater, Barry, 207
Granger, Bennie, 131
Graniteville Co., 5, 34
Graves, C. B., 107
Green, Clyde T., Jr., 87, 106, 107
Greenville Chamber of Commerce, 85, 98, 197, 216
Greenville City Council, 85
Greenville News, 138, 156, 184, 195
Greenville, Daniel Little Theater, 214
Greenville Piedmont, 146, 184, 196
Greenville, S. C., 23, 28, 34, 36, 37, 60, 66, 68, 84, 89, 93, 98, 101, 110, 111, 112, 113, 114, 143, 152, 167, 195, 199, 216
Greenville-Spartanburg Jetport, 68, 171-173
Greenville Symphony Orchestra, 214
Greenville Women's Club, 196
Greenwood Chamber of Commerce, 181
Gregg Dyeing & Finishing Co., 34
Gregory, P. C., III, 99, 107, 108, 109
Grier, F. E., 213
Grisby, Ernie, 65
Gunderson, Richard, 109
Gustafson, John W., 87, 108
Guy, Gerald E., 109

H

Hall, Wilton E., 14
Hammett, Lawrence, 38
Hampton County Guardian, 184
Harden, W. Frank, 218
Hardy, George, 38
Harper, Walter W., 79, 179, 180
Harley, J. Emile, 202
Harrison, Earle E., 108, 109
Harrison, James F., 41
Harrison, Wesley, 41
Harvard University, 49
Haynsworth, Clement F., 6, 7, 158, 214
Heller, Max, 196
Henderson, James M., 86
Her Majesty Industries, 119
Hickman, Robert, 218
Hitler, Aolf, 25
Hofacre, William M., 89
Holcombe, Neville, 171
Holcombe, Wesley, 68, 108, 113, 127

Hollings, Ernest F., 170, 175, 176, 177, 179, 197
Hollis, W. W., 39
Hopkins, James A., 109
Horton, Ralph M., Jr., 150, 151
Housman, Walter, 39, 108
Howey, J. Ronald, 108
Howie, Thomas, 142
"How To Lose $100,000,000 and Other Valuable Advice" by Royal Little, 41
Hruska, Roman, 157
Hudgens, R. W. 138
Hudson Valley Mgmt. Society, 163
Humbert, Richard B., 101, 102
Humphrey, Hubert, 207

I

Industrial Development Committee, 167
Irvine, Cal., 102
Isbell, Joe, 38

J

Jackson, Beaty, 15, 18
James Fabric plant, 116
James Lees & Sons Co., 39
Jeddah, Saudi Arabia, 99
Jefferies, Richard M., 185, 202
Jefferson County Hospital, 22, 33
Johnson, Lyndon B., 157-159
Johnson, L.D., 217
Johnson, T. C., 47, 65, 69, 83, 87, 88, 106, 108
Johnston, Olin D., 14, 157, 199
Jones, B. F., 38
Jones, Bob, 69
Jones, Wilfred, 71
J R.M. Roofing Review, 20
J. Roy Martin & Co., 20
Judson Mills, 34

K

Kansas City Light & Power Co., 103
Kansas Gas & Electric Co., 103
Kennedy, John F., 178, 197, 206
Kennedy, Robert F., 197
Keys, J. C., Jr., 31, 32
Keys Printing Co., 31
Killorin, George P., 107
Kimberly-Clark Corp., 40
King, Barrington, 39, 108
King, W. Mason, 158
Kliesrath, Jack B., 109
Knowland, William F., 159, 160
Kramer, William, 108
Kress, Tuscaloosa, 34

L

LaFrance Industires, 5
Lane, Hugh, 213

Lassister, Eugene E., 8-9, 12
Latimer, Carter, 138
Lees Cochran Co., 36
Lennon, Alton A., 157
Liberty Life, 24
Limestone College, 213
Lincoln, Abraham, 221
Lincoln, Freeman, 51
Lincoln, Samuel B., 10, 11
Linden, Van Der, 159
Little, D. D., 38
Little, Royal, 41, 61, 215
Littlejohn, Jim, 63
Lockwood-Greene, 10, 11, 33
Longcrier, L. G., Jr., 87, 108
Longcrier, L. G., Sr., 39, 64, 108, 127
Los Angeles Times, 102
Lyles, William G., 158

Mc
McCall, Howard, 71, 96, 106
McCarthy, Joseph R., 155, 156, 158
McCarthy, P. E., 109
McCauley, Chas. H., 33
McClure, Harlan, 147
McCormick, Thomas D., 99, 109
McCoy, T. Ree, 19
McCoy, Marcus G., 71, 107, 109
McDougall, George E.
    Canadian engineer, 26
    Director, 89
    Division manager, 108
    Eastern Hemisphere Group, 106
    Engineering, 117
    General manager, 66, 88
    Joined company, 26, 47
    Photograph, 127, 128
    Pilot, 68
    President, DISA, 99
    Vice-chairman, DISA, 99
    Vice-president, 89
McGovern, George, 207
McCraw, L. G., 71, 106

M
Mackey Mortuary, 217
Magill, Arthur F., 119
Magnolia Finishing Plant, 81-84, 186
Marks, Alfred M., 33
Mark Clark Hall, 141
Marsh, Charles F., 213
Marshall, Alan, 109
Marshall, Ralph, 38
Martin, J. Roy, 20
Martin, Thomas W., 211
Matteson, E. F., 70, 87, 88, 108, 127
Maybank, Burnet, 63, 138, 154, 157

Means, Cotesworth P., 169
Mefferd, George A., 102
Merchant, James A., 108
Mickel, Buck
    Assistant chairman, 65
    Chairman, 90, 95, 102
    Clemson life trustee, 146
    Director, 28, 89, 100
    Executive vice-president, 28, 65, 79
    Fluor board, executive committee, group
        vice-president, 102
    Greenville Chamber of Commerce, 98
    Joined company, 12, 47
    Milliken project, 83
    Monsanto director, 64
    Photograph, 128
    President, 87, 102
    WIS Daniel program, 220
Mickel Memorial Chapel, 213
Mickel, Viola Alston Carter, 213
Miller, Martin & Lewis, 33
Miles, James F., 152
Milliken Engineering, 82, 112
Milliken, Roger, 26, 27, 53, 61, 79, 81, 83, 84,
    112, 166, 171, 172, 213, 220
Mitchell, R. D., 37, 108, 109
Moncini, Renato, 123
Monsanto Co., 64, 215
Montgomery, Walter, 171, 213
Moore, E. W., 38
Moore, J. Ed., 13, 19, 21, 38, 113, 118, 129
Moore, Pearl A., 13, 18
Moore, Van, 92
Moose, J. Blake, 22, 24, 39, 87
Morrah, P. Bradley, 86
Morris, Earle E., Jr., 188
Morris, Edgar, 158
Murray, Walker, 109

N
National Association of Industrial Realtors,
    76
National Citizens Committee for Community
    Relations, 188
NLRB, 78, 192
Nazer, Reda, 99
Neill, Rolfe, 74
Newberry College, 213
Newton, Park, 73
New York, 23, 65, 66, 76, 92, 142, 176, 187,
    207, 216
New York Times, 167
New York Zoological Society, 215
Nichols, C. B., 38
Nickols & Co., 61
Nixon, Richard M., 76, 152, 157, 179, 187,
    206, 207, 208, 217

O

Oakley, O. R., 38
Oconee Mills, 22
O'Connor, Tom, 184
Odis-Clay-Poundstone Eng., 33
Odom, John P., 87, 117
Odom, L. A., 173
Ogden, R. L., 106
Oliver, Elmer, 44, 45
Outz, Hub, 38
Owen, Charles, 38

P

Page, Carey, 38
Palmetto Club, 218
Parker, E. Warren, 108, 127
Payne, Harry M., Jr., 70, 108, 115-117
Peace, Roger C., 213
Pearlstine, Milton A., 137
Peignage Amedee Provoust et Cie, 61
Pickens County Goodwill Club, 198, 200
Pickens Lumber & Mfg Co., 22
Piedmont Engineers, Architects &
    Planners, 110
Plumbing & Pipefitting, 192
Poinsett Hotel, 85, 117
Polytechnic Literary Society, 138
Potter-Shackleford, 24
Presbyterian College, 213
Prevost, F. Keith, 9, 14, 15, 17, 18, 22, 28,
    122
Prouvost, Albert A., 42, 157
Prudential, 5, 64, 79
PWA, 14

R

Ratteree, John, 173
Revenues chart, 133
Reynolds, Metals, 22, 29
Rice, Jim, 38
Rieger, Richard, 143
Rivers, L. Mendell, 183, 184
Rocky Bottom, 198
Rodgers Hosiery, 12, 34
Rome, Ga., 9, 10, 11, 34
Roosevelt, Franklin D., 14, 154
Ross Builders & Supplies, 32
Ross, George, 24, 32
Rothe, Greg W., 73, 89, 100, 102, 105
Rouse, Carl, 108
Rowland, Will, 38
Rubino, Anthony A., 32
Rubino, Mary Neese, 13, 15, 19, 30, 31-33,
    40, 44-45, 131
Russell, Donald S., 76, 185, 195, 216, 221
Russell, Richard B., 157

S

St. Paul's Cathedral, 217
Salomon Brothers, 102
Sanders, Paul, 145
Saudi Arabia Parsons Ltd., 99
Saudi Arabian Trading & Const., Ltd., 99
Saunders, Robert J., 158
Schroeder, J. J., 106, 108
Schultz, W. S. 33
Scovil, Roger M., 70, 108
Sears-Birmingham, 33
Sears Roebuck catalogue, 178
Seignious, George M., II, 99
Shafto, G. Richard, 218
Shelton, Don, 38
Shumate, Jeff, 16
Sibbert, Edward F., 33
Simpson, Alden, 158
Singer Company, 6, 22, 29, 59
Sirrine Company, 27, 29, 33
Sirrine, Joseph E., 32, 40, 60
Skidmore, Owings & Merrill Co., 172
Skrla Co., 91
Sloan, Alfred P., Jr., 76
Sloan, Allen P., 107
Small, Robert, 4, 80
Smith, Arthur, 108
Smith, Claude, 118, 119
Smith, Dresden, 156
Smith, Garry S., 39, 71
Smith, Leo R., 109
Smith & Norrington Eng. Corp., 90
Smyth, Norman, 70, 108
Society of Industrial Realtors, 187
S. C. Chapter, AIA, 148
S. C. City Magazine, 75
S. C. Development Bd., 56, 79, 149-151, 166,
    168, 179-180, 204
S. C. Electric & Gas Co., 72, 103
S. C. Farm Bureau Federation, 170
S C. Farm Market Bulletin, 14
S. C. Foundation of Independent Colleges,
    213
S. C. House of Representatives, 114
S. C. Magazine, 74, 218
S. C. National Bank, 5, 15, 16
S. C. Ports Authority, 137, 169, 170, 171,
    174, 199
S. C. Public Service Authority, 103
S. C. Tax Study Commission, 200
S. C. Textile Mfg. Assn., 170, 202, 204
Southeastern Shipbuilding Corp., 29, 30
Southern Airways, 34
Southern Bank & Trust, 115
Southern Bell, 5
Southern Industrial Supply, 99
Southern Paperboard, 40

Southern Railroad, 23, 44, 49, 220
Southern Research Inst., 211
Southerland, Philip J., 109
Southtown Housing, 33
Spartanburg Journal, 200
Sphinx Yearbook, 137, 138
Spivey, Currie B., Jr.
  Director, 102
  Fluor acquisition, 105
  Joined company, 47
  N. Y. Sales, 88, 108
  President, chief operating officer, 100, 105
  Southeastern Sales, 88
Springwood Cemetery, 216
State Newspaper, 186
Stellman, Harry, 64, 108
Stephens, James B., 41
Stevens Hangar, 168
Stevens Co., J. P., 5, 33, 36, 53, 60, 61, 77
Stevens, Robert T., 36, 37, 53, 157
Stevens Textile Plant, 121
Stipp, Peter A., 109
Stirm, Robert P., 73, 89
Stollings, Laurence, 139
Storey, Wallace, 82, 83, 84
Strauss, Peter, 109
Stroud, Joseph, 71, 108, 109, 127
Stuart, W. Preston, Jr., 108
Suitt, Howard, 50, 87, 109
Sullivan Hdw. Co., 17
Summerall Chapel, 142
Sutter, Thomas, 71
Swint, S. H., 38

T

Tappan, David S., Jr., 102
Taylor, Ed., 49, 50, 66
Taylor, Wm. M., 218
Tennessee Eastman, 69
Texaco, 100
Textron, 5, 41, 42, 53, 61, 215
Thomas, Albert S., 142
Thomas, Charles A., 215
Thompson, Harold, 116
Thomas, C. W., 30, 39
Thornton, Joel, 108
Thrash, Carl, 38, 129
Thrasher, C. A., 19, 23, 30, 39, 129
Thurmond, Strom, 56, 78, 130, 149-151, 156, 160-161, 166, 174, 195, 212, 217
Tillman, Benjamin R., 154
Timmerman, George B., Jr., 56, 166, 167-168, 170
Toal, F. C., 157
Tool Service Co., 89, 99
Townsend Lumber Co., 8, 9, 11, 12, 14, 15, 25, 28, 30, 32, 37, 38, 59, 111, 123

Townsend, T. P., Jr., 106
Traxler, David G., 56, 130
Truman, Harry S., 169
Turner, Harold, 158
Turner, LeRoy R., 95, 108

U

Ullman Adv. Agency, 33
Umstead, Wm. B., 157
United Negro College Fund, 213
U. of Alabama, 33
U. of S. C., 210, 215
U. of S. C. College of Business, 215
U. of S. C. Daniel Mgmt. Center, 215
U. S. Army, 8, 9, 139
U. S. Navy, 8
U. S. Navy Yard, 29
U. S. Senate, 63, 151, 154-161, 198
U. S. Supreme Court, 154
Utica Mohawk, 53

V

Vandiver, Thomas C., 115
Varello, Paul J., 109
Virginia Electric & Power, 72

W

Waldorf Astoria, 76, 117, 187, 207
Wallace, George, 207
Ware Shoals Mfg. Co., 33
Warren, Knight & Davis, 33
Washington, D. C., 155, 205
Watkins, Arthur U., 158
Watkins, Sherman S., 108
Watkins, T. Frank, 110
Watson, Phil J., 109
Watson, Thomas J., 76
Watt, W. Eugene, 23, 30, 33, 34, 35, 37, 129
Welch, Wm., 38
Wellman, Arthur O., 61, 157
Wells, Bobby E., 108, 109
Wells, George, 38
Westminster College, 215
Whisenhunt, J. Dan, 108
Wickes, 33
Wiget, Paul L., 108, 109
Wilkinson, Greg R., 109
Williamson, J. P., 198
Williamson, Wendell, 107
Winchell, Walter, 43
Winston Churchill Memorial & Library, 215
WIS Columbia, 218
Wise, Raymond, 108
Wofford College, 213
Wolff, Louis, 158
Wood, Henry, 38
Wood, John A., 106, 108

Wood, Wilbert, 38
Woodside Mills, 80
World War I, 3, 8, 59, 139, 140, 169
World War II, 55, 149
Workman, S. J., 173
WPA, 14, 110
Wren, Sir Christopher, 217

Y

Yale Univ., 49
Yeargin, Lawrence W., 13, 19, 38, 129
Yeargin, Robert, 50
Young, Bogue C., 17
Young, Joseph, 17
Young, Richard K., 67, 68, 113, 127
Young, T. B., 145

THE AUTHORS

The co-authors of this book are former South Carolina newspapermen whose careers began about the time Charles E. Daniel established his construction company.

Claude R. (Red) Canup wrote Part I, "Building a Business and the South." He held a variety of positions with *The Anderson Daily Mail* and *The Anderson Independent* from 1932 until 1960, ranging from reporter to sports editor. He was sports information director at the University of South Carolina (1960-62) and editor of *The Anderson Free Press* (1963) prior to joining Daniel Construction Company in 1964 as director of public relations and advertising. Canup was a Marine Corps combat correspondent during the latter part of World War II.

William D. Workman, Jr., author of Part II, "A Constructive Citizen," began his newspaper career with *The Charleston News and Courier* in 1936, but spent most of his 45 journalistic years with *The Columbia State*, of which he was editor. He graduated from The Citadel in 1935, served five active duty years with the Army during World War II, and retired from the Army reserve in 1965 as acting commander of the 108th Reserve Division. Workman is the author of two books — *The Case for the South* and *The Bishop from Barnwell* — and is co-author of several others.